Beyond Moral Fundamentalism

Beyond Moral Fundamentalism

Toward a Pragmatic Pluralism

STEVEN FESMIRE

OXFORD
UNIVERSITY PRESS

OXFORD
UNIVERSITY PRESS

Oxford University Press is a department of the University of Oxford.
It furthers the University's objective of excellence in research, scholarship,
and education by publishing worldwide. Oxford is a registered trade mark of
Oxford University Press in the UK and in certain other countries.

Published in the United States of America by Oxford University Press
198 Madison Avenue, New York, NY 10016, United States of America.

Library of Congress Cataloging-in-Publication Data
Names: Fesmire, Steven, 1967– author.
Title: Beyond moral fundamentalism: toward a pragmatic pluralism / Steven Fesmire.
Description: 1. | New York, NY, United States of America : Oxford University Press, [2024] |
Includes bibliographical references.
Identifiers: LCCN 2024013081 (print) | LCCN 2024013082 (ebook) |
ISBN 9780197763889 (hardback) | ISBN 9780197763902 (epub)
Subjects: LCSH: Ethics. | Pragmatism. | Dewey, John, 1859–1952.
Classification: LCC BJ1031 .F45 2024 (print) | LCC BJ1031 (ebook) |
DDC 170—dc23/eng/20240415
LC record available at https://lccn.loc.gov/2024013081
LC ebook record available at https://lccn.loc.gov/2024013082

DOI: 10.1093/9780197763919.001.0001

Printed by Integrated Books International, United States of America

For Rev. Dr. Charles Wayne and Jayne Fesmire,
in loving memory

Contents

Preface

Generations of intellectuals have found an inspirational taproot in John Dewey's (1859–1952) notion that practical concerns are not mere accessories to ultimate concerns. He summed up a spirit of public engagement a century ago in "The Need for a Recovery of Philosophy": "Philosophy recovers itself when it ceases to be a device for dealing with the problems of philosophers and becomes a method, cultivated by philosophers, for dealing with the problems" of humanity (1917, MW 10:46). Whatever the quality of a philosophical work's schematic form or of its erudite chewing of a "historic cud" (47), or of its promise for manufacturing academic citations, by Dewey's standards it is *philosophically* valuable insofar as it interprets the contemporary scene and sheds light "upon what philosophy should now engage in" (1949, LW 16:361).

In that applied and practical spirit, this is a philosophical book that deals with pressing social issues. Specifically, it focuses on problems with the way we make ethical and political decisions. I build on Dewey, but the basic lines of argument stand or fall independent of his pitfalls and promises. Inquiry into social problems was a prominent emphasis of Dewey's wider theory of experience. He embraced a philosophic turn that, in Naoko Saito's words, brings "our thinking back to life" (2019a, 12), and this includes but is happily not limited to the art of dealing with problems. I draw examples primarily from current moral, political, and educational problems in the United States, though my theoretical generalizations about ethics, education, and politics are directed toward a global audience.

The renascent scholarly interest in Dewey and pragmatism in recent decades has produced a highly articulated framework for clarifying and extending contemporary moral and political philosophy's achievements while critiquing its deficiencies. This book reflects thirty-five years of engagement with that scholarship. Some self-identified pragmatists would likely applaud Hilary Putnam's proposal of a third, Deweyan enlightenment, analogous to the Platonic and eighteenth-century ones. Others would deem such proposals overly idealistic, especially if decoupled from research to correct Dewey's own covert biases, presuppositions, and limitations. I count myself among the latter group, but I share the conviction of most pragmatists that critical reassessment of Dewey merits a central place in philosophical and educational research.

As Gregory Pappas (2011) has explored, pragmatism did not "grow up" in the United States. As a coherent philosophy it *originated* there, and it is still growing up through critical and mutually transformative intra-cultural dialogue (cf. Behuniak 2019a, 2019b). Among Dewey's greatest contributions to global dialogue was to show that we can live lives of deep moral integrity (cf. Rosenbaum 2015), courage, and commitment without sliding into what I herein call moral fundamentalism. This book develops Dewey's insights to argue that growth beyond moral fundamentalism is a possibility both for intellectual leaders and for the person-on-the-street. Both are deeply implicated in the problem.

Acknowledgments

Many friends, colleagues, and students helped to hone parts of this manuscript over the past few years. I am especially grateful to Guy Axtell and Jim Garrison for reviewing and offering thoughtful critical feedback on draft chapters. The manuscript was much improved through the diligence of Max Hayward and anonymous readers for Oxford University Press. Portions of the manuscript also benefited directly from critical feedback, dialogue, or correspondence with William Throop, Mark Johnson, Philip Kitcher, Peter Singer, Erin McKenna, Gregory Pappas, Thomas Alexander, Todd Lekan, David Hildebrand, Heather Keith, Kenneth Keith, Andrew Light, Bryan Norton, Kareem Khalifa, Heidi Grasswick, Lorraine Besser, John Spackman, Steve Viner, Martha Woodruff, Nobuo Kazashi, Naoko Saito, Eddie Glaude, James Campbell, Casey Haskins, Anthony Weston, Roger Ames, Len Waks, Al Frankowski, Larry Hickman, James Fesmire-Keith, and many others.

I extend a warm thank you to numerous students at Green Mountain College, Middlebury College, and Radford University who helped to fine-tune these ideas, and to Grace Anne Ankeney and Shailis Joplin for their feedback on early chapters.

The Society for the Advancement of American Philosophy continues to be a primary source for my intellectual growth and rejuvenation. The Center for Dewey Studies, and Special Collections at Morris Library, Southern Illinois University at Carbondale, were warmly hospitable and prompt in their assistance with archival sleuthing, as was the Wisconsin Historical Society. I am grateful to them for permission to publish the figures that appear in Chapter 5. Peter Ohlin at Oxford University Press was supportive and thoughtful throughout. Finally, thanks to Brent Matheny at OUP and Ganga Balaji at Newgen. Portions of this book were supported by a 2016 fellowship at the University of Edinburgh, Institute for Advanced Studies in the Humanities, and by a 2022–23 Dalton Eminent Senior Scholar award from Radford University.

I gratefully acknowledge permission to reprint, in substantially revised form, material from the following articles:

2023. "Democratic Decision-Making in Dewey's Ethics." In Deborah Poff and Alex C. Michalos (eds.), *Encyclopedia of Business and Professional Ethics*. Springer Nature.

2022. "Out of Plumb, Out of Key, and Out of Whack: Social Ethics and Democracy for the New Normal." Coauthored with Heather Keith. Eds. Eli Kramer and Giuseppe Spadafora. *Dewey Studies* 6, no. 1:480–520.

2022. "Environmental Pragmatism." In Hugh Lafollette (ed.), *International Encyclopedia of Ethics*. Hoboken, NJ: Wiley.

2020. "On (Not) Becoming a Moral Monster: Democratically Transforming American Racial Imaginations." Ed. Leonard J. Waks. *Dewey Studies* 4, no. 1:41–49.

2020. "Pragmatist Ethics and Climate Change." In Dale Miller and Ben Eggleston (eds.), *Moral Theory and Climate Change: Ethical Perspectives on a Warming Planet*, 215–237. New York: Routledge.

2020. "Dewey's Independent Factors in Moral Action." In Roberto Frega and Steven Levine (eds.) *Dewey's Ethics*, 18–39. New York: Routledge.

2019. "Beyond Moral Fundamentalism: John Dewey's Pragmatic Pluralism in Ethics and Politics." In Steven Fesmire (ed.), *The Oxford Handbook of Dewey*, 209–234. New York: Oxford University Press.

2019. "Ethics for Moral Fundamentalists." *Inside Higher Ed*, April 9.

2017. "Education Isn't a Commodity for Labor." *The Conversation*, August 31.

2016. Review of Bryan Norton, *Sustainable Values, Sustainable Change. Environmental Ethics* 38, no. 4:499–502.

2016. "Democracy and the Industrial Imagination in American Education." *Education & Culture* 32, no. 1:53–62.

2015. "What We Lose When We Treat Education Like an Industrial Sector." *Chronicle of Higher Education*, November 2.

Abbreviations

Citations of John Dewey's works are to the thirty-seven-volume critical edition published by Southern Illinois University Press under the editorship of Jo Ann Boydston. In-text citations give the original publication date and series abbreviation, followed by volume number and page number. For example, (1934b, LW 10:12) is page 12 of *Art as Experience*, which was published as volume 10 of *The Later Works*.Series abbreviations for *The Collected Works*:

EW   *The Early Works* (1882–1898)
MW   *The Middle Works* (1899–1924)
LW   *The Later Works* (1925–1953)

Citations of Dewey's correspondence are to *The Correspondence of John Dewey*, 1871–2007, published by the InteLex Corporation under the editorship of Larry Hickman. Citations give the date, reference number for the letter, and author followed by recipient. For example: 1973.02.13 (22053): Herbert W. Schneider to H. S. Thayer.

1

Ethics for Moral Fundamentalists

Even as we confront increasingly complex global problems that demand greater moral sensitivity and responsibility, a more popular approach beckons: a stark one-way mentality that assumes those going the right way ("us") are constantly endangered by others ("them") going the wrong way. Each is outraged that the other has misread the "one way" signs. I call this approach "moral fundamentalism," the habit of assuming that there is an exclusively right, accessible way to diagnose problems, along with a single approvable practical solution to any problem.

Moral fundamentalism is not the best way to show one's moral backbone. It causes people to oversimplify situations, neglect broader context, take refuge in dogmatic absolutes, ignore possibilities for finding common ground, assume privileged access to the right way to proceed, and shut off honest inquiry. This approach also makes the worst of native impulses toward social bonding and antagonism. This depletes social capital (Putnam 2000) and makes it impossible to debate and achieve contested *social goals* such as justice, freedom, public health, security, sustainability, peace, and democracy. These are superordinate goals. Unlike zero-sum games, we win or lose these goals together, even though our perceptions and motivations differ.

Meanwhile, exacerbating the one-way moral mentality, techno-industrial civilizations have arranged social networks and media communications into an infamous echo chamber that insulates "us" from having to learn anything new from "them" (Karsten and West 2016). With social media algorithms as their means and

Beyond Moral Fundamentalism. Steven Fesmire, Oxford University Press. © Oxford University Press 2024. DOI: 10.1093/9780197763919.003.0001

symbol, these ideological silos of the infosphere fortify the ancient yet still mistaken supposition that we have little choice but to oppose others' moral fundamentalism with our own. This assumption undercuts even short-term successes by driving us-them wedges deeper. The prevailing tendency to hyper-politicize social experiences, looking for politics around every corner, does not help (Talisse 2019).

Drawing from John Dewey's approach to philosophical questions, I develop in this book a pluralistic conception of moral and political life that is at once experimental, democratic, and pragmatic in method.[1] An alternative to both the tragic oversimplification of moral fundamentalism and the arbitrariness of relativism, pragmatic pluralism is an approach that is set up as a response to particular conditions and consequences, so it gains practical leverage with complex ethical, political, and educational problems without flattening variability among values or presuming that abstract theories can determine what we ought to do. In a style meant to be concrete, accessible, and engaging, this book clarifies and illustrates the promises and challenges of democratic decision-making in societies struggling to grow beyond moral fundamentalism.

Social goals like democracy are open possibilities that must be safeguarded and renewed through human choices and actions. This is a book about how to approach our choices and actions so that they are more likely to help. Unlike some popular political philosophies, I do not assume by default that social action is reducible to contests of will and power, but neither am I sanguine that bigotry and oppression can or will be ended entirely by means of pluralistic awareness, democratic communication, and a pragmatic methodology. I argue more humbly that, without these means, we are unlikely to make much progress toward our most important twenty-first-century superordinate goals.

A Moral Fundamentalist Pledge of Allegiance

I sometimes ask students if they would be willing to pledge the following:[2]

There's a single basis of moral life, and it determines the right way to proceed. I have access to this supreme basis. When others don't agree with me, it's because they have the wrong faith commitments, they aren't analyzing things properly, or they aren't letting conscience be their guide. Agreement with me is a prerequisite to solving our problems. Consequently, I have nothing to learn about these matters from those who disagree with me. Their participation is, at best, an irrelevant distraction and, at worst, an evil to be defeated. My diagnosis of the issue has precisely captured all that is morally relevant. It's exhaustive, hence beyond revision and reformulation.

I rarely get any takers. After the students and I swap stories about those who might blithely take such a pledge, we invariably conclude that the pledgers are outnumbered by their counterparts: conservatives, liberals, and radicals who would, upon conscious reflection, reject this outright as closed-minded arrogance. Moreover, it quickly becomes clear that this pledge does not speak to the sort of people they wish to be. (I later explain that "ethical monists" accept the first sentence, "moral fallibilists" reject the second, and almost all moral philosophers would reject the baselessness of the rest.)

And yet, our class conversation continues, how many of us certified broader-minded souls act as though complex problems come prepackaged with our interpretation of them? Do we prejudge and offhandedly dismiss alternative diagnoses of shared problems? However open-minded we may seem to ourselves, do we habitually react to others as though we are navigating with the one, universal

4 BEYOND MORAL FUNDAMENTALISM

moral compass? Are our real behaviors implicated in this pledge most of us would consciously disavow?

At this point, I introduce another classroom activity, inspired by pragmatist philosopher Anthony Weston's (2017) *A 21st-Century Ethical Toolbox.* Suppose we wanted to codify rules to sabotage democratic dialogue and make debates as fruitless as possible. The idea here is to spell out rules that maximize the distance between "us" and "them," ensuring that creative possibilities for cooperatively setting and achieving social goals go forever unnoticed. For example, consider things like "Be angrier and talk louder," "Emphasize disagreements," "Widen the gulf that separates our concerns," "Stereotype the other side," and "Approach any debate as a zero-sum game."

I divide students into groups and ask them to develop five more rules. Each rule, I tell them, should obstruct growth and communication, setting a context antithetical to mutually respectful dialogue and open-ended debate. They come up with an excellent toolkit for torpedoing public deliberation: "Be visibly offended by any questioning of your conclusions," "Prepare your comeback instead of listening," "Inflate certainty," "Be smug," "Gaslight," "Reject complexity," "Act as though your values and concerns invariably overrule theirs," "Ignore context," "Be uncharitable: always present your side at its best and the other at its worst," "Denounce pragmatic voices as sellouts," "Assume your interlocuter is clueless."

Gradually some of the fun fades, and the discussion shifts from a playful game to serious ethical reflection. Is there any link between the pledge activity and your new diabolical toolkit, I ask? The sense of the class is that the toolkit clarifies the practical upshot of the pledge, identifying legitimized behaviors. We end up recognizing some of these behaviors in ourselves, myself included. We purposefully drew up a malicious playbook for undermining democracy, and it mirrored the status quo. Many of my liberal-identified American students interpret the activity as a sendup of conservatives. Their imagined toolkit-users sport "Make America

Great Again" hats and threaten DEI advocates. Meanwhile, many conservative students interpret the activity as damning liberal wokeness, "virtue signaling," and "cancel culture." Through this discussion, the class gets an experiential introduction to work in moral psychology that bears on moral politics, such as Jonathan Haidt's *The Righteous Mind* (2012).

We conclude this introductory unit of the course with issues that tend to counteract fuzzy relativism by evoking strong condemnation, such as Martha Nussbaum's essay on female genital cutting (1999). Joining millions of ethics students before them, most conclude that extreme relativism leaves much to be desired as a coherent way to express the virtue of tolerance. Most want to show moral courage. Yet as they reach for their received language for thinking about morality, many are now unnerved by their own pledge-like tone. They are habituated to assuming that a kind of moral fundamentalism *is* the irreplaceable steam that powers activism and advocacy, that resistance to injustice is unintelligible without it, and that the virtues of moral clarity and conviction somehow imply a my-way-or-the-highway approach.

Shifting uncomfortably, we pause to explore our cognitive dissonance. Perhaps we are merely hypocrites, parading open-mindedness while betraying its opposite. Or perhaps we are beset with a neural vestige of moral tribalism, which some think might finally be enlightened by a universal morality (Greene 2013). Minimally, we are exhibiting what social psychologist Lee Ross studied as the illusion of objectivity, the error of assuming that *our* perceptions, motivations, and assessments are objective while those who disagree with us are irrational (Ross 2018). But there are additional philosophically interesting things at work. By exploring them, this book highlights social conditions that exacerbate our usual hypocrisy and attribution errors.

To clarify that there is much more than just hypocrisy implicated in our pledge-like behaviors, in the coming sections I introduce the terms *cultural lag* and *moral fundamentalism*, then define the latter by singling out two telltale features of *wicked problems*, a vague and overused notion that nevertheless has some practical traction for ethics, education, politics, and policy in complex systems.

Cultural Lag: Out of Plumb, Out of Key, and Out of Whack

John Dewey proposed soon after the atomic bombings of Hiroshima and Nagasaki that citizens of techno-industrial nations suffer from "cultural lag" (1945c, LW 15:199–200; cf. 1929, LW 4:203–228). He had in mind a condition in which most of the basic alternatives we have on hand to think and talk about moral and political life, from customary moralizing to sophisticated theorizing, were developed, canned, and pickled on a shelf so long ago that they now lag far behind the multifaceted problems that our values must speak to.

Some cultural lag is unavoidable because moral outlooks are mostly inherited from others at second hand. Humans are not disinterested spectators who choose whether or not to be involved in customary relations, values, and practices. "It is not an ethical 'ought' that conduct *should* be social," Dewey observed. "It *is* social, whether bad or good" (1922b, MW 14:16). There are psychological and biological drives that will express themselves no matter what, but moral character takes its distinctive form through sociocultural interactions. It is fine to live with accumulated moral wisdom, just as it is fine to live with hand-me-down clothes, so long as they fit and are not worn out. But when we fail to inspect habituated beliefs, values, and conceptual frameworks, many of them devolve into rationalizations for some group's dogmatic agenda or prejudices. These rationalizations make their way into theories and policies, arbitrarily lending them an air of inevitability. Economist Paul Krugman, in an essay debunking tax cuts for the wealthy, has called these pretexts "zombie ideas." In Krugman's variation on cultural lag, these brain-eating creeds of the living dead are "thoroughly refuted" propositions that "should be dead ... but won't stay dead" because they are self-serving rationalizations (2013). Conversely, some creeds are well-adapted ideas that *should* be alive but will not *stay* alive. They are ineffective because they are so sparkless, tenuous, and superficial. For example, if we think generosity a good thing simply because others prize it, or because of externally imposed discipline, then the efficacy of our generosity is fragile and incidental. As Dewey observed in *Democracy and Education* (1916), we all at one time or another robotically recite "the proper thing to say" absent the "urgency, warmth, and intimacy of a direct experience" that has deeply adjusted our attitudes (MW 9:241–243). Many do little but this, and scholars are not immune from espousing high-minded theories with shallow experiential roots. In part, this happens because long-preserved moral attitudes get out of key with the actual standards of value we live by.

Our moral imaginations are nourished in a conflicted social matrix, in which we habitually reach for values, beliefs, and conceptions that may be ill-suited to twenty-first-century "entanglements," to use Bruno Latour's (1993) term. Or reverting to the metaphor of cultural lag, it is as though thoughts and attitudes were formed in a distant time zone, yet we refuse to reset our watches. We rise with the antipodal sun, bent on maintaining, in poet Billy Collins's words, our "proper slice of longitude" (Collins 2005). The result is a curiously recalcitrant sort of moral jet lag.

The failure of many countries to effectively navigate climate change exemplifies this cultural lag. In *Reason in a Dark Time*, Dale Jamieson argues that the commonsense prototype of a harmful activity—one for which we ought to feel and be held responsible—is one that has negative consequences that are immediate, localized, intentional, and directed toward individuals (2014, ch. 5). But this conception of responsibility for harm, which is especially pronounced in the anglophone world, is eerily out of step with contemporary material developments and interdependent systems. For example, the greatest harm caused by local greenhouse gas emissions is long term, widely distributed, unintentional, and not directed toward individuals. Partly on this basis, Jamieson concludes that climate change presents challenges that "go beyond the resources of commonsense morality" (2014, 6). In this context, cultural lag is characterized by inherited moral and political concepts and frameworks that are too narrow, homogeneous, and individualistic to adequately meet global problems of techno-industrial societies, exemplified by a lack of fit with anthropogenic climate change.

Like many problems of twenty-first-century life, fueling a pandemic is likewise not intentional, does not deliberately target individuals, and has downstream and far-flung effects that are not immediately apparent. The globalized commercial and transportation infrastructure has dramatically increased the rate and scope of pandemics, even as modern epidemiological methods and techniques are placing in our hands some of the arts by which we can intelligently intervene in the spread of contagions. Yet the lagging idea that moral responsibility does not extend to systemic harms deadens moral and political perception. It abandons foresight and critical appraisal to the inertia of habits that are unsuited to the shifting intricacies of on-the-ground conditions.

Turning to an older example of cultural lag, we could prevent massive suffering if a positive *social ethics* (see Chapter 2), in Jane Addams's terms, predominated over lagging conceptions that stem from what Dewey called "ragged individualism" (LW 5:45). Within Addams's and Dewey's social ethics, individual freedom is expressed, to paraphrase Herbert Schneider, through our willingness and ability to make up our own minds and to take responsibility for our decisions (1966.03.07? [21808]: Herbert W. Schneider to Scripps College). Individual freedom may sometimes be in tension with social responsibility, but they do not have diametrically opposed agendas. To genuinely liberate individuality, we cannot ignore the wider canvas of social arrangements. Unfortunately, both hyper-individualistic and hyper-collectivistic conceptions are protected from critical reconstruction by the one-way mentality that is the focus of this book.

Cultural lag is also a factor in our stymied public discourse about racial justice. For example, building on both ragged individualism and the idea that people bear little to no moral responsibility for unintended harms, many white-identified Americans reason as follows: the institution of slavery and the worst of Jim Crow segregation ended long ago, so residual racial injustice is based on a lingering individual character defect called "racism." Many white Americans do not consciously *feel* racially intolerant anymore, and their introspective spotlight detects little racial animus in the Cartesian theater of their minds. So, they infer, racial injustice must be limited to a few bad apples who utter racial slurs, spew hatred, and blatantly discriminate. Those who commit hate crimes should be prosecuted, they agree, even as they may balk at actively desegregating their schools, democratizing single-family exclusive zoning laws, or otherwise disentangling themselves from large-scale social structures that differentially afflict or advantage racial groups (see Baca et al. 2019; Farmer 2004). In their view, structural-level racial injustice is water under the bridge, and advocates are stirring up trouble that would not otherwise be there.

James Baldwin wrote, "People who shut their eyes to reality simply invite their own destruction, and anyone who insists on remaining in a state of innocence long after that innocence is dead turns himself into a monster" (1985, 89). The easiest part of becoming what Baldwin called a monster is to cultivate only those beliefs and values that confirm preexisting desires and biases. The more complicated part is to construct a self-justifying consciousness, a lie (Glaude 2020, ch. 1), that allays doubts and minimizes the risk of an unsettling confrontation with others' life experiences. As Dewey observed in a 1916 essay titled "The Mind of Germany," this subtle work requires building up a system of beliefs that "effectively mask from view whatever would trouble action were it recognized" (MW 10:217). Today, once these self-justifying ideas are in place, they are fortified by social media platforms that rarely span boundaries. In this way, people avoid facing realities that might upend their pretenses, and they deny whatever they *need* to deny in order to maintain their familiar course. This is how people become ideally positioned to be, in Dewey's words, "profoundly moral even in their immoralities" (MW 10:217).

What is the route, if any, to moral recovery? Or as Baldwin pointedly asked in 1961 regarding racism in the United States, how might we achieve "the growing up of this dangerously adolescent country" (Baldwin 1985, 247–248)? Not by taking the low road of moral fundamentalism, which rarely rises above the level of self-justifying rationalization. Moreover, when we respond to moral fundamentalism with more of the same, we add fuel to the reactive wildfire that burns any communicative space between divergent life experiences and perspectives.

As these examples of cultural lag reveal, collective responses to widely shared problems are, in William James's words in *Pragmatism*, "out of plumb and out of key and out of 'whack'" (1907, 37). Crises such as pandemics, racial injustice, cycles of terror and retribution, gun violence, persistent poverty, warmongering, and the intensifying effects of climate change are catalyzing public recognition that we are indeed inviting our own destruction by continued failure to cooperate on paths forward. Public health, justice, security, peace, and liberty are social goals that must be worked for across intergroup conflicts (Sherif 1988). To the degree that we can grow beyond an inherited moral myopia and muster more public trust in pooled intelligence (see Chapter 2), guided by the disclosures of experimental inquiry, ideas and behaviors can get more in sync with the virtues required to improve troubled conditions.

What's the Matter with Fundamentalism?

Cultural lag is implicated in the uneasy relationship many people have with their inherited "moral fundamentalism." Confucius had something like moral fundamentalism in mind when he referred to "true goody-goodies" who are inflexibly principled in an obtuse way that stunts growth in relationships (Ames 2020). Or, in a popular quip attributed to Mark Twain, the moral fundamentalist is "good in the worst sense of the word."

This book explores six interrelated questions about moral fundamentalism: (1) What is it? (2) Is it really such a bad thing? (3) Is it good for motivating social action? (4) Can we educate beyond it? (5) Do many theorists inadvertently legitimize it? and (6) How might a pragmatic pluralism help?

Moral fundamentalism can be ostensively defined as the cluster of habits exhibited in "the pledge" and "toolkit" activities above. A more precise definition will emerge in this chapter. The term moral fundamentalism was used by Mark Johnson (2014) as a synonym for moral absolutism, and by Robert Baker (1998) as a broad-brush label for any principle-based moral universalism. But it is helpful to disentangle the term from just any avowed commitment to moral absolutism, for three reasons:

1. Philosophers who are moral absolutists generally condemn pledge-like traits, and their theoretical commitments do not necessarily imply fundamentalist behaviors.
2. A name is needed for the offending habits, whatever one's worldview. Rejecting self-certainty in theory does not imply rejecting it in practice.

3. Moral fundamentalist habits thrive today among groups whose outlook seems little troubled by the lack of a final mooring for their beliefs.

Although the word "fundamentalism" is contested (Peels 2022), it automatically suggests a helpful analogy to rigid religious dogmatism. For that reason, to better define *moral* fundamentalism, I first specify how its religious counterpart prevents us from achieving superordinate goals. Former US president Jimmy Carter observes that the rapid and deliberate spread of religious fundamentalism, especially among the world's worst-off, has made it much more difficult to work together toward solutions to problems (Carter 2005). Drawing from Dewey's analysis in *A Common Faith* (1934a, LW 9) and Kwame Anthony Appiah's (2018a) work on identity, I focus on three tendencies that operate as roadblocks to problem-solving. These general tendencies do not apply to all or only self-identified religious fundamentalists, and all are commonplace in the religious mainstream.

First, religious fundamentalism claims direct access to authoritative truths that are set up outside of experience and were once upon a time exclusively revealed to a credentialed few. These inerrant truths govern moral life, so complex forecasting of likely consequences of moral choices is deemed superfluous. Unfortunately, when we claim that cherished beliefs and values were dictated long ago from another world, we tend to quarantine them from public scrutiny and questioning. So we end up with walled-in faiths, each at least implicitly supposing that it has nothing to learn from—and much to oppose and fear in—other sects and creeds who have their own static truths that are immune from criticism.

This idea that some truths are final and hence beyond revision makes it especially difficult to create a culture of what Charles S. Peirce called "fallibilists." Peirce's term was born of his disgust with the doctrine of papal infallibility, defined by the First Vatican

Council in 1870. Dewey joined Peirce in embracing the idea that doubt can never be completely purged from assertions, that a "sceptical element" is involved in any claim that follows on the heels of inquiry. The opposite of fallibilism is dogmatism, the idea that some statements are inherently, self-evidently, and self-sufficiently true (LW 14:171–172).

Second, religious fundamentalism then drives a wedge between the saved and the damned in terms of exclusive commitments taken to be unchanging and hence closed to reform. This shrinks religious identity into nothing but a unified set of defining doctrinal beliefs divorced from interpretation of texts and traditions, evolving practices, and communal fellowship (Appiah 2018a, ch. 2). One narrow set of specifications is upheld as the admissions criterion into the identity group. Those who claim that existence has unauthorized traits are damned as outcasts. Brainwashing is inevitable. In moral education, the ardent dogmatist leader is contented only after a young member of the flock arrives safely at a foregone conclusion.

Third, religious fundamentalism speaks authoritatively about all-encompassing essences, including the essence of morality. By giving free rein to essentialist thinking, fundamentalists freeze creative *processes*, through which people may work things out together, into static *things*. When any group speaks for the universal essence of morality, they elicit what Appiah calls a Medusa-like reductive gaze that turns to stone what could otherwise be a collaborative project (cf. Appiah 2018a, 97). Fundamentalism turns moral artistry into moralizing.

To say the least, fealty to frozen essential doctrines is not a promising resource for public dialogue, restoration of trust, or reconciliation. When combined with nationalism, jingoism, xenophobia, racism, massive out-migration, and economic dislocation, it is a resource for reactionary oppression, rage, and fanaticism on all sides.

The way forward is not to categorically reject all religious life out of hand. Experiences of a religious sort may help people meet new situations in a way that expresses what is best in their whole characters, readjusting their attitudes and checking them from falling back on reactive habits. Dewey even argued that experimental intelligence attached to a democratic faith offers a direction for religious emotions that restores intellectual integrity, responsibility, and joy, without a trace of the fundamentalism that blocks the road of inquiry (Fesmire 2015, ch. 7). He wrote in *A Common Faith*: "Any activity pursued in behalf of an ideal end against obstacles and in spite of threats of personal loss because of conviction of its general and enduring value is religious in quality" (1934a, LW 9:27).

For many, the symbols and rites of religious communities have the potential to open new possibilities for growth, public dialogue, and humane solidarity, and even to help heal our estrangement from nature (cf. Auxier and Shook 2019). They also have a long track record of dividing and dulling. Nevertheless, religious attitudes will continue to be lived out through stories and practices of historic religions—it is moot to declare that they should or should not do so.

However, it is *not* moot to strive to uproot fundamentalist tenets wherever they take hold. I argue in this book that it is incumbent upon us to challenge *moral* fundamentalism. We must find our diverse ways beyond the hell we inflict in the name of righteous certainty. It is very well that we have living traditions and practices to guide and enrich experience. But misery clings to the idea that ancestral voices or institutional authorities have accessed self-sufficient truths that should be heeded without public investigation, critique, and reformation. It is a totalitarian idea. The fact that a community cherishes a code—say, the Ten Commandments or sharia law—does not on its own justify the conduct that flows from their interpretation of that code. Locally, nationally, and globally, in both religious and moral life we need the arbitration of wider outlooks to separate the recyclables from the refuse, empirically warranted propositions from the zombies, the well suited from the out of whack. The wider outlook I advance in this book is, in its outlines, the one Dewey proposed: a pluralistic philosophy that is at once experimental, democratic, and pragmatic in methodology.

Wicked Problems

In recent decades, the rejection of moral fundamentalism as a general outlook has entered design and policy studies in part through extensive research on "wicked problems," inspired by Horst Rittell and Melvin Webber (1973). The term is ubiquitous in the transdisciplinary field of environmental studies. Discussions about wicked problem are often clustered with research on "design thinking" (e.g., Whipps 2019), democratic decision-making and management (e.g., Norton 2015; cf. Sarkar and Minteer 2018), and proponents of deliberative democracy (e.g., Niemeyer (2013). Without canvassing the many senses of "wickedness" in the planning and policy literature, at least two necessary features can be identified that cut through the noise: when we say a problem is wicked, rather than benign and straightforward, we hypothesize *at least* that (1) there is no single definitive solution and (2) the way we formulate a problem, and the way we appraise success in dealing with it, are themselves at issue.

In Rittell and Webber's lingo, "benign" problems are those that can be tamed by objective answers that await computation. They may be easy, like solving a jigsaw puzzle, or they may be hard, like programming Einstein's equations for special and general relativity into GPS satellites and mobile receivers. Put the right pieces in the right places; get the math right. Only one way works, and conflicting values are secondary. We can typically solve benign problems without causing a lot of other problems.

In contrast, "wicked" problems are unique and heterogeneous. For example, if I buy an electric car to live more sustainably, the battery is linked to the environmental and geopolitical fallout of extracting rare earth metals. Given the cost of electric vehicles, I might do more life-saving good by purchasing a less expensive car, or eliminating it altogether, then donating the remainder to the Against Malaria Foundation to buy mosquito nets. Yet buying an electric vehicle supports the transition to a more sustainable transportation and energy infrastructure. My own values are colliding with each other, so what is the way forward? As US Supreme Court justice Stephen Breyer noted of intractable disagreements about how to construct criminal sentencing guidelines, there are "such good arguments all over the place pointing in opposite directions" (in Kahneman et al. 2021, 18).

To the degree that problems like these are wicked, the most rigorous and disciplined analyses and reasons can point in different directions, even in the absence of excessive "noise" or bias (cf. Kahneman et al. 2021). Moreover, every proposed solution causes other problems. Consequently, as Norton observes, when confronting wicked problems, "it is necessary to problematize problem formulation itself" (2015, 37), because in these situations even the most sincere and informed participants diagnose problems and interpret facts differently. Their diagnoses in turn affect choices and actions, turning problematic situations into moving targets.

From climate change and pandemics to racial injustice, most twenty-first-century social and environmental problems are wicked in the sense of having no straightforward and definitive formulation and solution. Unlike fixing a flat tire or solving a Rubik's Cube, these multifaceted problems are embedded in intricate and interrelated systems: for example, climate, ecosystems, healthcare, international relations, economic systems, food systems, legal systems, incarceration systems, governmental institutions, intergovernmental institutions, and educational institutions. These systems are implicated in social problems such as persistent poverty, gun violence, and substance abuse. They are also implicated in global anthropogenic problems like climate change, nonrenewable energy, habitat depletion, invasive species, nonpoint source pollution, antibiotic resistance, fungal blights, spillover of viruses, and an unsustainable food system.

The new normal of disruption in these networks is continuous with the older normal, such as the global wars, pandemics, and economic crises that marked Dewey's decades. In January 1919, toward the beginning of the 1918–1920 H1N1 flu pandemic that infected about a third of the world's population and killed fifty to one hundred million people (Johnson 2021), Dewey had to bail his son out of a San Francisco jail on the eve of their departure for Japan and China. Sabino had allegedly been caught without a mask (1919.01.21 [03858]: Alice Chipman Dewey to Evelyn, Jane, & Lucy Dewey). Some of the Dewey children caught the flu; all luckily recovered. A couple of months earlier, on November 11, 1918, the Armistice was announced ending the Great War. For the moment the Deweys breathed a sigh of relief, in part because this meant Sabino would not be drafted. The day before the Armistice, their daughter Jane wrote to her sister Lucy from San Francisco, "We still go around masked and all meetings are verboten so there is nothing doing and I may as well quit" (1918.11.10? [02269]: Jane Dewey to Lucy Dewey).

Most of these are familiar concerns, so despite shifting vocabularies it is unsurprising that there is nothing radically new in advocating for a shift away from culturally lagging moral narrowness, toward a more responsive and cooperative interdependence better suited to dealing with conflicting values within troubled systems. However, the adverse effects of staying the course have multiplied, not least because Earth's human population since the Armistice has increased from 1.8 billion to 8.1 billion, while annual greenhouse gas emissions have increased tenfold and the average human lifespan has doubled (Johnson 2021).

The recognition that most social problems are wicked entanglements gave birth to a recent cliché that "silver bullet" diagnoses and solutions must yield to pluralistic "buckshot" approaches. In Chapter 2 I follow the pluralist Isaiah Berlin's (1953) analysis of these respective approaches as hedgehoggish and foxlike. In climate ethics, perhaps there is no overridingly correct balance between a focus on vulnerable individuals (i.e., climate justice) and a focus on systems. In healthcare ethics, perhaps there is no unitary method or decision procedure that deals "correctly" with issues of risk and vulnerability. Triage decisions in a pandemic, for example, are based on contestable and incongruous values, as is the case when strict equity is traded off in favor of a utilitarian value of saving lives in the most efficient way possible. Favoring the latter may arguably save lives overall, but it leads to greater disparities in the healthcare system—say, for historically subordinated groups or those with disabilities. There appears to be no silver bullet approach that would inoculate caregivers from having to make "tragic, terrible, and haunting" decisions (Ne'eman 2020). Likewise, even granting Dewey's arguments against atomistic individualism, this does not dissolve the conflict between a negative conception of liberty rights, as freedom from interference (e.g., regarding mask and vaccine mandates), and a positive conception of our freedom to flourish.

Many widely shared problems have similar tensions. Observing this, Stephen Gardiner (2017) argues that wickedness is an unnecessarily vague concept. He is right that it is hopeless to circumscribe necessary and sufficient conditions to classify a subset of problems as essentially wicked. Gardiner might also have added that the concept can be misused to fatalistically defend the status quo: "it's too complicated, so don't waste your time worrying about it." Nevertheless, as Paul Thompson and Kyle Whyte (2012) argue, the concept of wickedness as the intractable dimension of many problems has proven useful in design and policy studies for highlighting that moral and sociopolitical life-as-usual is less straightforward than theorists have traditionally taken it to be.

Moral Fundamentalism

The literature on wicked problems offers a resource for anyone advancing non-absolutist approaches to ethics, education, politics, and policy. In light of this research, the term "moral fundamentalism" can be clarified as more than a synonym for absolutism. Moral fundamentalists may be more precisely defined, *minimally*, as those disposed to act as if they have access to (1) the exclusively right way to diagnose moral or political problems and (2) the single approvable practical solution to any particular problem. As with religious fundamentalism, this outlook is typically underwritten by a belief that one has privileged access to final authoritative truths. Nevertheless, as illustrated in the "pledge" activity, rejecting absolutism only in theory makes little morally apposite difference if this is not translated into conduct.

Is moral fundamentalism really such a bad thing? The preceding discussion clarifies several senses in which moral fundamentalism is a vice. A moral fundamentalist sees a moral, social, or political problem only as given, not taken. Consequently, the main problem is always presumed to be that others do not *get* the problem (Norton 2015), as though events carry their own meanings. Or the main problem is presumed to be the general failure of others to bow to our brilliant solutions. Never mind that these solutions are ideas that flow from values and purposes, and that have consequences which reshape subsequent facts to be interpreted. And never mind the unnoticed parts of the situation, aspects that are obfuscated by our way of casting the problem or occluded by our general principles. We too readily assume that, unlike *their* concerns, ours are value-neutral and free of interest-driven rationalizations and biases. *We* never doctor facts to predetermine results.

Moral fundamentalism is a drag on democratic social action. *This drag is to be expected when people feel backed into a corner, or when their social position limits opportunities.* But moral fundamentalism anywhere blocks communication and inquiry across differences. Whenever people suppose their reading of a problem is exhaustive, they autocratically predefine what is relevant and they covertly prejudge alternatives. They assume, as a matter of course, that others are stubbornly refusing to accept the interpretation that is staring right at them (1927, LW 2:38).

Philosophers earn their keep by striving to put questions well, and "as the saying truly goes, a question well put is half answered" (1933b, LW 8:201). Yet philosophers, no less than any other group, tend to disagree about the nature of the problems themselves. Neglect of cultural context makes communication even more difficult. Dewey observed: "A problem that appears to be the same problem when it is stated in general terms . . . has, in fact, different contents and directions according to the cultural situation in which it is bred and nourished" (Dewey 2012, 78; in Behuniak 2019a, 6). Nevertheless, he added, there are no "cultural block universes" that prevent intercultural communication across experiential differences (1950, LW 17:36; in Behuniak 2019a, 5). Moreover, uniform agreement about the nature of a problem is not a prerequisite to reducing its pinch (see Chapter 2), so long as our sharing of experiences does not devolve into reactive factions that stifle empathy (cf. Whipps 2019). The closer we are to each other in the specific way we experience a problem, the closer we are to agreeing. In Dewey's words, "our disagreements as to conclusions are trivial compared with our disagreement as to problems. To see the problem another sees, in the same perspective and at the same angle—that amounts to something. . . . To experience the same problem another feels—that perhaps is agreement" (MW 3:99).

When we disagree about problems, it is one thing to reflectively conclude that others are willfully refusing to face conditions (cf. Glaude 2020). It is quite another thing to start with the default assumption that we alone are taking the wide view. Despite these habits—not *because* of them—moral fundamentalists have historically done many good things through their dealings with opposing fundamentalisms. But what *else* have they done that might *in future* be minimized? Taking the longer view of these habits in action, what happens to opportunities for reflexively learning our way toward a healthier, more just, and more sustainable future across the dynamic spectrum of values, beliefs, and concerns?

Philosophy's Public Role: Creating a Culture of Inquiry

Is moral fundamentalism good for motivating social action? Does activism require and benefit from it? In order to restructure conditions and redress wrongs, must people harden their hearts and minds against the clamor of contradictory theories, both speaking and acting as if they are governed by final truths? If so, then perhaps a kind of incorrigibility is a virtue of public philosophizing.

To many intellectuals, the international resurgence of gaslighting demagogues and self-seeking cronyism is incontrovertible proof that we can *ultimately* expect very little of the public. It is assumed by some that the public switch is permanently set to dim, so it is up to us intellectuals to take up the civilizing burden of enlightenment. If this requires us to default to moral fundamentalism, then so be it.

Rather, we got here by expecting *too little* of the public. As explored in Chapter 3, we have long been running self-verifying social and educational experiments in low expectations. Electing or hiring competent executives who are accustomed to complex cognition can help, but it cannot solve the deepest problem of all: a failure to create a cultural context in which we may become, in Glaude's words, "the kind of people that a democracy requires" (personal communication).

Dewey argued in *Individualism, Old and New* (1930a) that as industrial civilization developed, philosophers and other intellectuals were among the many individuals who lost any coherent social function. By facing problems and guiding inquiry into them, intellectuals recover a public function. They can, and often do, help both experts and the public to engage problems in a way that aids deliberation and learning so that change is directed more intelligently and less haphazardly than it otherwise might be (see Kitcher 2019 and 2012). "Better it is for philosophy to err in active participation in the living struggles and issues of its own age and times," Dewey wrote, "than to maintain an immune monastic impeccability, without relevancy and bearing in the generating ideas of its contemporary present" (1908a, MW 4:142).

What sort of public participation did Dewey prescribe for philosophy? Did he expect too much of the public? Too little? Michael Sandel has observed that our philosophy of the public is implicated in our public philosophizing. It determines aims and shapes public discourse (1998). Journalist Walter Lippmann, whose aristocratic philosophy of the public Dewey famously critiqued in *The Public and Its Problems* (1927), wrote in *The Public Philosophy*:

> It is a practical rule that the relation is very close between our capacity to act at all and our conviction that the action we are taking is right. This does not mean, of course, that the action is necessarily right. *What is necessary to continuous action is that it shall be believed to be right. Without that belief, most men will not have the energy and will to persevere in the action.* Political ideas acquire operative force in human affairs when, as we have seen, they acquire legitimacy, when they have the title of being right which binds men's consciousness. Then they possess, as Confucian doctrine has it, 'the mandate of heaven'" (Lippmann 1955, 135).

In 1932, theologian Reinhold Niebuhr echoed Lippmann in an implicit criticism of Dewey. He argued,

Contending factions in a social struggle require morale; and morale is created by the right dogmas, symbols and emotionally potent oversimplifications. These are at least as necessary as the scientific spirit of tentativity. . . . No class of industrial workers will ever win freedom from the dominant classes if they give themselves completely to the "experimental techniques" of the modern educators. (Niebuhr 1932, xv)

In his opposing philosophy of the public, Dewey held that the appropriate vocation of public intellectuals is *not* the construction of dogmas for "the people" to follow, as though ready-made truths and an aura of absolute assuredness must replace experimental social inquiry in a pinch (cf. McAfee 2019). Dewey was not being overly idealistic here, and he was certainly not championing indecision. He built his theory of inquiry around the psychological insight that doubt disrupts action and spurs the search for a resolute way forward (cf. Fesmire 2003, ch. 2). Decisive action implies that inquiry on that subject is settled for the time being, but it does not imply dogmatic resistance to revision. Dewey often observed that in stressful times people incline impatiently toward dogmatism. "It is very difficult to satisfy people with an experimental liberalism in times of unrest," he wrote in a letter during the Great Depression. "They get in a hurry to find some harbor where they can be absolutely secure" (1935.04.24 [07751]: Dewey to George Catlin). But practical life does not offer unshakable security, only the fleeting feeling of it, which demagogues are happy to provide. We are left to "search for as much security as is humanly possible" (1929, LW 4:27).

People commonly assume, with Lippmann, that they can only express moral confidence, or rally people to just causes, through pantomimes of absolute certainty. I argue in Chapter 2 that this is mistaken and shortsighted, at least when coupled with pledge-like fundamentalist habits that conceal what James described as the "contradictory array of opinions" for which "objective evidence and absolute certitude" have been claimed (1979, 23).

Moral communication invariably includes expressions of confidence, and these will be expressed on a continuum. There are of course cases—contested, to be sure—in which decisive judgment minimizes or excludes a provisional tone. This may be due to a personal or social need to amplify strong moral approval or disapproval (cf. Lekan 2022), or it may be more a matter of rhetorical or cultural style than a rush to judgment. I am not taking a position in this book on whether, or under what conditions, such rhetoric might be justified, though this deserves more philosophical attention. I *am* arguing that absolutistic rhetoric has been normalized to ill effect, that it is implicated in moral fundamentalist behaviors that are obstacles for personal and political life, and (I will argue in the next section) that traditional theorizing has reinforced the single-right-way mentality.

Slavery and genocide are as wrong for a pragmatic pluralist as for a deontologist, though they are multifaceted wrongs (see Chapter 5). *Logically* speaking, strong moral judgments are as subject to continuous reframing as heliocentric cosmology or evolutionary biology. Dewey favored this analogy, arguing that people need immutable forms in ethics and politics to the same degree that Copernicus needed an immobile Earth or Darwin needed changeless species. *Moral confidence is not improved by impervious dogmas.* The classic quest for fixity is ill-suited to the moving and evolving world we actually inhabit (see 1929, LW 4:21–39).

In contrast with Lippmann, Niebuhr, and many twentieth- and twenty-first-century intellectuals who have normalized displays of moral certainty in order to motivate social action, Dewey did not think an enlighten-the-masses outlook reveals us at our philosophic or moral best (see 1927, LW 2; cf. Rogers 2008). As with doctrinaire rigidity in religion, he rejected as totalitarian the idea that "the mass of human beings cannot be trusted to judge and to believe aright in moral matters; that if they are permitted to exercise freedom of mind their policies and decisions will be so swayed by personal and class interests that the final outcome will be division, conflict, and disintegration" (1942, LW 15:177). In a letter to Chinese philosopher Hu Shih in the 1930s, Dewey summed up his position that policies must be determined through democratic action, not by elite rule: "for only by means of 'government by the people' can government *for* the people be made secure" (1939.10.27 [06907]: Dewey to Hu Shih).

Lippmann-esque critics of participatory democracy may retort that people happily weigh in on matters concerning which they are incompetent, so they need to be told what to think. Iterations of this old argument provoked Dewey's ire. Instead of lowering the bar on what we should expect from individual judgment, public incompetence clarifies the frustratingly uphill educational struggle to extend conditions for a democratic society that manifests a "method of consultation, persuasion, negotiation, communication, cooperative intelligence" (1939a, LW 13:187). If we measure success by the standard of a perfected future outcome—an ideally functioning democratic public that does not drift or backslide—our labors will appear Sisyphean. Dewey argued that this perfectionist standard misconceives the democratic ideal. Lippmann was correct that such an ideal public is a phantom. What he missed, Dewey insisted, is that pursuit and renewal of the democratic ideal is a labor that can grow, deepen, and expand inexhaustibly *in its present significance* if kept alive by experimentation that renounces pandering and debilitatingly low expectations (see 1922b, MW 14:144–145).

This "Deweyan" alternative is characterized by a hope that is, in pragmatist Eddie Glaude Jr.'s paraphrasing of W. E. B. Du Bois on American racial injustice, "not hopeless, but a bit unhopeful" (in Gilpin 2020). Pragmatist ethics and politics do not cradle Pollyanna optimism about the public. Democracy lives, and is undermined, through ideas, choices, and actions. Despite the inevitability of cognitive and motivational biases, reports of democracy's death are exaggerated, as are prognostications of its unavoidable ascendancy. Democratic hope is born of disappointment and expects more. It is not a call for lukewarm hesitancy, nor is it a timid providential faith that things will turn out for the best. It is a resilient and courageous disposition, in Christopher Lasch's words, "to see things through even when they don't" (in Westbrook 2005, 17).

Dewey made a point of the fact that no problems—such as willful ignorance (see Williams 2021), incompetence, gullibility, viral pseudoreasoning, an ideologically segregated infosphere, or susceptibility to political strongmen (Rorty 1999, 90)—are so bad that we cannot make them worse through our ways of dealing with them. Like Addams and George Herbert Mead, Dewey warned against a double standard when it comes to justifications for inflaming people to value moral and political ends irrespective of the results of the social means we use to achieve them (1939b, LW 13:229). He added in an essay on free societies during the Second World War: "Impatience has always made men want to take short cuts to attain ends they are persuaded are good" (1942, LW 15:177). When citizens of a society that is politically democratic divorce ends from means, they often fail to see that democratic ends have been most reliably secured cooperatively through democratic methods such as open inquiry, communication, discovery, and honest debate. "If there is one conclusion to which human experience unmistakably points," Dewey repeated in *Freedom and Culture*, "it is that democratic ends demand democratic methods for their realization" (1939a, LW 13:187). As with religious fundamentalism, totalitarian ends are secured through totalitarian methods such as uniform adherence to rigid and final doctrines, obedience to elite superiors, authoritarian dogmatizing, suppression of variability, and indoctrination of the young. Totalitarian methods of restricting free inquiry, intelligent participation, and open expression do not lead to democratic ends of extending these, no matter how good the ends (e.g., equality, freedom, security) are in abstraction. When people fail to "live up to their own professed ideals in the methods employed for achieving their ends," they fail morally and politically (179). Most of us do this more than we should, but the moral fundamentalist seeks to justify and reinforce it.

Moral maturation is a process of ongoing growth in which we evaluate and reconstruct our prior habits in response to circumstances, rather than simply parroting or reactively dismissing them. We are unavoidably entangled in relationships, values, and practices. The moral challenge—and *eo ipso* the educational challenge, for Dewey—is to engage these relationships more perceptively and responsively (cf. Fesmire 2003). "The choice," Dewey urged in *Human Nature and Conduct*, "is not between a moral authority outside custom and one within it. It is between adopting more or less intelligent and significant customs" (1922b, MW 14:58). To the degree that we disclose, evaluate, criticize, and redirect sedimented beliefs, values, outlooks, practices, and social structures, we can own them more imaginatively in the service of "growth of conduct in meaning" (1922b, MW 14:194). This is best brought about through nonreactive inquiry that sympathetically faces and intelligently responds to realities. Democratic discourse serves moral imagination by operating as a public check on exclusivity and knee-jerk partiality. In turn, to whatever degree habits own us mechanically, as in pledge-like fundamentalism and cultural lag, democratic discourse is a farce because choice in that case is indistinguishable from mere impulsion.

Dewey argued that the only reliable answer to failures of democracy is to reorganize, especially in education, to expect *more* of public intelligence, not less (see 1927, LW 2; cf. 1935, LW 11:39). But the ills of democracy are not cured by more democracy *of the same sort*, or by education that merely caters to the industrial economy (see Chapter 3). The prevailing formal mechanisms of political democracies, far from sacrosanct, are a mishmash of hypotheses and experiments that eventually coagulated. The erosion of democratic norms in the United States that erupted into an assault on the Capitol on January 6, 2021, along with further fragmentation into moral fundamentalist Twitterverses, is a reminder that democratic mechanisms are replaceable with forms that function far *less* democratically.

Dewey's democratic faith was bound up in the historical fact that the reverse also holds: because the political machinery of democracy is transitory, we can revise it with forms and procedures that enable more sensitive, expansive, and responsible communication across disparate groups (1927, LW 2:325–328). Philosophy's role in democratic life, in Dewey's view, is not to weave such new political machinery out of whole cloth, but to rigorously criticize the cultural and day-to-day conditions that either obstruct or foster critical democratic communication, while lending the same aid to grassroot advocates, nongovernmental organizations, and proxies struggling to remake democratic forms that are progressively responsive to public needs.

One way in which public intellectuals can help to regenerate the forms taken by democratic institutions is to spotlight and delegitimize speech in which the evaluative conquest matters more than improving conditions. Exorcise instead of exercising such speech. In public disputes, competing fundamentalist camps restrict the sympathies of in-groups to a single channel. This channel may be—and often is—*progressive* in one dimension of a problem, but typically at the cost of being *regressive* with respect to concerns that are off-the-radar of that group or political unit's idealizations. Better to set aside the notion that we can, even in principle, occupy a perfected standpoint (see Chapter 4). More can usually be done to minimize the way in which unconsulted concerns are illegitimately overlooked or relegated as moral externalities (see Thompson 2016).

Incorrigibility can shut down the communication that is needed to elicit thoughtful differences and give an appreciative hearing. People may not *wish* to freeze out others with a stake in the process, or presume them from the outset to be dull or irrelevant. But when this occurs, it increases the likelihood of failure to coordinate solutions in a way that inclusively develops individual capacities and durably modifies problematic conditions (see 1920, MW 12:192–193). This arguably occurred, for example, with the World Health Organization's and US surgeon general's discouragement of mask-wearing at the outset of the coronavirus pandemic in spring 2020. They announced that it was futile, when their more immediate practical goal was to deal with a medical supply chain crisis (Leonhardt 2021). When they later backtracked, it contributed to confusion and defiance.

In their single vision, moral fundamentalist clans exclude modest attempts to discover shared toeholds to set and achieve social goals. For example, in support of a pragmatic approach to the global food movement, Thompson observes how readily people violate the philosophical principle of charity: "Advocates of both biotechnology *and* organic systems too often compare the most advanced and optimistic interpretation of their favored approach to the least successful applications of the alternative" (2015, 252). The result, as Raymond Boisvert and Lisa Heldke have observed, has been dichotomized either/or thinking, attended by puritanical tendencies to ignore context, oversimplify, and dogmatize (2016). Such moral fundamentalism in the food movement is further explored through case studies in Chapters 2-3.

Wherever fundamentalist habits go unchallenged, they dig a deep channel for partialities and inclinations. This channel offers some security from wavering irresolution, and it obliges Lippmann by conferring the "mandate of heaven." But this mandate is gratuitous and profligate.

Lippmann did not limit himself to observing, with Dewey, that we require a Jamesian faith that affords us confidence to make personal contributions even when doubt remains plausible. He shortsightedly concluded that, in public, intellectuals should pretend that their enlightened perspective has a monopoly on truth—lest, in the haunting words of Yeats's "The Second Coming" (1920), "Things fall apart; the center cannot hold; / Mere anarchy is loosed upon the world." Dewey, in contrast, urged practical attention to the *overall* effects of dogmatizing: "Imposition of fixed principles may have temporary appeal and may give temporary relief. In the long run—and perhaps not so very long—it marks the road to collision and explosion" (LW 17:479). The sentiment of psychological certainty is purchased at a steep cost. In public and in private, indulging the quest for an invulnerable moral harbor encourages parochial antagonism toward excluded standpoints, closure to being surprised by the complexity of many situations and systems, neglect of the context in which decisions are made, obtuseness about one's own truncated framework, and a related general indifference to public processes and adaptive policies.

Beyond One-Way Ethics

Moral philosophers routinely reject any fundamentalism, but in the next breath they may speak for the essence of morality and thereby freeze "it" into a completed object instead of an imaginative and collaborative project. This props up moral fundamentalism by legitimizing its one-way feature, as a byproduct of monistic appeal to a supreme moral principle (e.g., Gewirth 1978), value, standard, law, concept, or ideal that foreshortens whatever is morally relevant in a situation. Needless to say, philosophers who identify themselves as monists reject the arrogance of popular fundamentalist habits that are antithetical to a philosophical methodology which has long championed ideals of doubt, humility, and open inquiry. And most contemporary monistic moral philosophers insist, against subjectivists and most religious fundamentalists, that we can and should make substantive determinations about what is good and bad, right and wrong, virtuous and vicious without falling back on the deus ex machina of infallible supernatural revelation.

But monistic moral theorists, alongside their counterparts in politics and policy, inadvertently legitimize moral fundamentalism's dogma that there is a unified conceptual home range that is adequate to all moral and/or political action. Or at least they give tacit consent to this view in their rhetoric. I explore and defend the hypothesis that, by assuming this often-hidden major premise, monistic theorists shore up the basis of a narrowing outlook that is alien to their own philosophic spirit, and they simultaneously set the stage for their antinomian antithesis. I argue, further, that classic traditions could gain traction and resilience by rejecting this unnecessary and unhelpfully thin reductive premise.

Moral fundamentalism cannot logically stand without its monistic premise. Or to approach it the other way, only a monist could be a logically consistent moral fundamentalist. This is because moral fundamentalism depends on the central dogma that some people have access to the right, ideal, or supreme way to diagnose moral problems. Some self-identified pluralists (pragmatists, cosmopolitans, deliberative democrats, etc.) may at times behave as moral fundamentalists, but they do so at the cost of metaethical coherence (cf. Coeckelbergh 2021).

The fact that ethical monism (as a highly articulated philosophical position) and moral fundamentalism (as a popular cluster of vicious habits) rely on a shared premise does not on its own negate that premise. A critic of pluralism might plausibly object that it is the right premise in the wrong hands, a golden truth turned to cyanide. Should we similarly reject Darwinian biology because it was used to prop up Social Darwinism's rationalizing of "natural" inequalities in industrial capitalism? The sociopolitical theory would indeed fall without the biological theory, but it would be a capricious epistemology that pointed to misuse of a theory as the final test of that theory's warrant. Analogously, the fact that moral fundamentalism rests on monism for its understanding of moral action does not *on its own* imply that pluralism is better justified.

Monists tend to uncritically suppose that moral experience forces a dilemma between universalism and "anything goes" relativism. In a variation on this impasse, the moral fundamentalist's mirror image is the reactionary nihilist. Dyads like this one earn their keep—if they do—as analytical and pedagogical tools. But binaries become dysfunctional dualisms when they are promulgated as forced options rather than as tools of analysis. When we see situations as intricate wholes, most circumstances do not require us to choose between a precise latitude and longitude of moral action, on one hand, or knee-jerk reactivity and whimsicality, on the other. Approaching the distinction as a forced option, monists almost invariably interpret pluralists as relativistic drifters. For confirmation, monists can point to self-described pluralists who offer thin rationales that are barely distinguishable from extreme moral relativists and skeptics. As an unfortunate result, Johnson observes, monists may prejudge Dewey's far more sophisticated metaethics and moral psychology (see Chapters 4 and 5). "Within this kind of absolutist framework, Dewey's account of moral deliberation will seem impossibly relativist and lacking in the very moral guidance we so desperately need" (2019, 190).

In that case, moral fundamentalism may be overzealous, but is that just an opportunity cost of upholding the moral life? It is not necessarily an indictment of monism's single-right-way mentality to observe that it gives rise to excesses that must be counteracted. Better to temper excesses than to give up on serious ethical deliberation altogether, monists may reply. If the one-way mentality were an unavoidable side effect of rejecting chaos, pragmatists like Dewey would be forced to side with monists. Humans are embodied organisms driven primarily by propulsive habits and impulsive desires, and this fact underscores how important it is to cultivate ethical reflection (see 1922b, MW 14:153). Apologias for a post-ethics world fail to comprehend the situation. However, actual moral experience does not force a choice between the absolute and the arbitrary (cf. Elgin 1997). The notion that we face this forced dilemma is a zombie idea, and I devote considerable attention to it in the pages ahead.

To set the scene, it may help at this point to introduce Dewey's philosophical modus operandi as the approach taken in this book. Dewey-inspired pragmatists rarely side with either contender in the conceptual prize fights that define "the problems of philosophy." They typically find that neither alternative is viable, as Dewey observed in "The Influence of Darwinism on Philosophy" (1909):

> The conviction persists—though history shows it to be a hallucination—that all the questions that the human mind has asked are questions that can be answered in terms of the alternatives that the questions themselves present. But in fact intellectual progress usually occurs through sheer abandonment of questions together with both of the alternatives they assume— an abandonment that results from their decreasing vitality and a change of urgent interest. We do not solve them: we get over them. (MW 4:14)

Instead of casting their lot with ethical absolutists or relativists, pragmatists reject both of the principal alternatives on offer: moral monism versus moral skepticism. By implication, as Philip Kitcher observes, pragmatists also reject a key assertion made by moral skeptics and subjectivists, namely that the futility of the reductive monistic quest spells the end of the ethical project (Kitcher 2014). Both monists and their nemeses tend to share a one-or-none mentality, yet ethics best serves moral life when we see beyond the disjunction that drives their debate.

Moral theory gets its social value as a form of generalized philosophical criticism by enlarging perceptions and awakening us to the world. Among the greatest obstacles to cultivating such perceptiveness are moral fundamentalism and its sidekick inversions: nihilism and extreme subjectivism. Theorists should avoid perpetuating these obstacles. The aim of ethics is to thoughtfully mediate objective difficulties, and no ethicist knowingly aims merely to banish doubt by resolving conundrums in the psyche. Ethicists best achieve their practical goal when they help us paddle, with our moral convictions, against the swift psychological current that propels people to automatically reject any position but their own. By sheltering our convictions from the questioning and revision that builds resilience, fundamentalism leaves them insecure. Confidence then veers into overconfidence. Moral commitments are better guides to practical life when they honestly embrace and reflect the dynamic, aleatory world of human experience.

Rejecting the one-way mentality does not pull the rug from beneath strong normative prescriptions. As shown in the following chapters, it is sensible and non-arbitrary to speak of right and wrong, good and bad, and virtuous and vicious ways to meet situations. In a theological parallel, Paul Tillich in *The Dynamics of Faith* (1957) understood that objects of "ultimate concern" are revisable and subject to ongoing questioning and doubt. He was far from implying that commitments are thereby tepid, hesitant, or wavering. Some of these commitments will doubtless be more central and tightly held than others. But *starting* with the notion that there is a theoretically correct way forward, one that determines the ideally right way to think or act (generally or in principle), only narrows practical deliberation about the means by which we can most intelligently meet the conditions we face.

Overview

This book argues for a pragmatic and pluralistic approach to ethics, education, politics, and policy. This approach checks moral fundamentalist habits that prevent us from collectively achieving superordinate goals. We especially need to move beyond moral fundamentalism when dealing with situations in which intergroup problem definition is itself among the key problems, as is true of most social and environmental issues. I criticize the single-right-way mentality shared by moral fundamentalists and traditional ethical monists, without losing sight of the need for a methodology to judge when people are being preposterous. I argue that the monistic premise that underlies moral fundamentalism is empirically unwarranted and morally constrictive, and there is little to be said in favor of the grand philosophical quest for a unifying principle that cannot be accommodated by reconstructing monistic insights within a wider pluralistic outlook. Although I have no pretense of presenting a comprehensive picture of Dewey's ethics, for which see Gregory Pappas's *John Dewey's Ethics* (2008), I build on Dewey to explain and illustrate how pragmatic pluralism can serve, at minimum, as a democratizing complement to mainstream theorizing.

A reader who renders the old Scottish verdict "not proven" in the case I present *against* traditional ethical monism can independently assess the case I make *for* a pragmatic approach to decision-making and a pluralistic standpoint on ethics in general. Some readers may favor more circumscribed forms of pragmatism and pluralism than the strong versions I am advancing (see Chapter 4). Pragmatism is *at least* a strategic method for navigating problems in complex systems (e.g., Norton 2015; Light 2017), and a pluralistic outlook is minimally an important virtue of moral and political inquiry in nominally democratic societies. Some readers may favor a more limited pragmatism, pluralism, or fallibilism that is compatible with their search for an ultimately unifying moral image. Nevertheless, I argue that setting the monistic starting premise aside—*at least* strategically to create a space for inquiry across conflicting values—places ethical and sociopolitical theory and practice on a footing that compensates for complicity in moral fundamentalist behaviors, regardless of which value theories capture our imaginations.

Chapter 2, "A Democratic Approach to Social Learning and Conflicting Values: Cases in Environmental Pragmatism," differentiates and advances a general pragmatist approach to ethics, taking environmental problems as test cases. The heart of the chapter is a study of pragmatic pluralism as a perspective on climate ethics, inspired in part by philosopher Andrew Light's work on climate diplomacy and by Bryan Norton's environmental pragmatism. After explaining the ends-means continuum to clarify what makes an approach "pragmatic," I turn to Isaiah Berlin's "The Hedgehog and the Fox" (1953) for metaphors to understand Dewey's democratic approach to social learning amid conflicting values. In opposition to technocratic rule in the vein of Walter Lippmann's *The Phantom Public* (1925), Dewey consistently warned against overreliance on autocratic, expert-driven decisions, and *where practicable* he advocated widening participatory processes that enlist communities in learning. His aim was to foster a "plann*ing* society" (as opposed to a "plann*ed* society") that is controlled internally by consulting stakeholders, uncovering troubles, and organizing the expertise to deal with those troubles.

Dealing effectively with contemporary entanglements requires a transformation of culturally lagging habits and institutionalized practices. Such a transformation appears a distant, and receding, hope to many who are dismayed by the resurgence of a populist misology in which thought, inquiry, and science are treated as an effete waste of time. Dewey did not have to be saved from excessive optimism regarding democratic processes. His later writings reveal a chastened philosopher who nevertheless doggedly advocated going as far as possible to educate cultures of shared inquiry. Building on Dewey, I argue that it is not a mere pipe dream to still believe we can democratically secure better lives (LW 5:269), especially by organizing formal education so that students gain direct aesthetic fulfillment even as they cultivate competent, forward-looking, open-ended, collaborative, and progressively specialized intelligence. Unfortunately, the increasingly dominant industrial model of education conceives service to the private sector as the overriding goal. It channels energies toward narrow workforce training. This approach takes the educative capacity of experience, our best hope for growing beyond fundamentalism, and uses it to reinscribe conventional practices. Chapter 3, "Educating for Democracy," explains, updates, and illustrates Dewey's alternative, which was to engage occupational callings in a way that contributes to a more humane culture.

Chapter 4, "Pragmatic Pluralism in Ethical and Sociopolitical Theory," begins by putting pragmatism in conversation with contemporary critics of "ideal theories," including critiques of John Rawls's idealized world of rational agents perfectly compliant with the demands of justice. I draw from nonideal theorists to argue that comparison to the ideal is valuable as a heuristic, but it is the wrong *starting point* for future ethical and sociopolitical theorizing (cf. Pappas 2019). A pragmatic outlook, in contrast, can elicit generative possibilities that are concealed by overly formal ideal theories, especially monistic ones. I argue in this chapter that traditional moral theorizing's zeal for unification standardizes moral life in a way that is poorly suited to navigating indeterminate systems. The monistic quest for a completely enlightened standpoint, secured in advance from the provocations and intractable tensions of particular contexts, increases cultural lag.

Chapter 5, "Dewey's Independent Factors in Moral Action," builds on Dewey's ethical naturalism to illustrate the way a deep pragmatic pluralism can accommodate traditional monistic insights in moral theory while delegitimizing moral fundamentalism's single vision. Drawing on archival and published sources from 1926 to 1932, this is the culminating theoretical chapter, programmatic though it is. Specialists in ethical theory may wish to turn here first, after reviewing the technical distinctions below. A primary focus is "Three Independent Factors in Morals," Dewey's address (1930b) before the French Philosophical Society in Paris. Exploring the pluralistic hypothesis that problematic moral situations are heterogeneous in their origins and operations, Dewey analyzed good, duty, and virtue as distinct moral categories that express different experiential origins. He traced these traditional abstract moral categories back to their generative experiential roots. An unpublished typescript clarifies his hypothesis:

> The three things I regard as variables are first the facts that give rise to the concept of the good and bad; secondly, those that give rise to the concept of right and wrong; thirdly, those that give rise to the conception of the virtuous and vicious. . . . What I am concerned to point out [is] that the concrete conflict is not just among these concepts, but in the elements of the actual moral situation that, when they are abstracted and generalized, give rise to these conceptions. (Dewey, undated ms, 2)

None of these three categories includes all that is morally relevant in the rest. For example, the fact that you are within your rights to do something does not on its own imply that it would be a good thing to do. Nor would it necessarily speak well of your character for you to do it. I suggest that a vital role for contemporary theorizing is to lay bare and analyze basic conflicts and frictions like these that constantly underlie moral action. We should foster a range of idioms, emphases, and identities which, while accommodating monistic insights, inform decision-making by (1) opening inclusive communication across diverse elements of moral and political life, (2) placing these elements in a wider context in which norms gain traction amid the discordance and friction of uneasy non-ideal conditions, and (3) expanding prospects for social inquiry and convergence on policy and action.

The conclusion recaps the book's main line of argument and offers recommendations for future ethical and political theorizing. Moral fundamentalist habits, and the reductive monistic assumption that mostly unintentionally exercises and reinforces them, are obstacles to cultivating virtues of inquiry that are suited to dealing with the predicaments that are rapidly transforming our planet. If philosophers and other public intellectuals are to speak to complex problems in a way that aids public intelligence, a critical focus on Dewey's pragmatic pluralism would be beneficial.

Some Technical Distinctions

A few technical distinctions upfront may help to clarify pragmatic pluralism for specialists in pragmatism or ethics. Other readers may safely turn the page without losing the main line of argument.

Pragmatism is herein treated primarily as a method of intelligent inquiry that guides action through experimental attention to ends and means (Chapter 2). It does not imply a universal, cover-all ethical theory, nor did the classical originators of the pragmatist tradition seek such a thing. Pragmatism does not logically imply pluralism, which emphasizes that value conflicts can arise from relative incommensurability (Chapters 4 and 5). Although this book takes steps toward a pragmatic pluralism, I agree with Scott Aikin and Robert Talisse that one can, in their words, "fully embrace" pluralism and not be a pragmatist. In "Why Pragmatists Cannot Be Pluralists" (Talisse and Aikin 2005), and more recently in their revised exposition Pragmatism, Pluralism, and the Nature of Philosophy (Aikin and Talisse 2017), they observe that one may, moreover, be a methodological pragmatist and not a pluralist.

Aikin and Talisse go on to assert, less persuasively, that pragmatists should reject pluralism because pluralists contend that

> the very fabric of value guarantees irremediable conflicts among goods. . . . Pluralism holds that some value conflicts are intrinsically beyond the power of inquiry to ameliorate. In contrast, pragmatism involves the commitment, or at least the *hope*, that ongoing inquiry, clarification, and experimentation can ameliorate all legitimate conflicts. . . . At the very least, pragmatists should regard pluralism as *premature*. (Aikin and Talisse 2017, 2)

I share Aikin and Talisse's general view that we should, to adapt a line from Peirce, reject the irremediable as a starting hypothesis. We cannot know prior to collaborative inquiry and action whether a problem can be ameliorated, so antecedently staking out a position of inevitable failure amounts to a self-fulfilling prophecy. If preordained failure were essential to pluralism, then pragmatists should indeed "regard pluralism as premature." However, as I illustrate throughout this book, relative incommensurability among conflicting values—which is an empirical matter, logically independent of our preferred methodologies— does not imply any advance guarantee of a situation's hopelessness. Finally, although I agree with Aikin and Talisse that social inquiry and hope are entwined, the pragmatic point is to find out how far inquiry and action may take us. There is no guarantee that intelligent inquiry and action will ameliorate a problem. In Sidney Hook's words, it increases the odds: "But that increase, however slight, might make all the difference in the world" (1925/ 1929, LW 1:xxiii).

In contrast to the intuitionist G. E. Moore's assertion in *Principia Ethica* (1929) that any candidate for a moral fact would have to involve a simple nonnatural property, I adopt Dewey's naturalistic and pragmatic view that there is no separate realm that marks off moral issues from those that are practical or factual. Hilary Putnam explains that Dewey developed

> a naturalistic picture of the way in which intelligence can be applied to ethical problems, and especially to social problems. For Dewey, . . . ethical problems are simply a subset of our practical problems, in the ancient sense of "practical"—problems of how to live—and it can be a fact that a certain course of action or a certain form of life solves, or better resolves, what Dewey called a problematic situation. (Putnam 2011, 52)

To say "the act ought to be done" differs only verbally from saying "this act will meet the situation" (EW 3:108–109). The statement

"You ought not to embezzle the money" is not essentially different from "You ought not to plant tomatoes outdoors in the Virginia winter." It is a truism in ethics that we cannot simply deduce how we ought to behave as an implication of factual descriptions, but we do constantly make inferences of a more inductive sort about how we should live. Moral judgments are distinct from scientific ones due to their concern with better and worse conduct, but logically speaking, both are provisional rather than final. In moral judgments we test practical inferences as hypotheses that are drawn from the available evidence, and we judge these inferences to be warranted or unwarranted by the consequences of acting on them (cf. 1938a, LW 12:424). In this respect, not only can one intelligently infer an "ought" from an "is," but one cannot responsibly avoid doing so.

Another truism in ethics is that people prize many things that are not, upon reflection, praiseworthy. In *Theory of Valuation*, Dewey logically distinguished the prized and praiseworthy, valued and valuable, desired and desirable. In his ethics, the former word in each pair highlights an impulsive or habituated motive, while the latter is a term of reflective judgment. Reflective value judgments are like maps that we have journeyed with and assessed. They have, in Dewey's words, "existential import" (1938a, LW 12:123), which means that we reshape moral situations for better or worse when we act on these judgments. Dewey observed that reflective value judgments are most reliable when they develop through the guidance and direction of colloquy with others, and through the use of moral principles and ideals, instead of in detachment and isolation. There are limitations of even the most refined moral understanding, so criticism is always necessary. Whether people are planting tomatoes or making reproductive choices, the test is in the reliability of their methods, not in whether they started with the right abstractions.

This book engages each of the four traditional categories of philosophical ethics: descriptive ethics (descriptions of moral thinking and behavior), metaethics (analysis of the nature of ethics through its most basic concepts), normative ethics (formulation and justification of moral values), and applied ethics (application of these norms to specific cases and areas of activity). These categories are often drawn too sharply, separating theory from practice and normative prescriptions from descriptive facts. But taking these categories as a practical division of labor, this book

- Infers that a strongly pluralistic and naturalistic standpoint is empirically warranted by the entanglements of actual moral experience. I argue that this metaethical standpoint accommodates the practical insights of traditional monistic theories.

- Reveals that Dewey was not a straightforward consequentialist. Pragmatism's methodological focus on the ends-means continuum (Chapter 2) is emphatically consequentialist in its way of replacing naive beliefs with experimental inquiry. Yet in his mature ethics (Chapters 4 and 5), he contextualized good consequences as one of at least three basic aspects of moral action.

- Argues normatively for a democratic approach to public education and problem-solving as the most effective antidote to moral fundamentalism. In turn, I criticize antidemocratic moral, political, and educational values. These normative criticisms depend on—but are not deduced from—descriptions of contemporary moral and political experience, including research in psychology and the social sciences.

- Sympathetically explains, expands, and updates Dewey's ethical theory. Almost a century on, Dewey's typology of ethical theories is inadequate to the diversity of twenty-first-century orientations. But his theory contains a sophisticated justification *for* moral pluralism and *against* the single-right-way mentality that reinforces moral fundamentalism. It merits rigorous criticism.

2

A Democratic Approach to Social Learning and Conflicting Values

Cases in Environmental Pragmatism

Soon after his ninetieth birthday, Dewey was feted at his alma mater, the University of Vermont. Too tired to rise and speak to the crowd in Burlington, he simply said: "I'm thankful for the privilege of living on this good planet, Earth. But living on this Earth has become the supreme challenge to mankind's intelligence" (1975.05.25? [22283]: Herbert W. Schneider to American Humanist Association).

Building especially on Dewey, this chapter explains, illustrates, and clarifies pragmatic pluralism through the burgeoning work of philosophers developing it as an ethical perspective on environmental problems broadly construed. I give some special emphasis to moving beyond moral fundamentalism in climate, animal, and food ethics. Prior to sketching a "house of theory" (in Iris Murdoch's words) for pragmatic pluralist ethics in Chapters 4 and 5, this chapter illustrates Dewey's democratizing corrective to traditional approaches. In their quest for an all-encompassing grand paradigm to govern human interactions with the rest of nature, monistic approaches inadvertently give succor to the "one way" mentality that sustains moral fundamentalism. My primary aim here is to characterize, differentiate, and advance a pragmatist *approach* to moral and political decision-making, albeit a broad and programmatic one, rather than to defend specific governing principles, formulate policy recommendations, or advance action items.

Beyond Moral Fundamentalism. Steven Fesmire, Oxford University Press. © Oxford University Press 2024. DOI: 10.1093/9780197763919.003.0002

The analysis of environmental pragmatism herein is inspired in part by philosopher Andrew Light's work on climate diplomacy (e.g., 2013; 2017) as assistant secretary of energy for international affairs in the Biden administration and as senior adviser and India counselor to the US special envoy on climate change in the Obama administration, and by environmental philosopher Bryan Norton's pragmatism (e.g., 2005; 2015), while drawing much more explicitly from classical pragmatist sources than either Light or Norton.

A Case for Pragmatic Pluralism: Animals and Food Ethics

To illustrate how a pragmatic and pluralistic approach avoids moral fundamentalism, I begin this chapter with conflicts between two out-of-the-mainstream diets competing for center stage in animal and food ethics debates: an omnivorous diet relying on grass-fed animal husbandry, and a vegan diet seeking to abolish animal agriculture. Each responds to problems stemming from our industrialized food system, such as chemical runoff, overuse of antibiotics, resource depletion, and animal confinement that suppresses natural behaviors. There is nothing extraordinary about this particular dispute among moral reformers. It is replaceable for purposes of illustration with any heated moral controversy in which disputants typify an outworn fundamentalism.

Debates over animal use and treatment have become standard fare in philosophical ethics since the 1980s, with special ferocity in the areas of biomedicine and agriculture. Returning to Thompson's, Boisvert's, and Heldke's observations about dogmatic tendencies in the food movement (Chapter 1), perhaps the touchiest topic concerns what we choose to eat, with many diets vying for "the best." With notable exceptions such as McKenna and Light's *Animal Pragmatism* (2004), McKenna (2018, 2020), and Thompson (e.g., 2010, 2015), scholars contributing a pragmatic pluralist perspective have taken a back seat to utilitarians and deontologists in responding to the far-reaching impact of human practices on other species and rising concern about animal use and treatment. As a result, ethical inquiries into dietary and other animal-related issues have been more anemic than they might have been. Unfortunately, unidimensional debates have done little to counter the livestock industry's broad-brush dismissal of all critics as harboring a "radical anti-meat agenda" (Tabuchi 2022).

The outlook of Virginia farmer Joel Salatin, popularized by Michael Pollan's bestseller *The Omnivore's Dilemma* (2006), offers a contrast with pragmatic pluralism.[1] Drawing in part from trail-blazing work on "perennial polyculture" by the agriculturalist Wes Jackson, Salatin advocates an approach to agriculture and eating that requires less tilling (hence less soil depletion) than exclusively vegetable-based agriculture, is well adapted to colder climates, and does not rely on long-distance transportation of conventionally produced grain. A pragmatic pluralist would approach perennial polyculture as a promising hypothesis that should be evaluated by how well it directs ameliorative action. But Salatin is no pragmatist in his ethics. He wields the sword of righteous certitude. For example, he argues that the "right" diet *must* be based on grass-fed animal husbandry if it is to mimic perennial natural cycles, so it must by natural law include meat. From his standpoint vegetarians are hypocrites (if they eat dairy and eggs), and the best that can be said of vegans is that at least they are not hypocrites. Unlike the ecocentric naturalist Jackson, Salatin self-identifies as a Christian fundamentalist who believes vegans and vegetarians commit a sacrilege against nature and God by refusing to enter the ordained cycle of eater and eaten.

Despite faddish proliferation of books and blogs proposing the correct, best, or "natural" diet, pragmatists reject the idea that such a thing can be determined in advance of the situations that require us to make dietary choices. There are multiple ways to pursue more responsive lives in relation to food, and no diet exhaustively deals with all of the often-incompatible exigencies inherent in agriculture and eating.

Salatin makes several typical moral fundamentalist assumptions. There is, he assumes, a right way to reason about moral matters, a single accurate way to conceive the relationship between humans and the rest of nature, and hence a right diet. Ironically, animal rights abolitionists share the same basic assumptions when they argue for their opposing vegan position that humans cannot ethically use other animals, that "meat is murder," and that all animal agriculture is slavery that violates their rights (e.g., Regan 1983; Francione 2021). For the vegan abolitionist, an animal's sentience or subjectivity grants it rights comparable to those Jefferson celebrated in the Declaration of Independence: life, liberty, and the pursuit of happiness (or, minimally, the right of a sentient being to maintain its bodily integrity). *Regardless of context*, vegan abolitionists argue that these rights trump any interest humans may have in killing, penning, or experimenting on animals, and violating these rights also degrades our shared environment and worsens human health. The purported analogy to human slavery highlights for abolitionists the dismal treatment customarily accorded to those we regard as property, emboldening their activism.

Notice that each dietary warrior starts with the same assumption about ethics: a bedrock, a correct worldview, an ultimate principle. They simply disagree about which, and this charges their polarization. When we reject this one-way mentality, we can disagree more productively. When polarized positions lose their winner-takes-all prescriptive force, there is a chance to liberate insights for accommodation in a broader-based inquiry. Instead of sabotaging communication across moral clans, we can create a context that facilitates a communicative conflict (cf. Gray 1996) that checks moral blind spots and grapples with the transitions ahead.

The absence of a right diet does not imply that institutions and practices are symmetrical in their justifiability. Dietary practices are pinched and constrained by objective factors, and many do not stand up to scrutiny. But, as illustrated, there is ethical leeway for dietary experiments that rely more *or* less on animal agriculture, and for champions of the same. The "moral" of this case is generalizable. The terrain of moral action is inherently unsettled. Although the avenues available to us are rarely ideally optimal or perfectly harmonious, there are usually more mutually traversable and ameliorative ways forward in any polarized debate than are rehearsed by mono-focused disputants.

In contrast with both Salatin and many animal rights abolitionists, practical ethicists such as the utilitarian Peter Singer generally agree with pragmatists that there is no such thing as *the* correct diet. We do not need a universally "right" diet to perceive that many choices and policies do little to objectively move us toward a more humane, just, healthy, and sustainable food system. Pragmatist and utilitarian approaches diverge, however, on whether there is a comprehensively correct way to *reason* about dietary ethics or other issues. Utilitarians routinely demand a fixed standard or principle that originates outside particular developing situations, a wholly impartial objective test of what it means to get things right. In Dewey's contrasting view, we do not require a universal moral compass or other fixed standard, law, principle, or ideal external to experienced situations in order to infer and exactingly test promising paths toward social goals. We need testable hypotheses to act upon, not finalities to swear by come what may (1929, LW 4:221).

Dewey insisted on operationalizing moral standards as tools (1929, LW 4:221–222). That is, they should be framed and assessed as instrumentalities to guide rather than govern inquiry and choice. What he was rejecting can be seen in analogous debates about the gold standard. Proponents of the gold standard once argued that paper currency was too arbitrary to serve as a standard of value in market exchanges, appealing instead to some property that gold magically has "in itself." Just so, in moral discussions it is still popular to assume we would wallow in subjectivity and con-fusion without some absolute metric to compare the fairness or goodness of actions. In practice, the fiat value of paper money ar-guably worked better for determining market value than the pur-portedly absolute gold standard. Adhering to the gold standard stymied development, and rejecting it led to some improvements instead of lawlessness. Fixed standards are antithetical to an exper-imental methodology. We can intelligently revise standards. Just as the English system of yards and pounds is more haphazard and less translatable than the metric system of meters and grams, we can also intelligently evaluate and revise standards for ordering moral conduct. To insist that a group's customary standard is holding up the sky is fundamentalism, pure and simple (cf. 1938a, LW 12:216–217).

In the case at hand, we can frame and adjudicate the respective hypotheses of perennial polyculture and veganism by what they secure and achieve *as means* to superordinate ends. Sidestepping their own incompatible gold standards, we can appraise the extent to which perennial polyculture and veganism reorganize experi-ence to "meet the situation," in Dewey's favored phrasing.

Again, utilitarian rules for "doing ethics" typically require an ex-ternal moral meterstick to assess whether a situation has been "met" well. Singer, for example, antecedently establishes an objective metric that aggregates good by counting each sentient individual one and no more. Absent this metric, he argues, judgments will be biased by physical and temporal distance, feelings, and empathy, which disproportionately favor the interests of those near and dear to us over those of strangers. Dewey agreed that moral judgments are subject to biases and distortions like these. But he insisted that these biases can be more effectively mitigated through delib-eration that uses principles, standards, and laws as instruments, without recourse to a supposedly wholly disinterested metric that replaces moral imagination and colloquy with objective reason (cf. Colapietro 2019). In this and later chapters, I will periodically return to these thoughtful utilitarian concerns as I build a case for pragmatic pluralism.

Naturalism, Pragmatism, and the
Ends-Means Continuum

> Life's but a walking shadow, a poor player, / That struts and frets his hour upon the stage, / And then is heard no more. It is a tale / Told by an idiot, full of sound and fury, / Signifying nothing. (Shakespeare, *Macbeth*, Act 5, scene 5)

A naturalistic approach to ethics will not fully satisfy what James called the rationalistic temperament. The rationalist conceives something unlovable about a world in which all purposiveness is finally vulnerable to contingency and chance. It seems to them to denigrate rather than celebrate human life. Yet a naturalistic ethics can be humble and inspiring. It can also be richly explanatory of human capacities. We may indeed strut and fret our hour upon the stage, as Macbeth despaired, but our lives as embodied valuing animals are more meaningful, purposeful, and value-rich than mere tales "told by an idiot, full of sound and fury, signifying nothing." Things and ends beyond us matter. As Mark Johnson and Jay Schulkin urge in their recent book on Dewey's *Experience and Nature*, we do not need to call down "supernatural or transcendent entities, agencies, forces, causes, or values" to "find meaningful ways to carry on and to throw in with the better, rather than the worse" (2023, 33, 234). Dewey himself lived as he counseled, using "thought to its utmost" and throwing his "puny strength" into the "moving unbalanced balance of things" (1925/1929, LW 1:314; cf. Fesmire 2015).[2]

What is a "pragmatist" in ethics? Like other ethical naturalists in the search for wisdom, philosophical pragmatists argue that we can deal more intelligently with problems and better direct ourselves toward justified goals, both personally and collectively, without transcendental standards or a priori deductions that hide from inspection even as they claim to guarantee the universal validity of judgments. Pragmatists are "postmodern" in the limited sense that they distrust grand metanarratives, spokespersons for superior reality, or conceptual skeleton keys that purport to unlock all difficulties.

More distinctively and controversially, though in common with many other strong pluralists, most pragmatists have long regarded the old quest for the single, central, and basic source of normative justification as myopic (see Chapters 4 and 5). In the sense that its approach to inquiry does not specify a single source of normativity or a coverall moral concept, being a pragmatist in ethics is not analogous to being a Kantian or utilitarian. The job of ethics, pragmatically understood, is to systematically work through, generalize, and guide inquiry into situations that call us to choose better over worse. Ethicists earn their keep when the way forward is not well lit, when multiple paths beckon, and when incompatible goods, colliding duties, and competing virtues "get in each other's way" (1932, LW 7:165).

Pragmatist ethics thus integrates moral intelligence with practical problem-solving, in contrast with the depreciation of prudential reasoning in an absolutistic ethics. Kant, for example, argued in *Grounding for the Metaphysics of Morals* that in a moral judgment "moral concepts have their seat and origin completely *a priori* in reason [Vernunft]" (1993, 22). He thus severed practical intelligence from a transcendental rationality that legislates eternal moral laws that are "unconditioned and indeed objective and hence universally valid" (1993, 26). Kant acknowledged the everyday wisdom of cultivating prudence about means and ends, but in stark opposition to pragmatists he denied its relevance to moral judgment.

The term "pragmatist" has done as much to muddle as to clarify. In his 1908 essay "The Thirteen Pragmatisms," intellectual historian and philosopher Arthur Lovejoy identified thirteen senses of pragmatism then in vogue among philosophers like James. Lovejoy objected to the "utter disconnection and even incongruity" of this "baker's dozen of contentions" that had arisen during pragmatism's first decade. He wrote: "The pragmatist school itself seems, thus far, more distinguished for originality, inventiveness, and a keen vision for the motes in the eye of the intellectualist, than for patience in making distinctions or the habit of self-analysis" (Lovejoy 1908, 5–6).

"Pragmatism" in colloquial English is less protean, with arguably two principal meanings. It primarily suggests the tempering of ideologies with practicality, the balancing of principles with achievable outcomes, or simply flexibility amid contingencies. To call someone a pragmatist popularly suggests a counterweight to pie-in-the-sky ideals, quixotic loftiness, or dogmatic ideology. Worldly pragmatists ensure that some portion of our ideals may be realized, which they presume is better than none at all. The word secondarily means, again outside of academic philosophy, pursuit of the most expedient means to satisfy a self- or group-centered desire, often associated with an outlook in which political actors take shortsighted gambles that may well backfire (e.g., Jotzo 2016).

If we shave off its anti-intellectual and anti-theoretical connotations, the first popular sense above may capture a hint of "Yankee pragmatism" in Dewey's theorizing. But this requires such a long string of qualifications that it may be best to approach philosophical pragmatism as semantically unrelated. Dewey's corpus thunders with criticisms of shallow practicality, unprincipled realpolitik, machinations toward fixed ends, atomistic individualism, acquisitiveness, the gospel of efficiency, and American swagger. His philosophical reconstructions cut much deeper than the narrowly opportunistic and extractive pragmatism of common parlance, as he developed a contextually sensitive method for anticipating consequences. Indeed, he wrote in a 1940 letter: "The word 'pragmatism' I have used very little, and then with reserves" (1940.09.06 [13667]: Dewey to Corliss Lamont).

Dewey expanded and rigorously systematized Peirce's and James's pragmatisms as a means for reconstructing philosophy to meet evolving difficulties. Dewey's pragmatism is, minimally, the critical attempt to replace culturally lagging ideas and beliefs, distorting prejudicial habits, and reactive impulses with intelligent inquiry that gains practical leverage because it is set up as as a shared response to concrete occurrences. Such natural human inquiry was the object of his "deepest faith and loyalty" (1925/1929, LW 1:325).

Had Dewey ever formulated a pragmatic maxim to clarify exactly what he thought made value inquiry more *intelligent*—which for him was one with specifying what makes it *experimental*—it might spotlight his emphasis on the ends-means continuum: always state your ends in terms of the means you plan to use to achieve them. For example, if you are ultimately aiming for climate justice, equitable distribution of greenhouse gas emissions, the right to sustainable development (Moellendorf 2014), or the rights of future generations (Gardiner 2011), then state these ends in terms of the means you propose for bringing them about.

Dewey analyzed the feedback loop that has always implicitly connected what people intend to do (an aim, purpose, or end-in-view, in Dewey's idiom), how they are going about it (means), and what they have actually done (an end, consequence, fulfillment, or consummation). These are inseparable, despite the familiar gulf between intentions and consequences, as when the US Soil Conservation Service vigorously incentivized kudzo in order to control erosion after the Dust Bowl of the 1930s.

Dewey antedated what Columbia University sociologist Robert K. Merton (1910–2003) influentially called the "unanticipated consequences of purposive social action" in a watershed article that cited Dewey (1936, 901). Later social scientists contracted this to "the law of unintended consequences," an insight that was pushed to its logical limit by Michael Scriven's goal-free evaluation model (Scriven 2000). As is well canvassed by moral philosophers debating the controverted principle of "double effect," side effects are often forecastable in light of past observations, even when bad effects are not intended, so moral choices must somehow reckon with the unintended fallout (e.g., McIntyre 2023). Dewey argued that, due to the inevitability of unintended yet practically relevant consequences (desirable or not), we must speak of the things we are consciously aiming for *in terms of* proposed actions and programs. In this way, Dewey urged, we can concretely specify actual spatiotemporal consequences of actions, direct and indirect. No matter how noble and brilliant our ideals and theories may be, they can never pin down the actual consequences (cf. 1922b, MW 14:154–163; cf. Hickman 1990, 2019). Such previsioning includes consequences for us as moral agents.

For example, if our aim is to check the growth of aquatic weeds without using noxious herbicides, then we might consider a nonchemical biological control, just as Rachel Carson advocated in *Silent Spring* (1962). Carson's solution was plausible at the level of abstract theory. But desirability in the abstract cannot determine how interventions will play out on the ground, so we need a reliably open-ended method for anticipating and tracking. Carson's proposal was the motivation behind the US Fish and Wildlife Service's breeding of Asian carp in the 1960s to control aquatic weeds. Unfortunately, officials were so concerned to solve the problem under their nose that they failed to take the next step in any intelligent inquiry, which is to confer and pool experiences (drawing on the current state of experimental knowledge) so that, ideally at an "adequate scale" (LW 2:379), we note and track the relevant looping first- and second-order effects of those means. Instead of studying the problem as a many-headed hydra, Fish and Wildlife officials were preoccupied by the focal or "first order" effects that suited their agenda. Soon the carp became ecosystem conquerors, outcompeting other species. The consequence for US waterways has been an ecological disaster, including a staggeringly costly ongoing effort by the US Army Corps of Engineers to prevent the carp from entering the Great Lakes (Kolbert 2021, ch. 1).

Tracking secondary effects of our chosen means may also lead to serendipitous breakthrough achievements, as with Alexander Fleming's unexpected discovery of penicillin. Regardless of whether the end results of experiments satisfy our needs, desires, or purposes, a pragmatic method of inquiry reckons with them without presuming that results are somehow determined by theories or research programs. According to Dewey, such reckoning is what makes inquiry intelligent (i.e., experimental). The opposite approach is to assume that "This end is what our theory or ideology has determined, so we can safely ignore extraneous results unrelated to satisfying our purposes." This is a moral fundamentalist maxim, reframed in terms of the ends-means continuum. It approaches problems from the wrong direction.

Dewey's methodological concern for tracing varied consequences far enough can be framed negatively as a cautionary maxim, following Mead: beware anyone's ends which are asserted ipse dixit or autocratically as finalities or absolutes rather than "in terms of the social means" being proposed (Mead 1930, 104–105).

For example, take security and justice as ends. Journalist Ronen Bergman's book *Rise and Kill First* (2018a) shows that Israel's long-standing practice of targeted assassination—drone strikes, bombings, shootings, and poisonings—has resulted in many "tactical successes" that have dramatically worsened diplomatic relations. Yet, in Bergman's view, the collective aspirations for effective security among conflicting actors in the Middle East can only be achieved through diplomacy, not imposed through the method of force. His approach to conflicts in the region parallels what Berlin called an "uneasy equilibrium which is constantly threatened and in constant need of repair" (Berlin 1998, 19; cf. Gray 1996). Bergman relates the tactics of Israel's Mossad security forces in an interview:

They felt that at the tip of their fingers, they can hit someone way beyond enemy lines, deep in the enemy state and solve the problem, and therefore, they do not need to turn to statesmanship or political reconciliation. And therefore I think the story of the use of these special means is a series of extraordinary tactical successes but, at the same time, a disastrous political failure. (Bergman 2018b)

When groups track only the isolated consequences that they consciously intended to bring about, such as eliminating an enemy, they do not usually feel responsible for collateral side effects of those means. The idea that the oppressed can do no wrong likewise presumes a holiday from moral responsibility. More generally, in the convective storm of terror and retribution, reactive fundamentalist habits prevail over patient experimental ones, so clashing sides double down on failed policies and tactics that inflict misery across generations.

To offer a contrastingly light, tractable illustration of how ludicrous it is to ignore collateral effects in our pursuit of fixed ends, I offer a scene from *Calvin and Hobbes*:

"Where are you going?" Hobbes asks.

Calvin, walking with a bucket in hand, replies: "I'm going to the other side of the lake."

"What's the bucket for?"

"I'm going to drain the lake" (Watterson 1988).

These choices by the US Fish and Wildlife Service, Israel's Mossad, Hamas, and Calvin illustrate the same life lesson: when making decisions about actions, public policies, institutional structures, or research programs, the only defensible alternative to singling out and favoring some fragmentary, abstractly desirable result as "the" end is to evaluate desires, ends, and consequences as themselves "means of further consequences" (1938b, LW 13:229).

Ever the advocate of democratic methods, Dewey argued that the most perceptive evaluations are achieved through colloquy that discloses troubled tendencies. Self-protective or in-group so-liloquy conceals any consequence that does not "correspond to our habitual courses" (1922b, MW 14:159). Once people have made a choice in light of its foreseen likely bearings (which are often legiti-mately contested), then they must review what they have actually—though perhaps accidentally—done beyond their immediate success or lack thereof. Then they must revise what they mean to do next accordingly. In Dewey's spirit, this holistic decision, review, and revision process is the most reliable way to rehearse and antici-pate unintended consequences, and it is the best way to experimen-tally note and incorporate actual results into future planning.

Upholding the moral correctness of an action merely because we intensely crave it, or because the other side deserves it, or because we mean well, without surveying unintended hazards and helps, is a mark of moral fundamentalism. It is more philosophically re-spectable to conclude that an action is justified because it squares with an ultimate end that is abstractly desirable, or because it is im-mutably dictated by transcendental reason to constrain us across all possible contexts. But if we overlook the variety of second-order effects of choices, philosophical respectability amounts to little.

Dewey's Democratic Radicalism

Dewey's analysis of the ends-means continuum serves as his ex-periential justification for a democratic approach to conflicting values and to dissenting or disaffected voices. He rejected claims to moral expertise that are separated from attention to the ends-means continuum. Moreover, he concluded that such attention can only be secured by extending perception through democratic processes. He did not derive the democratic ideal from what Rawls called an "ideal theory" (see Chapter 4). Nor did it spring from ignoring stupidity and groupthink. Most tend to overrate the war-rant of their assertions, so we are rightfully wary, in George Eliot's words, of "those who are too certain of their own interpretation to be enlightened by anything we may say" (Eliot 1876/2002, 600). Nevertheless, Dewey's approach is rooted in the practical demand for people to anticipate consequences together.

If perceiving the need for deep structural changes makes one a radical, then as Dewey observed in the middle of the Great Depression, "today any liberalism which is not also radicalism is irrelevant and doomed" (1935, LW 11:45). He was a thoroughly pragmatic radical. But his pluralistic liberalism was tethered to an experimental methodology that makes it a radicalism for grown-ups who urge courage and patience to secure the "democratic means to achieve our democratic ends" (332). Or as Jane Addams earlier made the point in her 1922 book *Peace and Bread in Time of War*: "Social advance depends as much upon the process through which it is secured as upon the result itself" (quoted in 1945b, LW 15:195). Delegitimizing the one-way moral mentality, and instead democratizing decision-making in a way that simultaneously educates the public—overlapping publics, to be more precise—in the critical method of experimental intelligence, is radical because it gives no succor to the moral fundamentalism that is perennially part of the problem wherever it is enacted as part of the solution.

To whatever degree they are fundamentalists, self-styled radicals can be tiresomely conventional. "I know of few radicals as yet who are radical enough," Henry David Thoreau wrote. He was implying, in an implicit jab at Emerson, that those who are nominally radical do not dig deep enough to inspect their roots in order to transform their own lives (in Walls 2017, 168–169). Some of today's radicals might be surprised at how little they must dig to reach the level of their moral and political conceptions. These conceptions are often noble in the abstract, but to gain practicality they must be rooted in the tangled conditions we mean to change. The best way to disclose those conditions is to attend to the ends-means continuum, not to rest on good ideals and intentions alone.

In this respect, Dewey was more radical than Marxists such as Chairman Mao or Leon Trotsky. For example, in a staggering failure of ecological imagination during China's Great Leap Forward in the 1950s, Mao called for eradication of sparrows as a means to protect the grain harvest from a pest. The subsequent campaign "worked" to almost extinguish sparrows, eliminating their impact on the harvest—a model of pragmatism, according to caricatures. But by ignoring ecological context, Mao's anti-pest campaign backfired. China thereby removed sparrows as the keystone predator of locusts and other insects, resulting in a population explosion that decimated the harvest. The resulting famine killed millions. By 1960, Mao heeded Chinese ecologists and reversed course (Shapiro 2001).

Dewey's fealty to the ends-means continuum was the heart of his response to the Soviet revolutionary exile Trotsky. Dewey chaired what became known as the "Dewey Commission" in Mexico City in 1937, which was organized to investigate spurious charges made by Joseph Stalin after ousting his brilliant Soviet co-revolutionary Trotsky. The commission cleared Trotsky of all charges, angering apologists for Stalin on the American radical left. Dewey wrote to a friend: "It was the most interesting single intellectual experience in my life" (1937.05.12 [08424]: Dewey to Max Eastman). Yet Dewey concluded that Trotsky was not *philosophically* radical enough.

On the face of it, Trotsky agreed with Dewey regarding the interdependence of means and ends, and they agreed on the goal of liberating humanity. Neither had patience for righteous indignation dressed up as eternal moral truth (e.g., see 1927.07.06 [06663]: Leon Trotsky to Wendelin Thomas). Both criticized unfettered capitalism, class-based education, and individualistic consumerism (see Chapter 3). The two quickly developed intellectual and moral respect for each other. Trotsky, however, was beholden to dialectical materialist dogma regarding the invariable law of all social development. The liberation of humanity was for Dewey an end-in-view set up within experience rather than a

sclerotic ideal descending from on high. He was a practical revolutionary. Meanwhile, Trotsky followed Marx in treating it as the
absolutely ordained social law. From this ideology, Trotsky deduced
his unquestioned doctrine that the sole and inevitable means to liberation is violent class struggle. Ultimately, the means he advocated
for social action were not the results of a wide survey of the situation and an empirically informed forecast of consequences.

According to his secretary, just after arriving in Mexico Trotsky
dismissed the experimental methodology of American pragmatism
as a curse and an infection (Novack 1937). This is unsurprising,
as Dewey was out of step with the ideology of violent upheaval in
Russia and China. When Dewey gave a lecture series in 1921 toward
the end of his two years in China, a young Marxist philosopher, Fei
Juetian, wrote a scathing review in which he summed up the view
that would prevail a generation later: "If I tell the world that we
should experiment with socialism and see if it works, people would
think that I am crazy and would oppose this experiment. If I proclaim that socialism holds the ultimate truth to solving problems in
today's society, that there is no better theory than socialism, people
will become interested in its practice and help transform the theory
into a reality" (in Wang 2007, 50). Fei added that "the experimental
method would not *work* in reality because no one would want to
risk their lives and their properties simply for the sake of experiment" (50–51, italics added).

People cling to the illusion of ironclad certainty, and Fei consciously exploited that illusion. Dewey was committed to uprooting
it, freeing intelligence to creatively and competently direct change.
He deeply respected persons, *with* their sane doubts, as equal
participants in projects.

Fei was, ironically, making a narrowly pragmatic argument.
It is a "schizophrenic" argument in the "self-effacing" sense
analyzed by Michael Stocker (1976): Fei assumes agents should
not be motivated by the (pragmatic) reasons he gives to justify
his prescriptions (cf. Parfit 1984, 23). Was his argument for the

workability of moral fundamentalism justified? More generally, is Fei right that, all things considered, it is better to motivate people by unquestioned absolutes than by experimental considerations? Dewey asked, as he would later ask of Trotsky: "Work" for what end? Fei's capricious pragmatism utilized moral fundamentalism to generate the will to achieve a prefabricated end of absolute equity taken to be valuable in itself. Proclaiming finalities worked to stoke revolutionary fervor in China, just as it had in Russia. But was it the only or most complete fulfillment afforded by the circumstances? Did it bring about the goods for which the revolution was fought? Did it lead to what Marx called the dictatorship of the proletariat, or did it lead to a "dictatorship over the proletariat" (LW 11:331)?

Liberalism and Social Action (1935), which Dewey wrote as Marxist ideology was gaining momentum over liberalism among those on the American left, grapples with indictments "from those who want drastic social changes effected in a twinkling of an eye, and who believe that violent overthrow of existing institutions is the right method of effecting the required changes" (LW 11:5). Fei and Trotsky implied that Dewey's experimental pragmatism is an ineffective, fair-weather, milk-and-water philosophy that should be repudiated by tough-minded radicals who are willing to take a stand on the barricade. Dewey replied, in effect, that we can purchase freedom from doubt with the coin of moral fundamentalism, but beware the hidden costs. In the fight for structural changes to secure the blessings of liberty, do not shortchange the democratic spirit that is being championed.

Trotsky adhered to a doctrine of final ends, complete in themselves and fixed in advance. In that important respect, he differed little from Salatin's vegan-bashing God. Trotsky famously dismissed religious dogmatism, but his adherence to unconditioned truths beyond the reach of honest examination and criticism was old-fashioned fundamentalism. Trotsky was a powerful analyst of social relationships, but much of his prowess was channeled into retelling history as a Marxist morality tale. By deducing and importing the social means (violent revolution) a priori from a superempirical source, he failed to empirically examine which social interventions would more likely lead *objectively* to desirable results (1938b, LW 13:351–352).

Absolutist pacifists are subject to the same pragmatist critique insofar as violent force is precluded a priori as an exceptionless prohibition. There is, after all, no "pragmatist" position on violence and nonviolence. Addams, who was honored with the 1931 Nobel Peace Prize, was a pacifist. Dewey, to the dismay of antiwar progressives during the First World War, was not. They agreed, however, that *"The fundamental principle of democracy is that the ends of freedom and individuality for all can be attained only by means that accord with those ends"* (1935, LW 11:298).

We Can Never Do Merely One Thing: Navigating Means and Ends in Complex Systems

The mad, antipragmatist maxim "the end justifies the means" arises from the warped idea that ends are to be valued as givens irrespective of the unplanned effects of problem-solving. We can imagine a fictional universe in which this is not absurd: by way of advice to fantasy writers, it would have to be a universe in which miracles intervene to keep the means we consciously employ from having their usual extensive side effects. In such a universe, to mean well is to do well. Moral agents could crave fixed ends without bothering to think peripherally, and things would turn out fine. In such a universe, moral agents could be single-mindedly absorbed in intended outcomes without bothering to forecast unintended perturbations cascading through the entire network of relationships in which their lives are embedded, because these consequences would never be "intrinsically obnoxious" (1938b, LW 13:228).

Returning to *our* universe, perhaps a suitably broad, multiscalar, pluralistic, and long-range conception of ends could be framed as justifying the means. I will leave that Pandora's box closed except to caution again that Dewey's deeply pluralistic approach does not neatly fit most familiar forms of consequentialist ethics, as will be explored in some depth in Chapter 5 (cf. Pappas 2008). For instance, Dewey joined Kantians in criticizing utilitarians for downplaying the practical thrust of attitudes and predispositions, of will (1932, LW 7, ch. 12). Nevertheless, he thought that his deconstruction of "the end justifies the means" was far more plausible than the pervasive antipragmatic notion in deontological ethics, echoed even by Rawls (1971, 31), that some objectives are ends in themselves. From Dewey's perspective, the notion of a self-justifying end—good wholly in itself, independent of context and consequences—is dangerously shortsighted about the way events naturally relate to one another over time and scale. There is indeed something more basic to honesty than that it is the best policy, and far more to kindness than that it is reciprocated, but this does not entail that honesty and kindness are coherently defended as ends in themselves. "Not *the* end—in the singular—justifies the means; for there is no such thing as the single all-important end" (1922b, MW 14:158), Dewey argued. When we erect an end such as justice, happiness, liberty, or the like into *the* overarching end, we put "a pseudo-stamp of moral justification upon success at any price" (1922b, MW 14:159).

The observation that "we can never do merely one thing" was formulated by conservation biologist Garrett Hardin as the first postulate of ecology. His second postulate was that "no effects are truly side effects." Strictly speaking, Hardin observed, there are no side effects, just as there are no "externalities." "All effects are effects, period. He who wishes to control the perceptions, and hence the actions of others, labels as 'side effects' those consequences he does not wish people to become aware of or to act upon" (Hardin 1985, 471).[3] For example, when I set out simply to eat a banana or make a cup of coffee, I may inadvertently affect the population of migratory songbirds whose winter nesting grounds in Central and South

America have been bulldozed and burned to plant banana and coffee trees. Recognition that choices are pregnant with unantici‐ pated connections, both proximal and distant, has more recently become par for the course in the field of ecological economics.

In short, we always do more than we mean to do. Some decades earlier than Hardin, in *Theory of Valuation* (1939), Dewey explored moral implications of such commonplaces from the physical sci‐ ences: "Nothing happens which is final in the sense that it is not part of an ongoing stream of events" (1938b, LW 13:229). "Ends are, in fact, literally endless" (1922b, MW 14:159). Whatever ends we bring about through a particular intervention will engender many existential connections and possibilities. So instead of loading the evaluative dice by noticing only what suits our grand designs, ends must be empirically evaluated as potential helps or hindrances in the struggle to disentangle and coordinate conflicting factors.

Recalling Jamieson's observations in Chapter 1, we can say that any ethical outlook in sync with current problems must per‐ ceive and respond to a wide range of harms, the causes of which are frequently systemic. Ethics and education today need to extend perception deeper into the tangled sociocultural, ecological, and in‐ terpersonal relationships that bring meaning and a renewed sense of responsibility to what is otherwise no more than the "flickering inconsequential acts of separate selves" (1922b, MW 14:227).

Whether this means the basic alternatives we call "morality" have failed, as Jamieson argues (2014), is an open question. What is clear is that, even amid rising global awareness of the unplanned effects that radiate from human actions—such as pandemics, cli‐ mate change, violent reprisals, alienated work, resource depletion, massive animal suffering, mass incarceration, and institutionalized discrimination—many still think of themselves as "contained" in the world like scissors in a drawer. Concurrently, as utilitarians such as Jamieson and Singer (2015) have long argued, people too rarely imagine consequences beyond the dramas in which they, or those dear to them, feature as the central figures. Resigning ourselves to this approach leaves us demoralized and ignorant of the social and environmental hazards posed by business-as-usual behaviors.

Philosophers and other intellectuals can aid our dealings with complex systems without toeing a single line, contemporary pragmatists insist. Nevertheless, it is vitally important for them to model and cultivate a sort of "relational virtuosity" (Ames 2007, 55ff.) to perceive and navigate entanglements. Such virtuosity has become paramount for dealing with anthropogenic drivers of global disruption. For their part, educational institutions must help youths to see beyond simple relations of consumers to commodities (see Chapter 3) if they are to respond to an economic milieu in which affluence sanctifies the innocence of consumers—an innocence maintained by disregarding the ends-means continuum (see Fesmire 2010, 2012).

Kyoto Hedgehogs and Parisian Foxes: A Wicked Case for Climate Pragmatism

Without staking out a position in the foundational values debate that has typified environmental and animal ethics since the 1970s, pragmatists inspired by Dewey struggle to create a context for more effective environmental decision-making. Adaptive decision processes are informed not only by well-vetted principles, but also by wise ecological perception of the complex nature of problems. The virtues of adaptive decision-making include cultivated empathy for those affected by choices, imaginative probings for technological and communal solutions, sensitivity to cultural traditions, and rich aesthetic responses to natural and cultural landscapes (e.g., Alexander 2013).

Norton (2015) clarifies the pragmatist approach to decision-making, planning, and goal-setting in the playful spirit of Berlin's "The Hedgehog and the Fox" (1953). In a tongue-in-cheek riff on Archilochus's saying that "The fox knows many things, but the hedgehog knows one big thing," the pluralist Berlin proposes that there are two kinds of intellectuals: monistic hedgehogs and pluralistic foxes. He contrasts the "centripetal" (centralized) actions and ideas of the hedgehog with the "centrifugal" (decentralized) ones of the protean fox. Norton picks up the image here.

This binary heuristic would amount to caricature if applied in toto to any individual moral or political theorist. But it serves as a rhetorical simplification. The monistic hedgehog—with its big, all-encompassing idea—looks for moral answers and progress in the wrong place. Instead of taking problems as they come, hedgehogs want a theoretic superstructure that solves everything at once. They want to get the bulk of the inquiry out of the way in advance. To see that this is a mistake, we might imagine a physician, Dewey prodded, who seeks to heal patients in light of some ultimate, final, complete, and universal ideal of optimal health, when the medical situation calls the physician to aid living processes of recovery (1922b, MW 14:196). In the face of dynamic complications, the physician's failure to meet existing health needs would be quackery. In contrast, the pluralistic fox avoids ethical and political quackery by approaching matters in medias res. Whether in medicine or morals, the fox starts with the problem as it is experienced, tracks it as it evolves, and actively remakes the situation through reflective choices and deeds. Instead of disengaging as a calculator, hovering jurist, or distant legislator, the fox is an active, imaginative, and experimental participant who sustains the suspense of inquiry.

Practical differences between hedgehoggish and foxlike decision-making are clarified by asking an educational question: Do we serve ethics, politics, and policy students well if we mostly cultivate their ability to judiciously weigh matters so that the balance tips toward a purportedly optimal policy supported by general principles derived prior to inclusive participation in real situations?[4] Economizing deliberation with a predetermined, rule-governed metric can be helpful for many purposes, and it is at least an antidote to excessive moral lability. But no matter the amount of data plugged in, or how well argued our principle of justice, insofar as an approach to ethics, politics, and policy fails to *also* prioritize sensitivity to context, creative social inquiry, and experimental understanding of complex underlying structures, its end result is too often reminiscent of an offhanded criticism that Dewey once made about "popcorn" solutions: put the right amount in the right mechanism and you get some "unnutritious readymade stuff" that will not sustain anyone for long (1951.02.14 [14090]: Dewey to Max C. Otto).

Exemplifying a foxlike approach, a pragmatist starts with the concrete situation as experienced by individuals in their unique contexts. No matter how egalitarian in spirit and belief, a pragmatist does not *start* with an abstract concept such as equity. Take the responsibilities of countries for reducing greenhouse gas emissions. Light highlighted in the buildup to the 2015 Paris climate agreement "a problem for any treaty that includes a notion of equity that conceives of the atmosphere as a global commons in which individuals, groups, or nations may claim shares." Many countries had been following India in advocating for equity in *historical* per capita emissions as the best way to determine a country's fair share of allowable emissions. Light observes that this abstractly defensible allocation placed the United States in a severe "carbon debt" (2013, 33). Moreover, there is no clear path in US federal law to restrict its emissions to accord with such an allocation. This presents a domestic hurdle for the United States to join an ambitious agreement, even though American cooperation remains essential to achieving "some modicum of climate safety" (30).

In *One World*, Singer acknowledges that the historical version of the principle of per capita equity in greenhouse gas emissions is an internal political hurdle for industrialized countries (2004, 195). As a political compromise to bring about the best outcome, Singer proposes a forward-looking principle of "equal per capita future entitlements to a share of the capacity of the atmospheric sink"

(194). An emissions-trading scheme is compatible with this principle, and Singer thinks such an approach is politically plausible, though it may eventually require United Nations sanctions against the United States analogous to those in the 1970s to 1990s against apartheid South Africa (198).

The difference between Singer's and Light's approaches does not pivot on a disagreement about the "optimal allocation of global reductions in emissions in the abstract," nor on how this should be carried forward in a climate treaty that will hold everyone's feet to the fire (Light 2013, 35). Light does not deny that there may be a theoretically defensible optimal emissions allocation for countries, or more or less optimal ways to deal with high short-range costs that have uncertain long-range benefits (see Broome 2012, ch. 8). But he insists that we remain clear about the aim of such debate: to sort out what to do, not to agree in advance on justifications or on the single correct way to reason about the matter. This is analogous to Dewey's doctor who aids healthy recovery. As an approach to climate diplomacy, Light thus focuses pragmatically on a decision process to elicit the generative possibilities of an international community shackled by an overly legalistic approach that was insensitive to seemingly intractable tensions, no matter how equitable the emissions plan was in the abstract.

This focus on adaptive and generative decision processes may be clarified by counterposing the Kyoto Protocol with the Paris climate agreement. At the risk of oversimplification, the Kyoto Protocol took a top-down, punitive approach tethered to an abstractly justifiable principle of equitable emissions. According to Light, who was confirmed in 2021 as US assistant secretary of energy for international affairs, by emphasizing *ends fixed in advance*, with penalties attached, Kyoto precipitated a race to the bottom when it came to agreeing on binding targets.[5] In contrast, the Paris Agreement took a bottom-up, "pledge and review" approach (aka "shame and blame"), which Light regards as exemplifying a pragmatic emphasis on adaptive action that keeps an eye on the ends-means continuum. He argues that this makes it more likely that evolving situations will be met creatively *and* with higher ambition.

While retrospectively acknowledging the periodic unreliability of the United States as an international actor in non-binding agreements, Light argues that relying on the benefits and backlash of being judged a good or bad international actor—especially as the tragic stakes of climate change continue to rise—"will not guarantee success for achieving some level of climate stability, but it will create an environment in which that will be more likely" (2017, 495). Additionally, Light argues, this approach makes it more likely that climate justice issues will be effectively addressed. He urges that it is essential for the United States to remain part of a coalition that agrees on a high-ambition interpretation of "shared but differentiated responsibilities"—that is, recognition that those most to blame for climate change are generally least vulnerable to its harms (2017; cf. Caney 2005), so that wealthier countries shoulder greater responsibility for abating the impact of their emissions while subsidizing climate adaptation and resilience in poorer countries.

In Light's view, the Kyoto Protocol's general approach to the problem was monistic, while the Paris Agreement's approach was pluralistic and culturally contextual, at least in the sense that a country's pledge to the world has to make sense domestically. Light argues, for example, that India's nationalistic Prime Minister Modi understands dealing with climate disruption primarily as a religiously bound moral obligation tied up with Hindu scriptures, not primarily as a utilitarian problem about how to secure the aggregate welfare of India's growing population. By encouraging pledges to target specific actions and commitments in ways that are "embedded in their cultural" and political contexts, countries under the Paris Agreement need not share views about *why* independent actors should respond to the problems, any more than actors in the abortion debate are required to agree about *why* prenatal care is important as a shared end. But a pledge-and-review climate agreement can nevertheless create a new context of mutual social inquiry in which groups converge on effective policies due to common interests (cf. LW 2:377). Separate and often deeply conflicting interests, beliefs, and values will remain. Those who prefer to take these divisions on directly may feel justified in giving up, while adaptive pragmatists try to build *first* on commonalities.

This case illustrates that confrontation among relatively incommensurable values does not preclude creating common ground, nor does it rule out constructing new interests and aims together. Rawls (1993) *hoped* in his later work to achieve something similar with his weakly pluralistic politics of "overlapping consensus." While his Kantian conception of "public reason" accounted for the pursuit and justification of public aims, Dewey did a comparatively better job accounting for the *construction and transformation* of aims through public deliberation and inquiry. Roberto Frega has argued, for example, that the most influential notions of public reason in contemporary political philosophy—represented for him by Rawls, Jürgen Habermas, and critical theory—make room for aggregation and negotiation of contested monological aims and interests, but not for their collaborative, dialogical revision. He proposes that Dewey's problem-solving model of public inquiry overcomes these limitations (Frega 2010; cf. Ralston 2010, 30).

Light adds that Paris encourages the celebration of intermediate progress as part of five-year plans in which countries convene, report out, and pressure each other to be more ambitious. (The first five-year meeting was the November 2021 UN Climate Conference in Glasgow.) This assertion that a foxlike pragmatist approach is ameliorative, and can increase ambition, raises a question: What counts as "progress" for a pragmatist, in the absence of a final and ultimate good for measuring it relative to an ideal that rests outside experiential facts?

Light, like Dewey, agrees that there must be quasi-definite (albeit revisable) agreed-upon ends to focus our collective ambitions.

But both reject absolute standards for measuring progress in favor of what Kitcher calls "pragmatic progress, progress as problem-solving" (2019, 12; cf. Kitcher 2021). Dewey argued that achievements in our transitional dealings with problems are real, *relative to earlier problematic conditions.* Successes along the way are to be celebrated. But our rectifications are not measurable by any rigid "general formula of progress" (1922b, MW 14:196).

Dewey rejected the two most influential variations of the quest for an absolute standard by which to measure ultimate progress: (1) the juvenile notion that progress "means a definite sum of accomplishment which will forever stay done, and which by an exact amount lessens the amount still to be done . . . on our road to a final stable and unperplexed goal," and (2) the popular perfectionist fallacy that all achievements are negligible in comparison to ultimate and perfect goods (1922b, MW 14:197–198). From this angle, whereas Jamieson (2014) was inclined to see the 2009 Copenhagen climate meeting as a disaster from which no good would come, Light saw Copenhagen as a prelude to bringing together a "high-ambition coalition" of odd bedfellows in the Paris Agreement, an adaptive coalition that might take things to the next level.

There are some promising signs that Paris's pragmatic pledge-and-review approach to one-upmanship among countries is working, and is moreover helping to scale up public-private partnerships that will be required to radically reconstruct markets. For example, the April 2021 Earth Day international climate summit hosted by US president Biden was distinguished by countries boasting about their accomplishments and green economy innovations (e.g., carbon pricing). Countries competed with each other's greenhouse gas emission targets to mitigate climate change, and there was unrelenting pressure placed on wealthy nations to increase their financial commitments to climate justice to help poorer countries adapt. "The theme of this conference is raising ambition," said US climate envoy John Kerry in his wrap-up to the first session, and "raising ambition" was the leitmotif used throughout by heads of state, nongovernmental organizations, and corporate executives. French president Macron, for example, announced at that conference that "2030 is the new 2050" for achieving net-zero carbon emissions, positioning France ahead of Germany in its goals, even as German chancellor Merkel announced 55 percent reductions in greenhouse gas emissions by 2030, thereby outpacing President Biden's relatively aggressive announced target of halving the United States' emissions by the same date.

Returning with a grain of salt to Berlin's heuristic, the monistic hedgehog is at home in a settled world. The hedgehog asserts a priori that its job as a theorist is to show which antecedently justified principles should govern politicies and choices. So the incorrigible hedgehog focuses first on getting the theory worked out before impersonally deciding whose values measure up to its supreme metric (whether taken to be constructed or foundational). Start with getting the theory right, as though the rest follows! This is a recipe for popcorn solutions. Meanwhile, the fox is at home in wickedly complex systems and is aware of the incompleteness of any decision or model. The fox attends to adaptive processes through which we may interpersonally or intra-nationally decide what to *do*, listen, pursue creative leads, take stock, critique choices, and correct mistakes.

Hedgehog processes (akin to Kyoto) are expert governed to predetermine a metric that will yield the right, optimal, or ideal outcome. Meanwhile, foxlike processes (akin to Paris) strive to engage communities or their proxies in what Norton (2015) describes as Deweyan "social learning" (clarified later in this chapter), which in Norton's interpretation is a scientifically informed procedural feedback loop for intelligently adapting policies by incorporating representative stakeholders. Foxlike processes may thereby increase ambition toward achieving shared goals and, at least potentially, foster growth in the public imagination as both means and end.

We all have hedgehog habits, but it would help to have them take a back seat for a while, especially when it comes to wicked problems. Hedgehog habits can complement value inquiries without collapsing into moral fundamentalism. They can be useful backseat drivers when they cut decisively through extraneous noise so that we attend to problems. Unfortunately, when yielded the driver's seat, hedgehog habits can tend toward moral fundamentalism, which undermines their positive social role.

There is a hedgehoggish dimension to all argumentation, ironically including my own argument here for the virtues of foxlike inquiry. If we can occupy a liminal position between them that does not stabilize fundamentalism, the hedgehog and fox probably need each other. The hedgehog's unifying image of moral life is at least consoling, and everyone at times need to be shaken from complacency. Nevertheless, foxlike habits have been underdeveloped despite their compensatory value for dealing with intergroup conflicts and unexpected consequences in complex systems under non-ideal conditions. This is no less true when conditions call for coordinated resistance to oppressive power. We could use more foxlike theories of structural injustice, oppression, power, and privilege (cf. Stuhr 2019; Whipps 2019). Erin McKenna and Scott Pratt, for example, urge "a recovery of a Deweyan pluralist philosophy of resistance and freedom" that is democratic, fallibilistic, attuned to issues of power, and responsive to situated knowledge (2019). While acknowledging that hedgehoggishness has pragmatic value (see Dworkin 2011), and that hedgehog habits have historically lent aid in situations where we must resist vicious narrowness and redress injustices, there is no logical inevitability in their codification remaining the primary and overriding focus of moral and political theorizing.

Environmental Pragmatism: Toward a Plann*ing* Society

In their groundbreaking edited volume *Environmental Pragmatism*, Light and Katz define environmental pragmatism as "the open-ended inquiry into specific real-life problems of humanity's relationship with the environment" (1996, 2). Franks et al. add that environmental pragmatism is "an approach to environmental ethics that emphasizes the need for environmental activists and academics to open-mindedly engage with people's existing environmental attitudes and behaviors if they are to have any influence over them" (2017, 13). These definitions are accurate as far as they go, but more should be said to distinguish environmental pragmatism from other approaches and to clarify what is meant by "open-ended inquiry" and "open-minded engagement" (e.g., see Hourdequin 2014, ch. 8; Thompson and Piso 2019).

A standout feature of environmental pragmatism, as represented, for example, by Norton (1991, 2015), Weston (1991), Minteer (2011), Thompson (2015), Light (2017), Fesmire (2020), and McKenna (2018, 2020), is sidestepping of the mainstream attempt in environmental ethics to find a single defensible paradigm with which we must align ourselves. Perhaps most notably, whatever their own eco-ontologies, pragmatist ethicists do not tend to place a high priority on revolutionary attempts to convince doubters that natural systems, living beings, or sentient beings have intrinsic value. Nor do environmental pragmatists perpetuate the late nineteenth- and early twentieth-century American idea of wilderness as a place where affluent white sons of privilege go to restore their manliness (Cronon 1996). Instead, they tend to focus more than monists on ameliorative processes for resolving disagreements and on making workable, ecologically informed decisions (Minteer and Collins 2005). Monistic standpoints are not dismissed, but they are recast as tools to open up inquiry, which compensates for their unidimensionality. Environmental pragmatism's sidestepping of the monistic quest clarifies one sense in which it is an "open-ended" approach to making better decisions.

Self-identified pragmatists may or may not additionally concur with Norton's "convergence hypothesis" (1991) that, in practice, broad-scope anthropocentric arguments usually justify the same policies as ecocentric arguments. But they do tend to agree with Norton that it is defeatist to declare in advance that the *only* effective way to deal with our most urgent environmental problems is to usher in a complete cultural paradigm shift that radically transforms human value systems. We do not generate much general willingness to act together when we insist that others first convert to our value framework. Insistence on more expansive values is often desirable and unavoidable, as with the history of Jim Crow segregation in the United States, but the pragmatist urges colloquy to go as far as it can instead of *starting* from an ideal standpoint that autocratically sidelines discord and dissent. If the aim is to gain traction for collective action, better to hypothesize with Norton that, when the view of human interests is contextually sensitive and suitably long term, it may motivate policies that converge with those that would be adopted by reasonable environmental theorists regardless of their conflicting standpoints.

Though overstated in its strong version (cf. Henning 2023, ch. 8), Norton's convergence hypothesis applies to what Dewey called a plann*ing* society rather than a plann*ed* society. "There is a difference between a society which is plann*ed* and a society which is continuously plann*ing*—namely, the difference between autocracy and democracy, between dogma and intelligence in operation, between suppression of individuality and that release and utilization of individuality which will bring it to full maturity" (1933a, LW 8:76). Subjection to "leadership imposed from above" was an early historical development compared to the recent emergence of democratic ideas, and autocratic worldviews persist today in many families, religious institutions, schools and universities, and professions (1935, LW 11:219). Dewey contended that "experience shows that as long as they persist there, political democracy is not secure" (219). Whereas relatively incommensurable values across individuals, groups, and countries are an inherent problem for any planned autocratic society, such as in Plato's *Republic* or the former Soviet Union, these values are irreducible frictional

factors of a continuously planning society. The Paris climate agreement illustrates cooperative planning across values of diverse
communities. Unlike the planned Kyoto Protocol, Paris can strategically navigate discordant values *as long as* countries keep planning together.

Environmental pragmatists' emphasis on continuous cooperative planning does not imply that they ignore the evaluation of
principles, though the literature has arguably underemphasized
the pragmatic import of principles and affiliated and worldviews
(see Henning 2023). There are tensions, for instance, between the
precautionary principle and welfare-based cost-benefit analyses,
and there are debates in climate ethics underlying the discount
rate (Broome 2012, chs. 6–8). It is perilous to ignore principles,
as Broome observes. This leaves the consequences of following
divergent principles solely to those with technical expertise, and
it fails to shed any light on what citizens should demand of their
governments. For example, during Europe's third wave of the
Covid-19 pandemic, European Union countries such as Germany
paused shots with the AstraZeneca vaccine while studying a cor-
relation with seven cases of blood clotting (Fisher 2021). This
risked lives. The Hippocratic principle of doing no active harm
competed here with a principle of overall welfare maximization,
in the fashion of standard trolley problems ("Would you kill one
person to save five?"). The EU move, like a subsequent pause with
the Johnson & Johnson vaccine in the United States, also aimed to
promote public trust in the vaccination process. Broome is surely
right that citizens need to understand what is at stake in following
principles like these.

Nevertheless, whereas Broome's utilitarian "expected value
theory" seeks "the correct principle for coping with uncertainty"
(11), pragmatists focus less on hedgehoggish debates about which
general principles are the all-encompassing right ones for thinking
about and governing human relationships. This puzzles earnest
utilitarian and Kantian ethicists who equate "doing ethics" with

justifying crisp, principle-driven prescriptions about how we should act and assess. Pragmatists do not identify conformity with antecedently determined law, or ciphering aggregate well-being, as the mainstay of ethical decision-making, though these methods are useful tools for imaginative "dramatic rehearsal," as Dewey framed his psychological description of moral deliberation in *Human Nature and Conduct* (1922b, MW 14; cf. Fesmire 2003). If this pragmatist turn appears to evade "doing ethics," perhaps even happily so (West 1989), it is at any rate not muddled.[6]

The Breakthrough Institute's widely discussed 2011 report titled *Climate Pragmatism* (Atkinson et al. 2011) takes positions that stand or fall independent of environmental pragmatism as a philosophical orientation. Their "ecomodernism"—inspired in 2003 by Nordhaus and Shellenberger, of "The Death of Environmentalism" fame—is explicitly pragmatist in its foxlike approach, but there is nothing inherent in environmental pragmatism from which one can deduce cautious support for technologies such as agricultural intensification, GMOs, and nuclear energy, or from which one can deduce whether the emphasis should be more on adaptation to climate change rather than abatement of it (see Gardiner's critique, 2011, 257).

Participatory Social Learning and the Democratic Ideal: More Dewey, Less Lippmann

In *Sustainable Values, Sustainable Change* (2015), Norton draws inspiration from Aldo Leopold's "Thinking Like a Mountain" (1949) to study a cultural shift from the 1970s to 1990s in the Chesapeake region of the United States. During that period, the policy discussions in this region shifted away from object-focused "thinking like an estuary" toward multiscalar "thinking like a watershed" (250–257). The former cultural model was so tightly circumscribed that it hid the long temporal and wide spatial scales of environmental problems such as nonpoint source pollution. This cultural shift to a more holistic conceptual mapping has affected the ecological imaginations of millions who live in the Chesapeake Bay area, yet—and here is Norton's pragmatist point— the transformation from localized bay to regional watershed did not require a victor in the prize fight over foundational environmental values. Nor did the collective shift to a more expansive ecological model require any *prior* commitment to a view about the moral standing of natural systems. However, learning to "think like a watershed" *did* minimally involve what Norton characterizes as Deweyan "social learning."

Norton draws from "adaptive management" pioneer Kai Lee's (1993) analysis of Dewey's approach to democratic participation, conflicting values, and policy formation. Lee and Norton highlight the role of social learning in policymaking processes that are informed by both scientific expertise and representative stakeholders. They propose that direct participation of representatives in policymaking can pay the fringe benefit of helping communities develop the knowledge, resolve, and resilience to achieve superordinate goals. Norton explains Lee's appreciative critique of Dewey:

> Lee recognizes that Dewey was overly optimistic in thinking all citizens will participate actively in public deliberation and experimental management. But by recognizing that, under the right conditions, an inclusive group of more committed stakeholders, representing the range of opinions existent in the society, could be formed into an "epistemological community," Lee, citing Haas (1990), concludes that social learning can take place by the proxied representation of diverse interests in the society. (Norton 2002, 187)

Lee (1993) proposes that decision- making can be improved through scientifically informed public participation (e.g., Smith et. al. 1998). He is inspired by Dewey's participatory ideal in *The*

Public and Its Problems (1927). Lee and Norton may not have entirely escaped a common misperception of Dewey's position, but their argument for broadening participation is strengthened by clarifying it. Dewey agreed with Lippmann's *The Phantom Public* (1925) that the "ideal of the sovereign and omnicompetent citizen" is unattainably romantic. Dewey also agreed with Lippmann that experts must communicate with nonexperts by simplifying and interpreting complex events. What Dewey rejected was Lippmann's coziness with paternalistic rule by technocrats who oversimplify problems so that citizens will accept the reality that is bureaucratically packaged for them. Dewey saw prophecies of public incompetence as self-fulfilling, and nothing made his democratic blood boil more than this idea that inellectuals must lift the burden of inquiry from the provincial and parochial little heads of the masses while conferring the "mandate of heaven" on certain ideas. A century on, Lippmann's outlook plays all too well into the caricature of contemptuous liberals that right-wing demagogues are fertilizing in order to harvest working class resentment. We need less Lippman and more Dewey.

In Lippmann's view, in sharp contrast with Dewey, Lee, and Norton, there is no realistic hope that reorganizing education and decision processes can put citizens in a position to steer the public ship because "the real environment is altogether too big, too complex, and too fleeting for direct acquaintance" (Lippmann 1922, 16). Dewey and Lippmann agreed that the great question is how to bridge "the gap between the limited capacities of the citizen and the complexity of his environment" (LW 2:216). Dewey's famous riposte to Lippmann's pessimism about bridging this gap was to advocate, like Lee, cooperative planning for a creative and adaptive public that had no need for omnicompetence.

Philosophic pretensions have been chastened over the century since Dewey debated Lippmann, but Dewey's general line of argument still holds when qualified. By pooling accumulated knowledge, guided by experts skilled in bringing facts to bear on social affairs, citizens can and often do become educated *enough* to effectively participate at manageable scales to a degree that is sufficient for more-or-less reliable decision-making (1927, LW 2). Lippmann will find no mandate of heaven here, Niebuhr no right dogmas, and Fei no ultimate truth. But perhaps we have finally had enough incitement of moral fundamentalism.

Democratic failings are symptomatic of many troubles, but Dewey insisted that Lippmann was confused about the *cause* of those failings: they do not spring from democracy, but from "stupidity, intolerance, bullheadedness and bad education, whether these traits decorate a monarch, ornament an oligarchy or supply the moral insignia of the populace" (1925, LW 2:220). Dewey should have added that democratic failings also arise from a rigged system rather than from democracy per se. He recognized structural injustice, but he often wrote as though a fair economic deal coupled with greater tolerance would be enough to set things right (e.g., see Glaude 2007). Twenty-first-century Dewey scholars turn elsewhere for their muse on structural injustice, as Glaude (2020) turns to Baldwin. Nevertheless, to sum up what Dewey saw clearly and prophetically in *The Public and Its Problems*: when the problem is not democracy, the solution is not to reject it via liberal aristocracy or the empowerment of illiberal populist strongmen.

When a particular democracy is not working for people, yet at least some communication across stakeholder groups remains possible, Dewey urged democratic reconstruction of that democracy's structures. Humans are educable yet myopic, so emphasize the former by engaging the public in decision-making processes at manageable scales. The Chesapeake region's cultural shift toward "thinking like a watershed" exemplifies Dewey's position that public processes are integral both to effective policymaking and to growth in public understanding. Spurred on by the grassroots work of nongovernmental organizations in tandem with the top-down "hammer" of state and federal regulatory demands (a legal resource for moving recalcitrant parties to the collaborative table), a new public identity for the Chesapeake region gradually developed. This identity was marked by a shift from small-scale and short-term thinking—circumscribed by a bay's boundaries—toward longer-term, broader-scope thinking and valuing at the watershed scale. Norton argues that this sort of transformation, however modest, can happen as we grapple together with problems (2015). This revaluing occurred *because* of participation, not as a prerequisite to it. Contrary to Lippman's overreaching approach, which blocks social learning, decision-making was not limited to experts who have proven their mettle.

Dewey first learned the importance of democratic processes from his work with Addams in Chicago in the 1890s. Addams cofounded Hull House on the West Side of Chicago as a settlement house for European immigrant women in 1889, and Dewey joined its board of trustees in 1894. Addams argued for a social ethics that swims *with* the current of social interactions and psychology. In her 1902 book *Democracy and Social Ethics*, she asserted that only those oblivious to actual circumstances fill themselves with pride in their personal morality in the face of the acute need for a social morality in which we join forces for practical reform of institutional structures (Addams 2002a, 6). Amid rapid population growth, she came to see social ethics as an essential mode of conduct for the flourishing of individuals, families, and states.[7]

Dewey later wrote that Addams and Hull House underscored for him the happiness to be "found simply in this broadening of intellectual curiosity and sympathy in all the concerns of life" (LW 5:422). He came to see democracy not just as a way of formally arranging political and legal machinery through elected representatives—as a "substitute for war," Rep. Richard Gephardt once remarked—but as a "personal way of life" (1939, LW 13:288) that breaks down exclusionary social barriers and opens up intersecting points of contact and communication.

Dewey nowhere weighed in on a finally "best" way to institutionalize democracy.[8] For example, during his two and a half years in East Asia (1919–1921), he recognized local and civil conditions that were ripe for social experimentation, but he did not hold up the specific forms of American or European democracies as standards for measuring Japanese or Chinese success. As Sor-hoon Tan observes in a recent essay on China's potential for democratization, Dewey was a fallibilist "about the political institutions of democracy" (2019, 608). Taken as "conjoint communicated experience" (1916, MW 9:93; cf. Mostajir 2022), democracy as a way of life creatively reinterprets, reevaluates, and continually transforms its own machinery, regardless of which organizational forms political democracies take.

Dewey argued that we should see how far it may be practicable to make decisions about public affairs through the give-and-take of open communication. He rejected as a false dilemma—stemming from a lingering dualism going back at least to Plato—the idea that we must choose between aristocratic command-and-control decisions, on one hand, and extreme populist rule, on the other.

Against the aristocratic view, Dewey urged that back-and-forth communication across differences is necessary if cooperative intelligence is to function as a method of problem-solving. As discussed, he embraced decision-making informed by experts, but he criticized overreliance on decision-making that is *determined* by them. For example, detached calculations of optimal welfare by policy analysts (see 1922b, MW 14:139–145) can aid public deliberation. But policy analyses should not merely be hung on a rack for the public to take down and wear without thought. Nor should expert analyses merely be translated into directives to those wielding executive power.

At the same time, Dewey rejected populist rule, in which we make choices based on how forcefully one group can drive home their point or sell it in the marketplace of ideas (cf. MW 8:443–445). Public processes fail to meet problems when power is bestowed upon individuals or groups who pretend to diagnostic expertise that they do not have. Even worse, a free democratic community cannot be maintained by populist masses, as these trend toward authoritarian regimes.

Democratic communication about problems, independent of the formal political and economic institutions such communication may plan and prescribe, maximizes the chance that we might find paths that respect legitimate interests, evaluations, and evolving identities of individuals, institutions, and groups. Inherent frictions are brought to the fore; empathy is enhanced. Meanwhile, merely reactive friction and inertial resistance to innovation are reduced (cf. Nordgren and Schonthal 2021). When "the decider" ignores stakeholders, this has unintended consequences. It raises suspicions about aims, interests, and background assumptions. It also raises issues of transparency and accountability, and it predictably leads to myopic, unworkable policies (1927, LW 2:235–372). When a decision-making process is more than nominally democratic, it seeks out points of friction and divergence, and it gains legitimacy and direction by evaluating them for their instrumental bearings, criticizing them, and incorporating them. "The man who wears the shoe knows best that it pinches and where it pinches," Dewey wrote in *The Public and Its Problems* (1927), "even if the expert shoemaker is the best judge of how the trouble is to be remedied" (LW 2:364).

Dewey is here distinguishing the pinch of the problem (and those feeling it) from the ways we formulate the problem (and those with relevant expertise). The way we concretely undergo a problem can be distinguished from the ways that we symbolize and inquire into it when we stop to think. In *Experience and Nature*, Dewey framed the distinction as one between primary experience and secondary experience (1925/1929, LW 1:15ff.). He had no dichotomy in mind and would agree with Johnson and Schulkin that "the distinction is trying to capture the need for a nonreductive, context-sensitive description of the richness of our lived experience. It is not meant as a fixed categorical framework" (2023, 18). When these two phases of experience form a feedback loop, secondary products of inquiry (such as the cobbler's craft) are able to nourish primary experience, so that the latter serves and reconstitutes the former. This distinction is pivotal for Dewey, as evidenced by his frustration with Bertrand Russell's misinterpretations: "Mr. Russell has not been able to follow the distinction I make between the immediately had material of non-cognitively experienced situations and the material of cognition—a distinction without which my view cannot be understood" (1939, LW 14:33).

Like the wearer who knows where the shoe pinches, stakeholders (and their proxies, Lee hopes) are better positioned than detached experts to speak for themselves (cf. Rogers 2008). Those who directly experience problems legitimately demand inquiry and a response, and they are vital contributors to embodied social knowledge. However, their preferred explanations and proposed solutions are not the final word. Being a shoe wearer does not qualify me as a cobbler; being a patient does not qualify me as a physician or healthcare policy expert. But these perspectives *do* qualify me as a player in expert-informed inquiries about means and ends.

As Richard Bernstein explained Dewey's critique of the historical quest for unmediated, noncontingent knowledge, "a good slogan for Dewey would be: Qualitative immediacy—yes! Immediate knowledge—no!" (1966, 92). Long before philosophy's "linguistic turn," Dewey joined Peirce in observing that we make sense of the world and its problems through representational signs and symbols that network together to form conceptual frameworks. These frameworks are selective, so we need conjoint, organized, and sustained experimental inquiry to highlight what they hide. No process of inquiry offers a perfected standpoint, and all inquiry is susceptible to the full range of cognitive biases in perception, assessment, and judgment (e.g., Kahneman et al. 2021; Ross 2018).[9] Add these to the long list of reasons that democratic processes cannot avoid failures.

Nevertheless, a method of moral and political inquiry that is both experimental and democratic has its virtues over placeless and faceless rationalistic demonstrations. Even when we fail, this method has the potential to be creative, critical, and self-corrective by raising questions, imagining alternatives, putting ideas to the test, and disclosing differences. At the same time, democratic participation can reduce apathy, build relationships across differences, and create consummatory value from what had been a Babel of meanings (see 1927, LW 2:324).[10] Dewey did not urge a democratic approach out of a misplaced overconfidence that success is vouchsafed to all who inquire earnestly enough. He urged it out of a practical belief that it is our only hope.

Democratic communication can offset the fraught tendency to predefine problems. Conversely, building on the moral fundamentalist "toolkit" activity in Chapter 1, if we wish to sabotage democratic planning, then we should act as though any well-intentioned and rightly informed person would formulate the problem or event *our* way. If we are simply unpacking the straightforward meaning that we found right inside what is happening, then the way we make sense of problems is not itself a problem. Dewey bet his life on a democratic faith that education has the mostly unrealized potential to curb this tendency *enough* to underwrite collaborative intelligence.

Conclusion

Dewey's idea of a democratic public as the medium of social inquiry and problem-solving is at once radical and genial. Closing his introduction to the critical edition of *The Public and Its Problems*, James Gouinlock acknowledges that Dewey's idea of democracy may not be fully realizable. "Like any theory," Gouinlock counsels, "its adequacy can be determined only by putting it to the test of practice. At this stage in our history, it would be premature to resign ourselves to lesser ambitions" (1927, LW 2:xxxvi).

A pragmatic turn that removes support for the "single right way" mentality would help philosophers and other intellectual leaders to speak more effectively to multifaceted problems on a warming planet in a way that aids public deliberation and promotes social learning.

Pragmatic pluralism challenges the destructiveness of those who act as though only their own concerns, socialized values, and received moral frameworks have overriding force when perceiving, diagnosing, and solving problems. Contemporary research in the ever-expanding American philosophical tradition that includes theorists such as Patricia Hill Collins, energized in part by critical engagement with the social ethics of Addams and Dewey, emphasizes that one's epistemic position is improved when one democratically inhabits the standpoint of intersecting identities (e.g., Collins 2019; Crenshaw 2017). Instead of developing theories that predetermine which valuational standpoints and idealizations are worth taking up, complex problems require the critical arbitration that democratic practices afford. Advocates for a broadly pragmatic, pluralistic, and democratic approach argue that through it we may mature together toward a freer, healthier, more just, more secure, more peaceful, more sustainable, and perhaps less lonely future.

3

Educating for Democracy

Are we stuck with moral fundamentalism? Yes, but its shape and extent are educable. Moral fundamentalism is a vice because it obstructs communication, constricts imagination, and underwrites bad decisions. Social inquiry and problem-solving are more honest, collaborative, rigorous, and productive when youths learn to be patient with the suspense of reflection, open to discomfort and dissent, resolute yet distrustful of tunnel vision, aware of the fallibility and incompleteness of any decision or policy, practiced in listening, and imaginative in pursuing creative leads. These are values of a democratic education (cf. Alexander and Kitcher 2021).

Over a century after the publication of Dewey's watershed *Democracy and Education* (1916, MW 9), trust in the educative capacity of experience remains our best hope for growing beyond moral fundamentalism and shrinking the problem of cultural lag. Dewey's book is the most widely cited, and perhaps the most rarely heeded, study of this capacity. The book is unified by a core question: How might formal education add something to informal and direct ways of learning? Formal schooling, he answers, "must provide genuine situations in which personal participation brings home the import of the material and the problems which it conveys" so as to evoke "attitudes of open-mindedness and concern as to the material symbolically conveyed" (1916, MW 9:242). Absent this, schooling will not speak to living.

"Making a living" captures a small part of the "living" to which schooling may speak. Educators can help students face the problems that most concern us, chart a course to clarify and interpret what is going on from a wide social and scientific perspective,

Beyond Moral Fundamentalism. Steven Fesmire, Oxford University Press. © Oxford University Press 2024. DOI: 10.1093/9780197763919.003.0003

and critically inquire into these problems with fresh hypotheses. In these ways, educators hope their students will be enabled to take part in directing events "instead of being overwhelmed by them" (MW 13:280). In the face of circumstances that overwhelm them, people tend to be reactive—like pinballs ricocheting around a machine. When schooling speaks to living by speaking to "intellectual and moral growth" (1916, MW 9:320), students can learn to guide changes through inquiry and communication instead of being tossed around or swept away. Educators can simultaneously contribute to wider public comprehension of what is at stake, and to habits that support the public in acting intelligently on that comprehension (LW 11:232).

Dewey's emphasis on democratic decision-making depends on a citizenry educated in experimental intelligence at a wide-enough scale. Given that some students betray a casual disregard for inquiry as a practical guide, even Dewey's admirers can find him quaintly out of touch. "Sure, Peter Singer is right that animal suffering matters and that we should make choices that decrease it," a student wrote in an undergraduate ethics class, "but I'm not going to do anything different." Teachers and professors sometimes despair of motivating students to improve their seemingly vestigial capacity to put reflection into practice.

Dewey argued that such alienation from competent inquiry is due in part to the pedantry that attends secondhand dispensation of isolated facts. By actively engaging students in open inquiry in an applied context, they can organically assimilate knowledge in a way that reintegrates them into communities and institutions. When we enlist students in inquiries that are personal, imaginative, and direct, what they learn is of value in the direction of life (MW 7:250). In that spirit, I open this chapter with a case study of Deweyan democratic pedagogy in education, before turning to a social critique of the industrial model that educates worker bees instead of experimental problem-solvers. I argue that this model is antidemocratic and blocks growth beyond moral fundamentalism, and I urge educational leaders and policymakers to embrace a holistic liberal education for all while continuing to support occupational callings.

The Strange Case of Bill and Lou: Educating Democratic Citizens

Democracy must begin at home, and its home is the neighborly community (1927, LW 2:367–368).

It is commonplace today to note that people are overwhelmed by momentarily exciting yet unfathomed information that is boxed for consumption—for example, through media exaggeration and social networking filters. As was already evident to Dewey over eighty-five years ago, people like prepared ideas as much as they like prepared foods (1938b, LW 13:95–96). In our dispersive age of mis- and dis-information, we should consider with Dewey whether the transitions we face might be better navigated by a citizenry that has learned to deal with problems at a more manageable scale, beginning with our families, neighborhoods, schools, markets, and local communities. And campuses.

Green Mountain College's oxen team, Bill and Lou, had plowed the fields of the small Vermont college farm together for a decade. Lou injured a rear leg over the summer of 2012 and became unable to support his own great weight. After consultation with the farm manager and with administrative consent, the college's farm crew decided to slaughter the team. Their plan was to "close the loop" between the farm and the college's dining services, providing two thousand pounds of meat from a high-welfare source.

As an expression of its environmentally themed liberal arts mission, the college's academic program in sustainable agriculture, led by Philip Ackerman-Leist, aimed to lift the veil that separates consumers from the sources of what they eat (cf. Murphy 2013;

Ackerman-Leist 2017).[1] That program typified a basic idea in the college's curriculum: change agents who are not fatalistically resigned to injustice, unsustainability, and disaffection need to understand the ins and outs of the socioeconomic context in which changes take place. This functional knowledge cannot be achieved by treating the classroom as a hermetically sealed space, or what Dewey called "a fenced-off sanctuary" (1933a, LW 8:58–59; cf. Waks 2019).

Through academic and co-curricular programs, faculty strove to bring food production, consumption, and distribution into the classroom so that students experienced firsthand the aesthetic, moral, and intellectual value of tracing the hidden relationships wound up with everyday choices. Chefs, farmers, and even slaughterhouse operators were not hidden away in their kitchens, fields, and abattoirs; they were brought into the educational process. This periodically meant that students made life-and-death decisions— guided by faculty, staff, and administrative oversight, along with a sheaf of policies which were hashed out in transdisciplinary classes and committees.

The farm crew's decision to slaughter was vetted by a packed "open class," a moderated campus dialogue that included many vegetarians and vegans.[2] The college's provost, philosopher William Throop, laid out arguments against slaughter, at least of the uninjured ox. He included a case for special obligations based on relationships formed over time with these animals. Farm crew members in turn presented their rationale. In addition to sharing some Jackson and Salatin-style arguments (see Chapter 2), they argued that the farm's mission was to be an educational model of sustainable agriculture, not a sanctuary or a petting zoo. The economic sustainability of animal agriculture drives a thorny logic of culling. Farmers work within a food system that does not typically include financial infusions to support unproductive animals. Additionally, the farm crew argued, simply euthanizing Lou would contaminate his meat, wasting a chance to replace industrial meat in the dining hall. Finally, they argued that it is more humane to slaughter both members of an oxen team that had been together since birth.

The ensuing discussion revealed discordant values and ambivalence among the students. The forum eventually affirmed the farm crew's plan with a near consensus that included most of the vegetarian and vegan students. If groupthink was involved, it would soon be challenged. After a news release announced the slaughter decision, the college moved unwittingly into the media spotlight. Journalists from the *New York Times*, NPR, the *Boston Globe*, and many other venues would pay a visit in the coming weeks to rural Poultney, Vermont.

"They're eating their mascots!" The international animal rights protest was led by a Vermont farm sanctuary, VINE (Veganism Is the Next Evolution), an organization publicly committed to the abolition of animal agriculture. VINE offered to pay for all expenses to relocate Bill and Lou to their sanctuary, an offer which the college declined. To say this angered protesters would be an understatement. Thousands of emails and phone calls—most civil, many derogatory, several alarmingly threatening—rained down on administrators, faculty, staff, and students who found themselves in the crosshairs. The onslaught continued for a couple of months. Due to sustained pressure from protesters directed at area slaughterhouses, the college was unable to carry out its decision. Instead, the college's veterinary service euthanized Lou, the injured ox. Months later, after the protest had quieted, Bill was slaughtered. The meat was not edible, confirming a speculation voiced by many protestors as well as some within the college.

I often share this case with students as an exercise in perspective taking, asking them to explore whether a decisive victory by VINE would represent moral progress. The case spotlights value conflicts between vegan abolitionism and sustainable animal husbandry. The former is individualistic and sentientist in its moral worldview, while the latter tends to extend moral consideration beyond individuals to encompass wider systems.

Prior to Green Mountain's decision, animal rights abolitionists had been seeking a photogenic target for a campaign against what they called "happy meat," animal protein procured from small, high-welfare farms. They argue for a moral identity between animal agriculture and human slavery. We can imagine, with Harriet Beecher Stowe, a Kentucky master who is kinder than a Louisiana master, but both traded in what the law declared to be monetized ambulatory property. Vegan abolitionists argue that since we agree that abolition of the institution of slavery was the only defensible option, we should equally agree that institutions and practices that treat sentient animals as fungible property must be universally dismantled. Scale does not matter. Small-scale farmers frequently name and care for animals like Bill and Lou who are eventually "humanely slaughtered." This pretense of moral defensibility, frequently voiced by omnivores on the opposite side of the food movement like Michael Pollan (2006), provokes special vitriol.

VINE's call for a one-diet-fits-all vegan revolution ruled out anything except their way forward. In their version of hedghoggish monism, they deduced that animal protein cannot be ethically sourced, so there is no room for educational institutions to experiment with sustainable options for producing eggs, meat, and dairy products. Meanwhile, a small minority in the college community wielded Salatin's opposing sword of righteousness (see Chapter 2). A year before the protest, Salatin gave a well-received talk at the college in which he argued that the "right" diet *must* be based on grass-fed animal agriculture, so natural law rules out ethical experiments in vegan or vegetarian living. In contrast to these fundamentalisms, a pragmatist ecofeminist ethicist such as Erin McKenna (2020) says "it depends" and opens herself to *critically* evaluating the particulars of various agricultural experiments.

Moral fundamentalism is at odds with the greatest educational need in any democratic society. As Dewey argued in *The Public and Its Problems*, that need is to improve "the methods and conditions of debate, discussion and persuasion. That is *the* problem of the public" (1927, LW 2:365). We should teach students to value friction and to be suspicious of both majority tyrannies and negative partisanship (Abramowitz and Webster 2018), and we should help them to become compassionate, active, and informed problem solvers who do not simply oppose others' moral fundamentalism with their own. Exercising moral fundamentalist habits gives those habits safe haven and feeds the underlying one-way mentality.

Thoughtful and well-informed people may reasonably disagree about how best to meet wickedly complex ethical problems. In the lingo of European cognitive psychologists such as Joachim Funke, dealing with such problems requires contextually sensitive "complex cognition" that goes beyond "simple cognition" (Funke 2010). Complex cognition names the kind of critical intelligence and creative imagination that is needed to deal with tangled problems in the food system. On the problem of Bill's and Lou's fate, the way forward was not crystal clear. It was far from a matter of unbounded subjective preference, but it could not be straightforwardly computed.

In class meetings during the protest, faculty strove—and sometimes failed—to counter the artificial clarity that arises in the face of intense public scrutiny. When a group has made a decision, it too often resorts to rearguard measures, shoring up defensive arguments and tidying up the details ad hoc. The resulting fundamentalist camps impede mutually transformative dialogue. Green Mountain College educators consciously steered clear of moralistic lessons, but they did selectively cultivate dispositions to help students become more resilient and a bit wiser in navigating life's terrain (Throop 2017). Students learned that every action has extensive consequences, but they did not merely learn it as a free-floating factoid. After all, having a great deal of information that hitches only to other information does not make one informed in any functional way (cf. MW 7:250–251). A student who develops functional knowledge is more likely to take active responsibility for the cascading effects of behaviors, choices, and policies.

Parochialism abounds, but students are better prepared to reform wider affairs and institutions when their perceptions and judgments have been expanded by problem-solving at a relatable level. They can imagine concretely and extensively the situation at hand, exchange and assess relevant information and observations, and confer about ways forward. Dewey proposed that such social communication, when scientifically informed, offers a participatory medium for quickening the public's slumbering democratic imaginations. Instead of leaving all nontrivial decisions to administrators, treating public deliberation as impractical à la Lippmann, the college opted for a more direct and inclusive process of social learning. This included many attempts by student and faculty to communicate with protesters. At least internal to the campus community, some were persuaded by others, and most got used to each other (cf. Appiah 2010). In end-of-term course evaluations, students reported that they grew in their ability to critically incorporate different and dissenting voices. They also witnessed, and some fueled, the ugliness of moral fundamentalism. It remains difficult to assess the learning that occurred beyond the college, but in later years, student stories encapsulated the meanings they had wrested from events. The episode neither embittered them nor left them with a lopsided and mono-focused moral outlook. It helped their growth beyond moral fundamentalism.

The Purposes of Education

Media fact-checkers promptly corrected US senator Marco Rubio when he called for more vocational education during the Republican Party's November 2015 presidential debate: "Welders make more money than philosophers," he said. "We need more welders than philosophers." It was widely pointed out in response to Senator Rubio's remark that, on average, those who major in philosophy at a college or university tend to have higher salaries than professional welders. But making this point, despite its possible utility for promoting philosophy as an academic major, sidetracks us from a more fundamental question: What is the mission of education in a democracy? We cannot, on a pragmatist approach, circumscribe a set of necessary and sufficient conditions that will single out *the* essential mission of education across all courses, programs, and institutions—from primary school science to dental hygiene programs. But we can meaningfully debate the aims of education and analyze conflicts in educational politics, with an eye to creating a more humane democratic culture.

In *Woman in the Nineteenth Century* (1845), Margaret Fuller admonished the practice of educating girls just to be wives and mothers. "A being of infinite scope," she wrote, "must not be treated with an exclusive view to any one relation. Give the soul free course ... and the being will be fit for any and every relation to which it may be called" (in Marshall 2014, 226).

Educational politics and policy are entangled in notions and practices as constrictive as the one Fuller criticized more than 175 years ago. For many, the mission of education is, in former Wisconsin governor Scott Walker's infamous words, "to develop human resources to meet the state's workforce needs" (Bump 2015). Walker's clumsy statist language faded with his national political fortunes, but his general outlook is far from an outlier. It is premised on a truncated education-as-job-training model that provides padded yokes for students to place around their own necks so they can be driven down a row that strictly prepares them for their careers. Walker's outlook typifies a popular view that education is mostly a way to fuel industry with skilled labor, and it is incompatible with Fuller's democratic goal of preparing students for "any and every relation to which [they] may be called."

The Industrial Model in Education:
Training Worker Bees

When it comes to recent debates in educational politics and policy, even a strident defense of the liberal arts that is diametrically opposite Governor Walker's dismantling of the public-spirited "Wisconsin idea"—such as George Anders's You Can Do Anything: The Surprising Power of a *"Useless" Liberal Arts Education* (2017) or Randall Stross's *A Practical Education: Why Liberal Arts Majors Make Great Employees* (2017)—may inadvertently reinforce the top priority given to market-driven values in educational policy and curriculum revision.

The priority implied by the "industrial model" is that teachers are first and foremost preparing students with the specific workplace skills they need to be good employees. Cultivating such skills is of course appropriate, especially as older students enter progressively specialized programs. The risk, however, is that students may achieve at best "a machine-like skill in routine lines" (320) that suits them for rigid jobs that keep them busy, subordinate, and easily replaceable.

Thoughtful pedagogy is not enough. What matters even more is how workplace aims are connected to wider educational goals. Beyond conveyance of information or skill acquisition, a wider goal is "to enlarge and enrich the scope of experience, and to keep alert and effective the interest in intellectual progress" (242). The core of Dewey's approach to vocational education in a rapidly changing techno-industrial society is his conviction that "The dominant vocation of all human beings at all times is living—intellectual and moral growth" (320). When educators lose sight of that expansive goal, they too readily become servants to an inflexible outlook that externalizes moral and citizenship education as somebody else's job. A putatively employer-serving industrial outlook is evidenced, as Diane Ravitch and many other critics have observed, in the narrow business model that drives for-profit universities, and in ongoing closures of humanities programs. This narrowing outlook is also implicit in the economic challenges facing American liberal arts colleges.

Sidestepping debates about what some philosophers of education have called the "factory model" or "corporate model" (e.g., Leland and Kasten 2002; McDermott 2013), I suggest that we also focus on the moral, social, political, and pedagogical consequences of understanding education as just another industrial sector. I avoid staking out a position on the growing literature on "academic capitalism" (e.g., Jessop 2018) or on the "corporate" or "neoliberal university" (e.g., Seal 2018). This important literature is highlighting ways in which universities have reorganized education as a fungible good efficiently marketed to Homo economicus, a species of atomistic individuals seeking to advance their human capital through incentivized competition.

But discourse on the corporate university is too often mired in a traditional humanist critique that claims to defend spectatorial "truth" and humane learning from encroachments that valorize practical outcomes and specialized performance. I reply below to what I take to be misguided about that traditional humanist outlook, while acknowledging points of convergence with my own critique. In sum, it is helpful to analyze the industrial model of education more precisely, getting clearer about the way it informs both educational discourse and delivery, so that ill-considered aims and priorities can be clearly and forcefully targeted. I argue that the industrial model is, to repeat James's words, "out of plumb, out of key, and out of whack" with the kind of formal schooling that will help us to achieve superordinate goals.

Over a century ago, Dewey saw that the then-rising consumer economy of enclosure and commodification channeled our imaginative energies into thin and superficial personal dramas. Commercial interests have "interwoven our destinies" (MW 10:193), he observed, and these interests have been shaped and directed by a dangerously narrow individualism that lags behind contemporary needs. In order to grow beyond moral fundamentalism toward a more adaptive culture of collaborative inquiry, we need to educate "cooperative individualities" (LW 5:75). Job skills matter, but scaffolding a curriculum on individualistic consumerism and employer specifications does not fit the bill.

Rather than educating whole persons for lifelong growth, concerted problem-solving, and engaged social learning, the industrial model treats education as just another unstable, market-funded service sector of the techno-industrial economy, on a par with any other sector (Fesmire 2016). In this view, education's job is to manufacture skilled labor, and it is expected to do so in a way that is maximally efficient. Knowledge is seen as a market commodity, teachers and professors are delivery vehicles for knowledge content ("SMEs," subject matter experts, in the jargon of online for-profits and higher education consultants), and students are either consumers/customers or manufactured products marketable to employers.

Educational institutions that conform to the industrial model are seen as marketplaces for acquiring and delivering content. And when tuition and fees are involved, that is simply the fair price for accessing monetized content, while the high-to-low grade differential is the extrinsic means for incentivizing initiative and competition. Whether tacit or expressed, all or most of this is presumed by the faithful to be obvious and uncontroversial. Critics of industrial education are dismissed and broad-brushed as obsolete protectionists. Many students agree, at least until they reflect on the model's demeaning implications. They have come to see themselves as customers. They "vote with their feet" by majoring in the areas they perceive as promising the best economic payoff consonant with their test scores and personality type, and they resist liberal education as irrelevant to their career plans. The more thoroughly commodified the area of study, the more likely it is to attract faculty who are relatively comfortable with an image of themselves as well-compensated delivery vehicles for fungible content.

Analogous to the industrial philosophy that now dominates food and agricultural institutions in most countries (Thompson 2010), the industrial model of education has become a mostly unexamined prepossession. It keeps many citizens, educational leaders, educators, and policymakers from furthering their own best-justified values. When schooling speaks widely and deeply to living in all of its variety, not just narrowly to making a living, it respects students, teachers, and eventually employers by placing job skills in an appropriately multivalent and long-range context. This in turn creates a context for democratic citizenship.

What Do We Lose When We Reduce Education to an Industrial Sector? Cultures of Inquiry, Imagination, Growth, and Fulfillment

When described in this way, the industrial model of education seems cold and inhuman. Thankfully, on-the-ground experiences of teachers and students tend to be less bleak, tempered as they are by care, commitment, and practical life. Nevertheless, our conceptual frameworks have serious consequences for politics and policy, and hence for kids and adults.

Although the industrial model has a global reach, the United States offers a rich vein for illustrating effects on public inquiry. The nation's two political parties, Republicans and Democrats, are substantively divided on issues of educational delivery, content, and equitable access, but (in the main) they take the industrial model as a given. This obscures noneconomic values (Garrison 2012). Both parties tend automatically to identify investment in the future with the need to grow techno-industrial sectors and thus jobs. It is sane for people to vote for jobs when they have so little control over the conditions through which they and their children can make a living. But neither party consistently sees students as collaborators in analyzing, evaluating, and reconfiguring the economic regime.

Especially under current social, economic, and political conditions, non-market-driven values warrant a compensatory emphasis. It is not that economic values are irrelevant to education's purposes. Far from relegating organized callings or occupations, these can be reframed to respect the ends-means continuum. Unfortunately, those socialized to the industrial model tend to be oblivious to its shrunken framework and its distorting effects. My aim here is not to develop a theory that precludes their valuational standpoint a priori as having nothing legitimate to contribute. Instead, I clarify this model, show what its adherents are missing, and recommend Dewey's educational model as a democratic alternative better suited to twenty-first-century social needs.

When we reduce education to nothing but an industrial sector, then subordinate curricula to workforce specifications, something is lost. Let me highlight two areas of loss: the industrial model props up our social problems, and it sacrifices personal enrichment.

First, the industrial model props up social problems by training students to the status quo, and it narrows imagination. In his own childhood, Dewey regularly did chores on his grandfather's farm outside Burlington, Vermont. He later lamented that such occupational supplements to formal education were mostly eclipsed by urbanization and mechanization, and he sought ways to bring practical life into the classroom. He sought to infuse schooling with the interests students naturally have in adult careers, while building on thousands of years of informal vocational education that "furnished the social stimuli to knowledge and the centres about which it has been organized" (MW 4:189). "Education through occupations consequently combines within itself more of the factors conducive to learning than any other method" (1916, MW 9:319).

But there is an important distinction to be made. In Dewey's approach, as illustrated in this chapter by the sustainable agriculture program at Green Mountain College, you may steep a liberal education with occupational content that progressively and sympathetically acquaints students with careers—so-called real life. What Dewey wisely rejected was allowing the existing market-driven infrastructure to be the primary driving force behind all educational life. When the latter occurs, students and teachers are turned into "instrument[s] in accomplishing the feudal dogma of social predestination" (328). In essays during the 1910s, building up to *Democracy and Education* (1916), Dewey countered Massachusetts educational commissioner David Snedden's "socially efficient" trade-training initiatives. An occupation-rich education, Dewey argued, should have "as its supreme regard the development of such intelligent initiative, ingenuity, and executive capacity as shall make workers, as far as may be, the masters of their own industrial fate" (1915b, MW 8:411).

The industrial model lowers a student like a stylus into grooves predetermined by workforce routines. Dewey instead called for what most educators themselves hope for: helping students become flourishing participants in the imaginative, intelligent reconstruction of social conditions. As David Labaree observes, Dewey defeated Snedden in the intellectual debate. At least among educators, his more progressive rhetoric of "education for democracy" persists into the present. Yet beginning with the Smith-Hughes Act of 1917, which gave federal support to narrow trade-training programs, Sneddens's social efficiency gospel defeated Dewey in the practical "fight to set the broader aims of American education in the twentieth century" (2010, 164). Nevertheless, if there is cause for optimism in our century, it is that few educators would knowingly choose a career that trains students to fit predetermined roles so they can increase industrial profitability while "getting ahead" as bystanders to the status quo.

Many specific goals of education are, and should be, defined by a society's economic infrastructure and aims—such as the demand in techno-industrial countries for specialized curricular offerings in STEM areas. Meanwhile, access to occupational education needs to be more widely shared. But these facts do not imply that the overriding educational aim is to train students to conform to existing specifications. A narrowly workforce-oriented approach is *especially* a disservice to students in professional (e.g., business or healthcare) and STEM areas who face rapid technical and structural changes that require them to stand and think on their own feet. Such dependency is ultimately a disservice to employers, colleagues, patients, customers, partners, clients, and all others who rely on insight, interest, and constant intellectual growth among their associates. When education is dominated by narrow job training for "machine-like skill in routine lines" (320), it leaves everyone behind.

Dewey remains the most scathing philosophical critic of education as strict vocational training. Yet unlike many critics in literary circles, he celebrated the way occupational callings can organize knowledge and motivate attention far more effectively and vitally than even the most thoughtful and complete curriculum designed by a philosopher. For Dewey, learning begins when people encounter situations that engage, destabilize, and stimulate deliberate readjustment to enhance experience and navigate the surprises of a changing world. Individuals naturally reach out to assimilate and transform subject matter that may nourish and consummate their own concerns and life projects. When schooling respects these interests and the vital role that occupational callings play in these concerns, students are more likely to be active players in who they are becoming and in the world they are helping to shape. Trying to churn out efficient worker bees through strict preparatory training does not respect these interests.

Many corporate leaders agree with Dewey, at least in part. For example, as Apple cofounder Steve Jobs underscored every time he launched a new product "with an image of street signs showing the intersection of the liberal arts and technology" (Isaacson 2017, 3), mere workforce training can stifle imagination and innovation. It simultaneously directs students down the routinized channels that are implicated in our social, economic, environmental, and geopolitical problems. This reinforces cultural lag, replaces social learning with algorithmic technologies deployed mechanically to achieve commercial ends (Hickman 2019), and sacrifices our best hope for cultural transformation. Ilyse Morgenstein Fuerst, from the University of Vermont Humanities Center, made the related point that STEM education should be infused with the humanities in her succinct criticism of the university's 2020 plan to eliminate a wide range of humanities programs in response to budget cuts: "STEM without humanities gets you Facebook. It gets you this place where the algorithm drives all, regardless of the content, the ethics, the morals" (in Dougherty and Schwenk 2020).

It is culturally suicidal to educate imagination too narrowly. Imaginative activity is an irrepressible function of human interaction, but it can be left coarse, monochromatic, and tunnel-visioned by miseducation. As a capacity for "realizing what is not present" to the senses (LW 17:242; cf. 1916, MW 9:245), imaginative foresight enables us to creatively meet possibilities afforded by a situation— as when a gardener cultivates the possibilities of seed and soil, considering "what may be, but is not yet" (MW 9:153). Imagination, in Dewey's view, functions concretely, inescapably, and irreplaceably in the moment-to-moment life of the artist, the moral decision-maker, the scientist, the teacher, the STEM entrepreneur, the professional, and the student. It plays a formative role in thought and design by enabling us to stretch beyond the mechanics of our conditioning and to communicate with the past and present experiences of others. If continuous growing, readjustment, and publicly engaged inquiry are what we want for students, then cultivation of imagination through active learning is essential (e.g., Hanstedt 2018). If, however, we want students to become more submissive, susceptible, dependent, and predictable, then we should prefer an educational model that subordinates their present experience to preparation for remote vocational tasks in "the real world," and we should accomplish this by constantly covering ground prescribed by pat lesson plans.

In *American Philosophy in Translation* (2019a), Naoko Saito draws from Dewey and Stanley Cavell to explore ways to educate imagination to be more perceptive and responsive in a global context. She argues that *mutual* destabilization and transformation of imagination can arise through the difficult experience of standing on and crossing linguistic borders. Through such experiences, teachers and students learn to live with "discordant elements of human lives" by preparing and inhabiting a self-critical "space of disequilibrium" (122). She argues that where linguistic differences are involved, the experience of untranslatability is key to this kind of educational transformation. Saito laments that monolingual education does not expose students to dissonance across linguistic borders, so she urges creation of a cross-linguistic context for democratic education (2019a, 136; cf. Saito 2019b).

Saito implies that when we experience bidirectional transformation across languages, we can extend these lessons to "spaces of disequilibrium" across cultures and subcultures. As an example of such a space, consider the contested meaning of "inclusion" at American universities that are predominantly white. Many black and Hispanic students, Glaude observes in *Democracy in Black*, feel small and insignificant at these institutions and end up not flourishing (Glaude 2016). This is in part because students are too often "included" in a one-directional assimilative way, on the *terms* of those holding positions of institutional dominance. By creating an unsettling context for bidirectional transformation, Saito suggests, we serve the intellectual and moral growth of all students. Regardless of whether one agrees with Saito's position on the role of linguistic translation in an education that is receptive to diverse voices, the industrial model is so hegemonic that it ignores the sort of noneconomic educational questions that Saito raises regarding moral imagination, mutual growth, justice, and inclusion (cf. Striano 2019).

Second, not only does the industrial model narrow imagination and encourage submission to market specifications, but it also sacrifices personal enrichment. Is the principal mission of education today, if we may fictionalize such a thing, to provide a padded yoke for the state's workforce? Or is it, all things considered, to help us to flourish and to grow in our relationships at work and at leisure?

It is simply not clear how education as seen through a narrowly industrial lens might address personal growth, help us to achieve noneconomic goals, and holistically improve quality of life. If unaddressed, we risk building institutions that do a disservice to students by marginalizing these aspects of individual and social flourishing. An educational institution is capable of training more students with fewer or lower-paid teachers or professors—just as an industrial sector can produce more clothes, cars, or animal protein to meet market demands with lower overhead costs. These products can then be purchased through taxes or tuition at a relatively low price, and used or put to work to produce more things. The industrial imagination stops here, with efficient production and affordable consumption. This is a useful objective, right up until we ignore the ends-means continuum and fail to track unintended consequences (see Chapter 2).

In that pragmatic vein, what else do we produce when education—or industry, for that matter—is made "efficient" in the way the industrial model prescribes? Have we made narrower lives? Have we numbed sensitivity to relations? Has our desire for external possessions submerged our sense of wonder? Have we reinforced political fatalism? Have we left each other embittered and disabled? Have our curricula devalued ecological perceptiveness, moral imagination, and care? Have we, in Dewey's words, made life even more "congested, hurried, confused and extravagant" (LW 1:272)?

If we are obliged to answer with a qualified yes, then we need to repeat these questions in committees, policy discussions, electoral politics, legislative debates, school board meetings, and other public forums. Many still avow that the main point of education is to help people live better together, not just to churn out worker bees. In the United States, the dispiriting industrialization of education threatens to overturn a Jeffersonian ideal that, despite its long history of antidemocratic detractors and its roots tangled in racism, nevertheless penetrates the deeper soil of American yearnings and sympathies: namely that everyone should have the opportunity for an education that emphasizes growth and the pursuit of happiness, a happiness more rooted and lasting than fretful accumulation of external possessions (cf. 1930d, LW 5:422). Perhaps in coming years the democratic ideal will have greater power to adjust the attitudes and practices of those determining educational policies and curricula.

It bears adding that many criticisms of the "Common Core" and the standardized testing climate in US primary and secondary education should be viewed against the backdrop of the industrial model. Critical analysis of that model can make it easier to clarify educational priorities and values so that our assessments and standards can operate as means to justified ends. There is no reason to object, in principle, to a Common Core that views teachers as informed, skilled, and experienced facilitators and practitioners. Meanwhile, as educators have long been asserting, there are sound empirical reasons to reject the use of inflexible yardsticks to standardize measures of educational progress uniformly across all individuals, schools, school districts, state borders, and national borders. It is particularly appropriate to raise cautionary flags in an institutional milieu where teachers feel they are under the constant surveillance and regimen of an administrative bureaucracy, and where well-meaning bureaucrats are under pressure to prioritize easily measurable skills while outsourcing curriculum and instruction to for-profit digital platforms.

The Humanities, STEM, and Professional Education

Traditional defenders of the humanities as well as defenders of STEM education often overlook the way an education that integrates occupational "callings" can energize and transform cultural practices through more better public deliberation. It is difficult to date the outset of today's tug-of-war between the arts and humanities, at one end of the rope, and STEM, at the other. On the side of the humanities, Matthew Arnold's nineteenth-century argument that poetic intuition is superior to scientific discovery is perhaps as representative a place to begin as any, although Arnold was participating in a rationalistic modernist tradition that philosophers and historians trace back at least to Descartes (e.g., see Hammer 2019). A main assumption of the interminably reheated intellectualist strand of that modernist tradition was that human experience is essentially about knowing (cf. Hildebrand 2019; Alexander 2019). Noncognitive experiences were relegated to second class, while cognitive experiences reigned supreme. Intellectualists agreed that human experience peaks in cognition. That is, on their view cognitive pursuits answer to a *higher* calling. If so, the experiential quality of philosophical contemplation is intrinsically more valuable than, say, the experience of welding, trading, or lovemaking. But the *means* by which we know things are not created equal, according to modernists. The disagreement hinged on which sort of cognitive pursuit is superior: cognition directed at scientific objects, or cognition directed at "higher" humane knowledge.

Arnold grabbed the latter horn. There is, he held, a kind of knowledge accessible by timeless poetic intuition. This contemplative knowing-as-seeing is higher on the ladder than the kind of knowing that denotes tentative results and experimental investigations of scientific objects. Arnold's "aristocratic" mode of thinking, as Dewey called it, has tended to stand aloof from mundane, practical life—that is, the life of the vast majority of people caught up in accomplishing goals—and has retreated instead to the wide truths of the spirit. Unsurprisingly for a philosopher so disdainful of aristocracy, Dewey reserved his most scalding polemics for such views. In the recently recovered "lost" manuscript from the 1940s, published under Dewey's working title, *Unmodern Philosophy and Modern Philosophy,* he made what he called a "cynical" suggestion that the "writing class" suffers from an inferiority complex. We place our own cognitive activities atop a value hierarchy while relegating practical inquiry to second-class status, as compensation for the fact that our wider social environment consistently places narrowly practical activity above knowing (Dewey 2012, 345; cf. Deen 2019).

Whatever its many sources, the sharp separation of the humanities from STEM as well as from professional pursuits such as business has led today to an overall institutional life that is too fragmented and disintegrated to meet the holistic aims of a liberal education. Dewey held that a liberal education should be universal, guided by a working faith in the possibilities of the person-on-the-street when given the benefits of refined techniques and intergroup communication. It should not be designed to reinscribe existing social positions.

Specialization—say, in the arts and sciences, politics, religion, business, or recreation—is an apt response to demands on time, material resources, and diverse motivating interests. It is necessary. But under prevailing institutional politics in higher education, today as in Dewey's day, the "aim and animating spirit" of academic specialization is not always benign (1916, MW 9: 257). Proliferating new courses of study merely to meet market demands, with no more than a perfunctory nod at longer-term and wider-ranging educational aims and methods, has tended to drive the wedge even deeper between studies we deem instrumental (often disparaged by humanities faculty) and those we deem intrinsically worthwhile (often regarded as expendable luxuries by presidents and boards). As each discipline, field, or preprofessional area strives to gain or retain its piece of the curricular pie, argue for tenurable lines, defend budget proposals, and justify its continuation, advocates of the humanities come off as self-interested agents struggling to hold onto their rightful old market share. Meanwhile, their better-funded colleagues may parrot that "business is business" as a province peculiarly its own while they add high fees from corporate content providers to their courses. Alas, Dewey writes, "In the multitude of educations education is forgotten" (1916, MW 9:255).

Dewey argued—rightly, in my view—that there is a way beyond this impasse, and it is not to enjoin one side of a misguided battle. The way forward is to actively infuse the arts and humanities throughout curricular and co-curricular life, while simultaneously bringing all fields and professions into the arena of engaged humane study. To make Dewey's proposal clearer, it will help to clarify his pragmatic approach to the distinction between instrumental and intrinsic values in education, as he rejects the tired idea that there is an inherent superiority of one over the other.

By way of illustration, Sam Cooke's 1960 classic "Wonderful World" may be the most famous twentieth-century song in English about academic disciplines: "Don't know much about history / Don't know much biology / . . . maybe by being an A student, baby / I can win your love for me."

What is the value of studying history or biology? This question about the valuation of studies points to a dual sense of the word "value." Studies may be appreciated as intrinsically worthwhile, or they may be valued as a means to something comparatively advantageous that is enjoyed for itself. Cooke's delightful, love-besotted persona hopes that his studies will help win a lover, so they are taken as instrumental goods. His schooling is bathed in the light of a happy possibility that motivates him to subordinate present enjoyments, and his studies have just that much immediate significance. The same logic holds for students pushing themselves to impress a college admissions committee, or studying for a standardized admissions exam. Consider Dewey's advice to educators in that light: "In general what is desirable is that a topic be presented in such a way that it either have an immediate value, and require no justification, or else be perceived to be a means of achieving something of intrinsic value. An instrumental value then has the intrinsic value of being a means to an end" (1916, MW 9:251).

Some spark of direct interest in history or biology might coincidentally flare. It happens. Cooke's studies would to that extent be appreciated for themselves. This would be a fine thing, but contrary to Arnold's view, this is not because academic pursuits have some inherent snobbish superiority or aristocratic purity in comparison to consummated love or other practical affairs such as fixing a car or making a good deal. Enjoying the studies for themselves could be doubly good, because studies that become the immediate fruit of personal enrichment also become available for dealing with other life situations. In Dewey's words: "Never having been realized or appreciated for itself, one will miss something of its capacity as a resource for other ends" (1916, MW 9:249). Cognitive pursuits often do have longer-range and more diverse instrumental bearings than, say, welding or trading or arguably even lovemaking, but Dewey rejected as elitist poppycock the notion that cognitive experiences are inherently superior in their immediate quality. Moreover, as even a cursory reading of *Art as Experience* makes plain, Dewey would side with Cooke, against Arnold, if given a choice between even the most refined academic training and the immediately felt richness of life's consummations in love, art, family, friendship, and nature.

Absent direct enjoyment, Cooke's academic pursuits are less likely to help when the need by and by arises. Human existence is, after all, a scene of instability and risk in which diverse goods compete, and we need to draw from all the intellectual resources we can muster. Cooke's passionate dedication is meaningful. But akin to narrow workforce training, taking the most expedient straight line to a goal can make us heedless of other opportunities and aims (Hickman 1990). It is from this wider practical standpoint, and not from an Arnoldian mismeasure of the inherent worth of Cooke's pursuit, that we might ask whether his lovestruck imagination has fallen short of "a warm and intimate taking in of the full scope of a situation" (1916, MW 9:244).

More to the educational point, Dewey argued that we need to organize schooling so that students gain direct fulfillment even as they anticipate future goods and cultivate competent, forward-looking, and cooperative intelligence. Teach toward fulfillment, so that the subject matter becomes "an end in itself in the lives of students—something worthwhile on account of its own unique intrinsic contribution to the experience of life" (1916, MW 9:249). We can teach toward fulfillment by infusing the arts and humanities throughout community life, and remaking all fields into subjects of humane study.

Democracy and Educational Values

Dewey believed in the pedagogical value of integrating head, heart, and hands (cf. Carver and Enfield 2006), and he held that a genuinely educative activity is not just another damn thing to be checked off on a list of intrinsically worthless tasks that teachers feel obliged to cover in the prescribed way at the prescribed time. He also kept a watchful eye on the political upshot of such integration for a healthy democracy: when we split the head from the hands, or isolate humane studies from practical life, we unfortunately tend to suppose that a liberal education is the right of only an elite few—the privileged heads. Dewey rejected as antidemocratic and foolhardy the notion that we need one distinct educational approach for vocational trainees who will be led, and an essentially different one for elite intellectuals who will lead (cf. Noddings 2019).

In a 1909 address to the New York City High School Teachers Association titled "The Meaning of a Liberal Education," soon-to-be president Woodrow Wilson, then president at Princeton University, baldly asserted, "We want one class of persons to have a liberal education, and we want another class of persons, a very much larger class, of necessity, in every society, to forego the privileges of a liberal education and fit themselves to perform specific difficult manual tasks." Some elements of manual and liberal training may mix in both classes, he said, but "we are either trying to make liberally-educated persons out of them, or we are trying to make skillful servants of society along mechanical lines, or else we do not know what we are trying to do" (Wilson 1909).[3] Snedden and others quickly followed up with a system of trade-training that separated rank-and-file "producers" from liberally educated "utilizers" (Labaree 2010, 164). This evolved into a "tracking" system for mechanically sorting social classes. In comparison to Wilson's and Snedden's master-servant model, the current industrial model is more monolithic and perhaps less classist: workforce training for both rank-and-file and executives.

Dewey countered that everyone should have the ongoing opportunity for an education that emphasizes experimental inquiry, moral growth, emotional development, imaginative engagement, aesthetic vitality, and social responsibility. From primary education to university, "getting an education" in this broad sense can establish conditions for personal enrichment, critical inquiry, and democratic participation. Decades of lip service to the rhetoric of democratizing education have too often mired Dewey's reputation in practices that narrowed and lowered expectations (cf. Lasch 1991), but every page of his educational writings called for high expectations, depth, and rigor.

If democracy is reduced to the formal mechanics of "one person, one vote," with duties exhausted at the polling booth, then perhaps a democracy can treat students—or a majority of them à la Wilson and Snedden—as serfs to the consumer economy as-is, not as social learners in an ever-evolving economy. Yet Jefferson's spirit is reflected in those who also cherish democracy as an inspiring moral ideal. As such, the democratic ideal *legitimates* the polling booth. The *moral* meaning of democracy, Dewey argued, "is found in resolving that the supreme test of all political institutions and industrial arrangements shall be the contribution they make to the all-around growth of every member of society" (MW 12:186).

In neither the electoral nor the moral sense is democracy a static inheritance that we can simply live off of. It must be renewed through vigilance and active effort (LW 13:298–99). Dewey made the point succinctly in "Education and Social Change" (1937):

> The trouble, at least one great trouble, is that we have taken democracy for granted; we have thought and acted as if our forefathers had founded it once for all. We have forgotten that it has to be enacted anew in every generation, in every year and day, in the living relations of person to person in all social forms and institutions. Forgetting this, we have allowed our economic and hence our political institutions to drift away from democracy; we have been negligent even in creating a school that should be the constant nurse of democracy. (LW 11:416)

Schools are our cultural means for educating free citizens who can intelligently—creatively, critically, and competently—participate in democracy's perpetual rebuilding effort. Education is how we invest in the future of democracy, both at the polling booth and as a way of life.

Under today's economic and social conditions, what then does it mean if "education for the state's workforce" has become the primary mission of schools and universities? It further destabilizes liberal education, but what else? Taking the democratic ideal in its moral sense, the industrial model of education is antidemocratic. It sacrifices the quality of a student's present life for the sake of a promised good that may never be realized. It confines imagination and inquiry, along with the fine arts, to consumer specifications and profitability. It conceals complexity. It uncritically perpetuates zombie ideas that fuel cultural lag. It supports plutocracy, a frozen system of privilege, frantic and unsustainable consumption, and deadening efficiency. At the university level, it diametrically opposes the Dewey-steeped 1915 American Association of University Professors' declaration that a higher education institution should serve as an "intellectual experiment station" (cf. Dea 2024).

Ubiquitous references to economic prosperity only weaken the case for the industrial model. It is true that a healthy economy is a public good. It is equally true that this good is not served when students, educators, and policymakers treat each other chiefly as servants to the workaday system of adult business-as-usual. Nor does it serve economic health when we treat each other as interchangeable functionaries.

Indeed, Dewey proposed, an educational institution dedicated to the growth of free inhabitants of a democratic culture may reveal in microcosm the refinement that is possible in other cultural institutions (1916, MW 9:257). We live best and serve the public good when our various professions, occupations, and leisure pursuits are energized by schools that are cultures of imagination and growth. It also serves the public good when teachers, instead of being asked to hoe the straightest line toward testable skill acquisition, help students to imagine the conditions and challenges they face in light of what is possible. Absent such engagement, both a student's and a teacher's career become stories of lost possibilities.

As part of this engagement, an emphasis on artistic-aesthetic experiences, far from being a luxury when time can be spared from the chop-chop of graded academic rigor, is central to a democratic education. In experiences that we call aesthetic, there is an immediately felt quality that does not ask to be a means to some extrinsic end. The prevalent assumption that there is an inherent separation between this quality and the instrumental quality of "real," assessable academic achievement leads to an anesthetizing attitude toward reading, writing, math, and technical skills. Yet as Dewey observed, "Every subject at some phase of its development should possess, what is for the individual concerned with it, an aesthetic quality" (1916, MW 9:258). Perpetual bliss in schoolwork is a fantasy, but a richer fulfillment is an ideal worth striving for, something beyond mere toil and extrinsic reward. Let us discover together what is possible, Dewey urged, instead of setting out with unrealistic and untested assumptions about the stick-and-carrot nature of student motivation.

The fine arts throw into relief the tragedy that so much human experience is shallow and narrow, incomplete and underdeveloped (Alexander 1987). Many experiences are too loosely organized to give expressive form to much of anything—for example, consider the perfunctory way some high school and college students approach writing, unguided by sympathy for any ideal more inspiring than word count. If that is writing, then it is sensible to turn it over to artificial intelligence. The fine arts offer an inspiring ideal and a riposte to the so-called threat of emerging technologies. The fine arts are "organs of vision" (1916, MW 9:247) that reveal engrossing possibilities to excel beyond the alienating, self-absorbed, trivial, despondent, or humdrum. They can be a source of intensified fulfillment that reverberates through life (cf. Haskins 2019). "They are not luxuries of education," Dewey urged, "but emphatic expressions of that which makes any education worth while" (1916, MW 9:247). As Andrea English and Christina Doddington (2019) argue, the fine arts should not be marginalized or eliminated merely because the labor of educating for humanity is occluded by the industrial imagination.

Artistic production and aesthetic experiences offer a resource, standard, and hopeful reminder that we are not limited to merely passing through. Even amid the troubles, regret, and fretting that subdues so much of life, experiences that are refined in the arts remind us of the potential for the rest of our experiences to be fulfilled. They serve as models and inspirations for establishing conditions that improve the educational odds that our students' experiences may become as complete as those peak experiences we justly celebrate in the fine arts.

In *Art as Experience*, Dewey clarified the "instrumentalist" aspect of his philosophy accordingly: "I have from time to time set forth a conception of knowledge as being 'instrumental.' Strange meanings have been imputed by critics to this conception. Its actual content is simple: Knowledge is instrumental to the enrichment of immediate experience through the control of action that it exercises" (1934b, LW 10:294). Without the methods of science, we drift at the mercy of natural forces. But without lives rich in aesthetic punctuations and fulfillments, he portended a century ago, we "might become a race of economic monsters, restlessly driving hard bargains with nature and with one another, bored with leisure or capable of putting it to use only in ostentatious display and extravagant dissipation" (1920, MW 12:152).

Educational Pragmatism

These reflections on diverse public goods suggest a strategy for educational politics and policy, akin to the development in Chapter 2 of environmental pragmatism as an orientation toward environmental issues. Democratic decision-making is not doomed without a cultural shift away from the industrial model in education, desirable as that would be. Many educational problems can be ameliorated by creating solidarity with others who agree that current conditions are unacceptable, yet disagree about why.

I have argued that democratic societies should not conceive service to the private sector as the overriding goal of education. Nevertheless, there is broad agreement that careers are vital to educational aims. Early in a child's education, Dewey urged in *Democracy and Education* (1916), we can start with the idea that being well educated for future careers is largely a second-order consequence. Later, gradually support diverse student aptitudes by progressively refining and focusing knowledge and skills to responsibly and sympathetically meet increasingly specialized career interests and prospects. Choosing a calling, such as engineering or healthcare, simply outlines a trajectory. "It is a sort of rough sketch map," Dewey suggested, "for use in direction of further activities. . . . Future explorations of an indefinitely more detailed and extensive sort remain to be made" (1916, MW 9:321).

As with the Green Mountain College example, we can educate *through* occupations, as Dewey put it, so that careers enliven the educational process while opening pathways. Start from the standpoint of education as growth, then fine-tune. Meanwhile, Dewey warned in 1916, an era when many held careers for life, always be "on the lookout to see that their calling does not shut down on them and fossilize them." "When educators conceive vocational guidance as something which leads up to a definitive, irretrievable, and complete choice, both education and the chosen vocation are likely to be rigid, hampering further growth" (321).

Dewey's approach is flexible, supports mobility, and is above all experimental, fallibilistic, and open to continuous revision. His approach differs from intellectual leaders who subordinate growth and imagination to economic purposes, even as they appropriately pause to consider effective means to economic ends. For example, editors of the *Harvard Business Review* may be unlikely to approach Carol Dweck's research on "growth mindset" from a standpoint beyond serviceability to industry, as evidenced in their article "How Companies Can Profit from a 'Growth Mindset'" (2011). The article starts with the industrial model of workforce preparation and notes that adequate preparation includes things like imaginative thinking, team deliberation, and a growth mindset. These are shared concerns that can be built upon, suggesting that the gap is not insurmountable between the industrial model and an education-as-growth outlook.

Clashing educational models have far-reaching practical consequences. The conflict is not a hair-splitting subtlety. Nevertheless, some convergence is possible. Education is much *more* than a supplier for the economic sector, but it is at least that. Building on this commonality, we can discuss the imagination and creativity needed for careers without losing sight of the way heightened intellectual vitality, discernment, care, and aesthetic consummations contribute to human flourishing and help us to achieve social goals. We can also mutually recognize that one-size-fits-all content delivery is ineffective, regardless of discipline or area. Prioritizing education as growth helps businesses and professions, and a flourishing private sector can contribute to the commonwealth. Even as we continue to debate educational values, we should not insist upon a shared pre-alignment of ends, diagnoses, and justifications as a political prerequisite to engaging in public deliberation. Even when irksome, participating in decision-making processes in nonideal conditions has the potential to catalyze cultural shifts, as Norton and Lee reveal (Chapter 2).

Conclusion

In *Democracy and Education,* Dewey closed his chapter on educational values with hard questions, left unanswered, regarding "that organization of schools, materials, and methods which will operate to achieve breadth and richness of experience." He asked:

> How shall we secure breadth of outlook without sacrificing efficiency of execution? How shall we secure the diversity of interests, without paying the price of isolation? How shall the individual be rendered executive in his intelligence instead of at the cost of his intelligence? (1916, MW 9:257)

Philosophy can go only so far. The questions set and defined by the problems of education are among the most momentous we face. Hypotheses for dealing with them must be tested, modified, and settled in that experimental medium. Nonetheless, it is a practical necessity to reflect philosophically on what we are really aiming for as we discuss elimination of university programs such as the fine arts and humanities amid fiscal exigencies, secondary school spending and priorities, consolidation and mergers, school budget caps, student-teacher ratios, affordability in higher education, active learning, education for the green economy, the future of the liberal arts, and so on. It would be a tragedy that undermines all of our successes if educational politics continues the lockstep march down a path in which educational institutions—or industries, for that matter—gain economic efficiency and increase productivity by sapping democratic engagement and frustrating growth, inquiry, imagination, and fulfillment. These are the very educational values required for a society to mature beyond moral fundamentalism.

4

Pragmatic Pluralism in Ethical and Sociopolitical Theory

The problem with wallpapering an old house is that the lines vary from room to room, so wallpaper neatly squared by the eye in one room appears crooked from the next.[1] The effect is jarring. The well-tested solution is to square the first strip of wallpaper to the world, not to the room, by following the vertical line of a weighted string called a plumb line.

It is a common presumption that one's own moral or political understanding has been impartially adjusted by *the* all-inclusive plumb line of reason, direct intuition, or divine authority. Instead of just another peculiar brand of rectitude, this presumption accords an exclusive logical space to our understanding. Descartes ran with a related image in the *Discourse on Method*, as a metaphor for adjusting his opinions *au niveau de la raison*, to the level of reason. In both scholarly discourse and popular culture, Descartes's seventeenth-century assumption that we can square our individual judgments to the fixed geometry of God's creation persists today as a latent recurring habit, even where it is openly rejected. Whatever their metaphysical stances, philosophical pragmatists argue that no plumb line of pure thought or transcendental reason is required as a leveling reference to orient scientific or value inquiries. Nor has such a universal level ever been available. The dream of an impartial state or act purified of natural interactions is itself a delusional partiality, all the more obnoxious for its evasive self-concealment (see 1925/1929, LW 1:324; cf. Johnson and Schulkin 2023, 204;

Beyond Moral Fundamentalism. Steven Fesmire, Oxford University Press. © Oxford University Press 2024. DOI: 10.1093/9780197763919.003.0004

cf. Margolis 2019). It is wiser to chart a course to make the best of humanity's inescapable contingency and provincialism.

The plumb-line metaphor highlights the fact that we use improvable intellectual instruments to enlighten judgment and regulate inquiry (cf. Hickman 2019). Tools are forged in response to situational needs, and they are evaluated and refined by how well they meet those needs. We need all the help we can get to square our judgments with our most generous ideals, and to square our inquiries with the highest standards of open scrutiny. As explored in Chapter 1, it *matters* when our normative outlook is, in James's words, "out of plumb." But the practical problem, which I earlier discussed in terms of cultural lag and zombie ideas, is not that our outlook is out of plumb from the utilitarian Henry Sidgwick's "point of view of the universe" (Lazari-Radek and Singer 2014; cf. Williams 1995). We get in a jam when our outlooks are out of plumb with the particular circumstances we face.

An old-fashioned plumb line remains the best tool for wallpapering a house. But anything resembling the pursuit of a universal level of normative reasoning is out of plumb with today's ethical and sociopolitical problems. As explored in Chapters 1 and 2, that monistic pursuit yields homogeneous outlooks that do not effectively square value judgments and policies with the wicked entanglements of techno-industrial societies. Dewey proposed that we approach these entanglements through participatory decision-making by a citizenry educated for democracy. As examined in Chapter 3, it is realistic to educate in that direction, even though antidemocratic training of worker bees will not get us there.

In this chapter, I contribute a pragmatist voice to the chorus of contemporary theorists who argue that "ideal theories" deal badly with nonideal conditions when they begin their ethical and political inquiries with abstractions, as with the search for a universal plumb line of moral reason. Pragmatism offers a pluralistic, experimental, and democratizing corrective. In Chapter 5, I turn to

Dewey's pluralistic hypothesis that there are at least three independent experiential roots of moral life that cannot be brought under the logical scope of a single blanket concept. These two chapters conclude my case for moving (1) away from the culturally lagging single-right-way habits of moral fundamentalism, and (2) toward a pragmatic and pluralistic approach that operationalizes the wisdom of ethical traditions without succumbing to monistic narrowness.

Pluralism and Nonideal Theory

In the terminology of philosophical ethics, pluralism implies affirmation of multiple values that cannot be reduced to a single value. Strong pluralists such as Williams (1985), Taylor (1982), Noddings (2013), and Appiah (2017) go beyond simple fallibilism to argue that traditional ethical monism abridges moral life and edits out the diversity of situational tensions that mark real, unsettled circumstances.[2] Accordingly, strong pluralists agree that moral problems often admit of more than one reasonable diagnosis and approvable solution.

Should a soldier shoot upon command? Should a security analyst blow the whistle on government intrusions into privacy? Values typically get in the way of each other, and, according to the strong pluralist, it would be an atypically easy case in which tensions could be satisfactorily resolved or frictions negotiated—to whatever extent they might be resolvable or negotiable—by appealing to a value, principle, standard, law, concept, or ideal that telescopes whatever is of moral worth in the rest of our concerns. A strong pluralist position is well stated by Haidt and Bjorklund: "Monistic theories are likely to be wrong. . . . If there are many independent sources of moral value . . . , then moral theories that value only one source and set to zero all others are likely to produce psychologically unrealistic systems" (2008, 215).[3]

Strong pluralists also tend to reject the quest for a self-contained "ideal theory," as Rawls (1971) called his idealized approach to a well-ordered society in which we envision what should be done by free, equal, and autonomous rational contractors who fully comply with the requirements of justice. The now-traditional "ideal theory" approach to moral and political theory is exemplified by Rawls, Nozick (1974), and arguably Dworkin (2000). Rawls proposed a division of labor between ideal and nonideal theories. The former's job is to determine "what a perfectly just society would be like" (1971, 8–9), whereas nonideal theories are tasked with discerning principles to handle nonideal conditions in which people do not comply with the principles of justice, as with war or racial oppression, or in which circumstances make perfect fairness unrealizable. We need to start by constructing an ideal theory to discern the principles that would be rationally agreed to in a perfectly fair society, Rawls thought, if we are then to construct a moral compass for dealing with imperfect, nonideal conditions that are closer to home. His critics argue that he was mistaken, not in clarifying ideals worth striving for, but in his point of origin.

Recent critics of "ideal theory" approaches to moral and political theory include, to various degrees, Mills (2005, 2017), Anderson (2009, 2013), Pappas (2008, 2019), Sen (2009), Valentini (2012), Medina (2013a, 2013b), Gaus (2016), and Appiah (2017). Anderson, for example, has influentially argued in *The Imperative of Integration* that Rawls's color-blind approach to an ideal society blinds us to race-based, gender-based, and other social injustices to a degree that is "epistemologically disabling" (2013, 5). Gaus's title alone makes the point: *The Tyranny of the Ideal: Justice in a Diverse Society.*

These critics propose shifting to a nonideal point of departure. They do not, of course, object to idealizations in ethics, a subject canvassed in *Appiah's As If: Idealization and Ideals* (2017), but most insist that values have to be appraised in light of the particular experiential contexts and purposes that generated them. To meet the morasses we face, we need the moral clarity (see Neiman 2008) of idealizations. But clarity can be robbed of its virtue by theorizing that is not integrated within the complications of social, natural, and interpersonal experiences

Many critics of ideal theory also advocate, in Pappas's words, a radically empirical shift "toward a more nonideal, contextualist, problem-centered, and inquiry-oriented approach." What should be the starting point of value inquiry, Pappas asks? If we reply with some kind of empiricism, then what does it *mean* to take experience seriously, and what are the implications for ethical and sociopolitical problems? Taking experience seriously, he concludes, implies that "there are as many problems of injustice, as there are problematic situations suffered in a particular way" (2019, 235). Start with the bleeding, distress, disaffection, sweat, grind, and struggle. Start where the problem pinches, then idealize and persist to deal with it.

Pappas takes Dewey as his model for a radically empirical point of departure, though he recognizes that Dewey did not historically fare notably better than Rawls as an incisive theorist of race and racial injustice (e.g., see Glaude 2007, Sullivan 2019, and Carter 2024). Pappas argues that Dewey's approach to moral and sociopolitical theory was more radically contextual and problem-centered than many of his twenty-first-century allies who are today finding common cause with pragmatist critiques of ideal theorizing (cf. Myers 2019 and Hildebrand 2019). For nonideal theorists working in the tradition of French poststructuralism, Jim Garrison adds that Dewey's empirical pluralism and contextualism is an alternative to Jacques Derrida's "quasi-transcendental apriorism" (Garrison 2019).

The division between ideal and nonideal theories can be overstated, and they often converge more than is acknowledged in the current debate. For example, in climate ethics, Darrel Moellendorf's *The Moral Challenge of Dangerous Climate Change* singles out an "Antipoverty Principle" (2014, 22) that is a variation on Rawls's worst-off principle (that inequality is justified only when it improves conditions of the worst-off). In justifying this principle, Moellendorf rejects separating theoretical justifications from practical applications (4), though he is far less pragmatic in his Rawlsian ideal starting point.

Appiah enjoins that even a plausible and practically informed ideal theory "doesn't help much in the circumstances of an actual non-ideal world" (2017, 120).[4] Ideal fairness and equity, and theories about them, apply to ideal worlds, of which ours is not an example.

Pragmatism as Nonideal Theory: Experiments in Living Together

In the general spirit of Hume's *Treatise* (1739), the full title of which was *A Treatise of Human Nature: being an Attempt to introduce the experimental Method into Moral Subjects*, Dewey sought to bring experimental method to bear on value inquiry. "The growth of the experimental as distinct from the dogmatic habit of mind," he asserted in *Experience and Nature*, "is due to increased ability to utilize variations for constructive ends instead of suppressing them" (1925/1929, LW 1:7). He thus approached the natural human fact of variability in valuing and valuations as a useful starting point for constructive inquiry, rather than as a troublesome deviation to be suppressed or intellectually standardized in the name of systematic rigor.

If embracing divergences means that sometimes competing claims will not be resolvable, then so be it, so long as we do not predetermine the result. We cannot put hospital corners on moral life. Following a naturalistic and empirical methodology, there is no providential guarantee that reason will be sufficient. Despite the rationalistic ghosts that imperceptibly draw theorists away from the doings and sufferings of moral experience toward self-evident truths, the point of reflecting philosophically on normative tensions across individuals and cultures is not to gratify a misbegotten sense of entitlement to ethical truth. Nor is it to flatten variability once and for all by sorting out the logical relationship between ethical ideas. Neither is it, at the other extreme, to revel in banal relativistic claims about undermining the universalist's standardizing quest (cf. Appiah 2010, 3). The point is to conduct ourselves better.

Among most pragmatist moral and sociopolitical philosophers inspired by Dewey, such as Kitcher (2014), Johnson (2014), McKenna (2018), Pappas (2008), Thompson (2015), and myself (Fesmire 2003), pluralism's acknowledgment of deep divergence among values is incorporated into a method of inquiry. But pragmatic pluralism is not necessarily "a method of ethics" in the sense crystallized by Sidgwick: "a rational procedure for deciding what we ought to do" (Lazari-Radek and Singer 2014). Norton's "heuristic proceduralism" comes close (2005, 2015), but, like other pragmatists and unlike many contemporary utilitarians and Kantians, he is critical of rational procedures that fail to fathom the extent to which we are inescapably limited and guided by our particular standpoints, contexts, and purposes. We are all frogs looking at the sky from the bottom of Zhuǎng Zǐ's well. We can compensate, but we cannot escape. As Peirce observed in his 1868 rejection of Descartes's absolute starting point: "We cannot begin with complete doubt. We must begin with all the prejudices which we actually have" (1992, 28).[5]

Like Dewey, Norton is focused on ethical inquiry as an experimental process rather than conceiving it as incessant verbal argumentation. For classical pragmatists like Addams and Dewey, ethical and political theorizing was not understood on analogy to logical or mathematical problems that have a correct formulation and computable solution. In tandem with twenty-first-century discussions of wicked problems, design thinking, adaptive management, and systems thinking, Dewey and Addams approached decision-making as part of a pluralistic experiment in "living together in ways in which the life of each of us is at once profitable in the deepest sense of the word, profitable to himself and helpful in the building up of the individuality of others" (1938, LW 13:303).

The disanalogy between moral problems, on one hand, and logical or mathematical problems, on the other, spotlights what is perhaps the most distinctively "pragmatist" (from Greek *pragma*, action) feature of Dewey's ethical outlook: his insistence that our choices and deeds (i.e., the means we select) are essential players that change the moral situation. Out of love for moral certainty, we may demand guarantees "in advance of action" (1922b, MW 14:163). But in contrast with British empiricism's influential notion of a receptive mind behind a veil of ideas—an assumption within John Stuart Mill's associationist psychology which persists in much utilitarian thought—Dewey argued that our encounters with the world are creative (cf. Alexander 2019). This creativity is integral to Dewey's view that what is good or bad, right or wrong, virtuous or vicious cannot be completely ascertained prior to acting and reviewing. In his epistemology and metaphysics, Dewey rejected the stubbornly recurrent assumption common to most idealisms and realisms, of an *unaffected mind* that mysteriously "knows" an *uneffected world*. He had little patience with idealism's vaporous internal magic or with realism's finished and changeless world, and even less indulgence for post-truth skeptics who reasonably proclaim the obsolescence of such dogmatism but who have never learned to love the search that doubt funds (e.g., see 1929, LW 4:182). From the temporalized standpoint of Dewey's experimental method, mind "is an agency of novel reconstruction of a pre-existing order" (1925/1929, LW 1:168) rather than an aberrant epiphenomenon à la crusty empiricism or an "independent creative source" à la equally crusty idealism.

In the ambit of Dewey's critical understanding of moral intelligence as a participant in directing change (1929, LW 4:170), what Kitcher (2014) calls "the ethical project" is a process in which, as Johnson explains it, we actively try out "various modes of behavior (verbal and nonverbal), various institutional structures, and various life strategies" (Johnson 2014, 126). Verbal argumentation remains important for ethics, but theorists have by and large neglected the way *experiments in living*, as Mill phrased it (Mill 1986, 65; cf. Anderson 1999), also constitute "arguments" for and against various practices, in the sense that these practices objectively provoke, address, or fail to meet problems (cf. Putnam 2004). These facts are controverted and value laden, like all spatiotemporal facts. It is better to acknowledge this than to tilt at the windmills of eternal facts and final truths (see LW 2:377).

Johnson argues that experiments in living are enactive, embodied, and embedded, and arguments incorporating them should play a more central role in future theorizing (2014, 126). Such enactive arguments comprise the most forceful and honest reply to critics who suppose that regulative moral principles must be based on absolute authority, lest chaos ensue. "Next they'll be inviting Nazi experiments in living!" Setting aside this caricature of experimentalism, the Nazis' totalitarian view was that a system of fixed principles must be inculcated to avoid moral disintegration. Any reference to their atrocities should chillingly remind us that a commitment to open inquiry, free communication, and tolerance must be nurtured, rediscovered, renewed, and stabilized by each generation.

As explored in Chapters 2 and 3, Dewey urged experiments in democratic social inquiry, especially in education, to replace one-way moral and political approaches. Such inquiry involves not just verbally arguing, but also "on-the-ground experiments in living" (Johnson 2014, 126; cf. Kitcher and Keller 2017) in which we steer between the Scylla and Charybdis of what Catherine Elgin aptly calls "the absolute and the arbitrary" (1997).

As Appiah (2017) has argued, experiments in living necessitate ideals and idealizations, such as Dewey's advancement of the democratic ideal, through which we appraise alternative avenues for acting. These idealizations are often provincial, but they have *always* proceeded in the absence of a noncontingent perspective.

Humans have never had access to an ideal standpoint untainted by particular human drives, habits, and choices. Recognizing this, we can put ideal theories to work for specified purposes, but this usefulness is obscured when we presume to speak as representatives of the essence of morality. Along the same lines,

to echo a point made by feminist theorists regarding universalizing (e.g., Noddings 2013; Heldke 2019), the usefulness of epistemic inquiry is diminished when we presume to speak for transcendental rationality, as though our vantage point is mysteriously unlimited (cf. Morton 2012). Philosophers do their best theorizing by studying, communicating, forecasting, experimenting, listening, assessing, and revising. The best moral judgments are made in the same way, not by presuming an enlightened standpoint that turns morality or rationality into a static thing that can be spoken for in toto.

Ideal theories can focus and economize reflection, but they are not the last word. Ethical inquiry is imaginative, communicative, and unending. What we count as progressive or regressive is *ultimately*, in Kitcher's words, "something people work out with one another. There are no experts here" (2014, 286). Instead of yet another iteration of the old escape through faith or reason to an antecedently established "aperspectival position" (Johnson 2014, 120), pragmatic pluralists embrace in their methodology the fact that when we ask different questions, we see different connections and possibilities. Partiality is inescapable. Some pragmatists argue, accordingly, that theorists should shift away from beating the dead horse of impartiality and toward distinguishing virtuous from vicious partiality, perhaps especially in relation to those near and dear to us (Axtell 2023).

Dewey's theory rejects aperspectival positions and is marked by a naturalistic emphasis on the embodied context of moral action as a need-search recovery process (see Johnson 2019). As a naturalistic empiricist or cultural naturalist, he emphasized virtues of conscientiousness and courage, not native conscience, and he rejected the split between a moral realm sharply marked off from a nonmoral realm, observing that actions are so interconnected that any choice potentially has moral significance (1932, LW 7:170).

Nevertheless, as Kitcher and Johnson also observe, Dewey's rejection of perspective-free ethics and his wide interpretation of the moral realm "in no way keeps us from making reasonable claims about" the relative suitability of certain "values, principles, and practices" over others (Johnson 2014, 129; cf. Kitcher 2014, 210ff.; cf. Silverman 2023). And these are *reasonable* claims—not merely constrained by the rationalistic demand for consistency, as prescriptivists argue, but constrained and guided by worldly features that we need to perceive and meet. Much that we in retrospect judge to have been morally retrograde was at the time supported by rational arguments that seemed persuasive, and much that is now saluted as progress has been due to people getting over outmoded mores and getting used to unscripted arrangements. Theorists can participate in this process so that it is less haphazard. Consequently, the expert theorist's primary job is not to tell us the right thing to be doing in advance of consultation and colloquy. There is no finally right or ideal way to think *in advance* about moral or political problems, and hence rarely a complete "theoretically correct" diagnosis of any particular problem. But there is room for experts to inform the decisions we make, and to critically reflect on those decisions after we have made them. In sum, given our contingent starting point, facing nonideal conditions, Kitcher and Johnson follow Dewey in recommending an experimental, democratic, and pragmatic pluralism as a strategy for conscientious normative inquiry into what we *ought* to deem progressive or retrograde.

Dewey's Moral Psychology I: Deliberation as Dramatic Rehearsal

Dewey's democratic and experimental method is especially effective, I have argued elsewhere, when deliberations are informed by broadly attentive imaginative rehearsals and moral artistry

(Fesmire 2003). Our best choices are not typically marked by detached accounting, disembodied cerebrations, or radical separation from the intimacy of our own yearnings. Reliable moral choices, Dewey argued, mark the closing phase of attentive and communicative "dramatic rehearsals" of alternatives for acting.

Whatever else may or should be involved in human deliberation, it must at least be compatible with our moral psychology. Dewey's theory of dramatic rehearsal is gaining a foothold in twenty-first-century philosophy and neuroscience (e.g., Johnson 2014, 2019). Lacking an account of neural connectivity, his descriptions were more phenomenological than "experimental" in the contemporary sense (see Johnson and Schulkin 2023, 143). In his skeletal description of the psychology of deliberation, thought "runs ahead and foresees outcomes, and thereby avoids having to await the instruction of actual failure and disaster" (1922b, MW 14:133). When we are presented with only one alternative for dealing with perplexities, we act on it without further reflection. But when alternatives contend with one another as we forecast the consequences of acting on them, the ensuing suspense sustains deliberation (1933b, LW 8:200).

Anticipating contemporary research on the predictive brain (e.g., Hutchinson and Barrett 2019), for Dewey dramatic rehearsal is not a formula, recipe, flow chart, or decision procedure for deliberation and judgment. Whether we are plotting the next chess move, planning a trip, or struggling over a reproductive choice, our evolved neural adaptation for experimental simulation is a native psychological activity, on its own morally neutral. We dramatically rehearse for better or worse. When Dr. Seuss's Grinch has a "wonderful awful idea," he is tentatively rehearsing ways of acting. When open-world video gamers explore the land of Hyrule in Nintendo's epic Legend of Zelda series, they imaginatively forecast and evaluate alternative scenarios. Ideally, this indirect and vicarious mode of acting opens the way for critical assessment and redirection of conduct. Dramatic rehearsal is our means for plotting and scheming, but it is also our natural resource for intelligent and inclusive foresight of the consequences of alternative choices and policies.

Catechisms and formulas are often dispensed by moral authorities (clergy, parents, teachers, etc.) as though moral thinking is a recitation or "mechanical rehearsal" rather than a predictive dramatic rehearsal (1916, MW 9:244). Yet in order to deal responsibly with unique situations, we need to survey the consequences that will follow if we make this or that choice. Arguing that people already deliberate by crystallizing possibilities and transforming them into directive hypotheses, Dewey proposed that we can piggyback on our own psychology to deliberate more democratically, experimentally, and conscientiously.

Dramatic rehearsal may be hegemonic, or it may provide the cognitive scaffolding for what José Medina calls "resistant imaginations" (2013a). To nudge moral education toward the more encompassing view, we need what Johnson and Schulkin call "an account of the virtues of inquiry" (Johnson and Schulkin 2023, 139). Careful ethical reflection upon ideals and principles is a vital tool, but conscientious deliberation is typically harder work than applying an abstract principle to the events at hand. No rehearsed option will perfectly harmonize tensions, each will spawn new questions, and each must be evaluated in relation to other problems, social positions, identities, and goals.

Rawlsian comparison to an ideal world of rational agents who are in strict compliance with the demands of justice may make us more sensitive to the particular pinch of an injustice. It may help us singly or collectively hunt for ways to settle difficulties, creatively scope out alternatives, and picture ourselves taking part in them. To that extent, it may make deliberation more expansive and intelligent. But it is the wrong starting point for future ethical and sociopolitical theorizing.

Dewey's Moral Psychology II:
Making Intelligent Choices

Ethics is popularly taken to be about getting people to do the right thing when they are inclined to do otherwise. This is why straightforward and uncomplicated cases such as "Should he embezzle the money?" are often spotlighted as prototypical of ethical subject matter, even though such cases are not usually occasions for much deliberation. Dewey recognized untangled cases in which habituated rule-following is best and excessive deliberation amounts to dawdling. Or worse, deliberative excess may signify a manically imbalanced character that shirks responsibility for choosing, like Hamlet in his apparent indecision, "sicklied o'er with the pale cast of thought" (Shakespeare, *Hamlet*, Act 3, scene 2; cf. 1932, LW 7:170).

Dewey observed a related disposition to slough off responsibility for decisions among intellectuals who retreat to remote abstractions even when circumstances require more than begrudging notice. Those who "devote themselves to thinking are likely to be unusually unthinking in some respects, as for example in immediate personal relationships" (1922b, MW 14:137). Mike Parker humorously wrote in *Map Addict*: "I'm the one in the car with the map in his lap, . . . often at the expense of seeing the actual landscape it depicts rolling past on the other side of the window" (2010, 2). Like Parker, philosophers tend to be more map-oriented than terrain-oriented. There are consolations of retreating from the ambient buzz, but at their *philosophic* best they do not escape from peril into symbolic formulations and indulgently remain there when situations demand choices and action. When practical demands loop back into symbolic conceptions, philosophic theorizing speaks to living. Theorizing can help us to be more conscientious, at least if it is not separated from the courage to act. Thoughtfulness in isolation may be paralyzed by a kind of "anxious scrupulosity which is so fearful of going wrong that it abstains as much as possible from positive outgoing action" (1932, LW 7:259).

Dewey also understood that ad hoc rationalizations can masquerade as conscientious deliberation. This is a problem that virtue theorist Elizabeth Anscombe countered in "Modern Moral Philosophy" (1958), where she argued for an exceptionless prohibition against murdering the innocent (cf. Appiah 2017, 132). More recently, in their development of the dual-process or dual-track model, moral psychologists have documented the extent to which so-called moral reasoning can amount to little more than an ineffectual "rider" presuming to steer the headstrong "elephant" of habituated intuitions (Haidt 2012; cf. Hauser 2006, 86). As Johnson explains, the elephant (which personifies our habituated setup for moral appraisal) typically makes snap judgments, and then "the rider (our conscious rational processes) makes up a good story about how he or she was actually planning and controlling the elephant's appraisals and movements" (Johnson 2019, 181). Such dual processing is often circular and self-deceptive, and it frequently gives a self-justifying "rational" stamp of approval to automated impulsiveness. People make an appraisal on autopilot, then they "gin up allegedly rational justifications for what they have already" decided (181).

The mechanisms we use to hide things from ourselves have fascinated psychologists and social scientists for decades. Dewey, who in 1899 was elected the eighth president of the American Psychological Association, anticipated many of these insights into the propulsive power of habit over a century ago (e.g., 1922b, MW 14). Despite his anticipation of twenty-first-century dual-process theorists, Dewey would reject their dualistic schism of reason from habituated intuition, and he would reject their reduction of intelligence—"a short name for competent inquiry at work" (LW 15:41)—to nothing but the slave of intuition. Even more importantly, he would regard dual-process theorists' understanding of moral deliberation as impoverished due to neglect of imagination.

Imagination is not merely a faculty that forms images in isolated minds and is prone to frivolous fancy. As Medina observes,

"Imagination is not a luxury or a privilege, but a necessity" (2013a, 268; cf. Medina 2013b; cf. Paris 2016). For that reason, Johnson critiques and augments the dual-track model by arguing that dramatic rehearsal in deliberation is "a third track of moral cognition" (182). This third track is expansive, embodied, and active in a way that can counteract, albeit imperfectly, our penchant for being taken in by ad hoc rationalizations and for earnestly imputing meanings to events using ideas that others can barely conceive without caricature. Our imaginative capacity for tentative rehearsal is educable and responsive, whereas the traditional plumb line of principled rational justification tends to be ineffectual and self-deceptive. Johnson argues that Dewey's pluralistic and dialogical approach compensates for our autopilot system better than a monistic and monological approach, so that we can more competently reconstruct problematic situations and grow in our understanding of diverse others.

Pragmatism Does Not Give Away the Moral Store

Favoring a nonideal, context-steeped starting point seems to many ideal theorists, especially deontologists, to endorse an appeasing attitude. Analogously, the Compromise of 1850 in the United States ushered in measures such as the Fugitive Slave Law, which bartered away human rights and dignity for the sake of mealy-mouthed half-measures that protected and strengthened despicable practices. Do we need an ideal theory to justify moral condemnations?

Take the Fugitive Slave Law. In the historical case of the 1850 compromise, Massachusetts senator Daniel Webster sought to prevent southern secession while peacefully preserving the westwardly expanding union. Webster, a tepid abolitionist, held that the ends of Union and Manifest Destiny justified the law as "a measure of pacification and union," despite the fact that it would cement the institution of slavery. As discussed in Chapter 2, Webster's guiding principle that the end justifies the means is colloquially dubbed "pragmatic," but it is at odds with the philosophical school that included thinkers such as James, Dewey, Addams, and Mead (see Campbell 2019; Huebner 2019). As Dewey makes the point in *Theory of Valuation* (1939b), when we identify, evaluate, and revise our ends in light of means and consequences, we avoid "the absurdity of any 'end' which is set up apart from the means by which it is to be attained and apart from its own further function as means" (LW 13:227).

Ralph Waldo Emerson bitterly opposed Webster and other partisans who favored the Fugitive Slave Law. In his address to the citizens of Concord in May 1851, the first of several lectures he gave on the topic, he began with arguments about eternal rights, divine laws, the principle of respect for mankind, and the natural sentiments of mankind. Then he subtly shifted to largely pragmatic arguments that began not with abstract eternal verities but with an evaluation of means and ends in this particular historical situation. For example: a law that "fines pity, and imprisons charity" will be disobeyed because it runs against the grain of humane sympathies; it rewards mischievous and dishonorable behavior and thereby lowers and contaminates society; it systemically chains and subordinates everyone by hitching them to "the chariot of the planters"; it reduces the function of government to the protection of property. If the only way to save the union is to enact a suicidal law that "orders disunion," Emerson continued, then the United States is a union in statute only. He condemned preservation of an *unreconstructed* union, along with expansion of a country cemented by that union, if it had to be paid for at the monstrous moral cost of stabilizing an infrastructure that reduces human lives to legal property. The "practicable course" for the union, Emerson concluded, is to "exterminate slavery" by compensating southern planters. We should "acknowledge the calamity of his [the planter's] position, and bear a countryman's share in relieving him" (Emerson 1851).

A decade later, Emerson eventually supported deployment of political violence, and he again did so on mostly pragmatic grounds, his transcendental idealism notwithstanding. Emerson abhorred the hydra-headed monster of violence, and he rejected Hegel-steeped arguments about the inevitability of violent conflict as a means to social progress. He did *not* argue generally and abstractly that the end of abolition and freedom justified any means whatsoever. Nor did he fall back on an a priori ranking of freedom over peace (see Stamant 2012). Instead, he identified and evaluated means and ends.

Whether Emerson's pragmatic evaluations were sufficiently expansive is up for debate. Twenty-first-century scholarship complicates any "good war" tale of the American Civil War, given its massive morbidity and upheaval along with the subsequent history of white supremacist oppression (e.g., Horwitz 2013). As a telling lesson about moral fallibility and the perennial need for reckoning and revision, Emerson's support of the Union cause was coupled with naively idealistic prophecies about the Civil War as America's final chapter of political violence (Stamant 2012), just as Dewey in 1916—to his later dismay and regret—naively supported President Wilson's war that would end war.[6]

When values compete for our moral and political allegiance, judging the best *way* to work things out with one another is more reliable *and durable* when it involves dramatic rehearsal and experimental colloquy about means and ends, economized by ideals, principles, standards, and laws that help us to map out moral terrain. This depends on relatively civil conditions, even if adversarial, when communication has not entirely broken down. Establishing, sustaining, and renewing dialogical conditions must be an essential aim of education in any democratic society.

Pragmatic pluralists operationalize principles by interpreting and evaluating the vital experiential legs on which they stand. For example, it is difficult to imagine a classroom conversation about the Kantian practical imperative that fails to bring home that principle's practical durability. (My own students recently applied it to social media influencers who turn themselves into products and whose self-worth is keyed to the number of "views.") Moral principles and rules are shorthand; their job is focus us on salient situational features. They are not arbitrary. To borrow from Sherlock Holmes, princpiles can keep us concentrated on what is vital instead of being dissipated by what is incidental. As Nussbaum observes, they also help to guard against partisan bias, summarize prior wisdom, and establish intellectual parameters (1990, 99). In this respect, acting consistently with principles is more than what Oscar Wilde dismissed as a mere "refuge of the unimaginative." Nevertheless, to loosely paraphrase Henry James, it is a *foolish* consistency that fails to sacrifice a dictum or code when considerations of a finely perceived situation demand it. Laws are pragmatically justified as, in Cheryl Misak's words, "provisional punctuation points in a democratic process of inquiry" (2019). But no codified rule, principle, law, or concept can replace a flexible, discerning, and democratically engaged imagination. In Emerson's famous words, albeit penned as an argument for self-reliance, "A foolish consistency is the hobgoblin of little minds" (1965, 263).

Beyond Monism

Akin to Dewey's pluralistic account of the tangled terrain of moral action, Latour (1993) argues that "imbroglios" typify moral experience: that is, moral predicaments are entanglements of often-incompatible forces. When making decisions, we are routinely pulled in multiple ways, none of which has overriding moral force. This relative incommensurability of discordant situational factors presents a *practical* problem (not primarily a theoretical one):[7] if diverse factors are already in tension with each other, then monistic decision-making can lead to overly simplistic normative prescriptions that ignore or relegate factors that are relevant to making responsible choices. This oversimplification is analogous to the logical fallacy of causal reductionism, assuming a single cause for a complex outcome and ignoring multiple conjoint variables.

For example, rapid vaccination programs during the Covid-19 pandemic brought down hospitalization rates with some sacrifice in equity, whereas a loss in aggregate welfare, at least in the short term, was seen in states and countries that rolled out restrictive yet more equitable processes that may have cost more lives (Galston 2021; Rubinstein 2021). Relatedly, as vaccination lagged in the United States while cases rose from new variants of the virus, some cash incentives were offered. This was not fair to those who had already been vaccinated, but as long as policymakers are mindful of unintended consequences of such inducements, economic incentives may serve public health when reaching out to people who do not already identify their welfare with the general welfare (Van Vugt 2009).

Healthcare ethics should be multidimensional because it must grapple with many competing intractable factors, including overall social welfare, equity in the system, virtues such as social responsibility, issues of fairness (e.g., relating to resource scarcity—such as ventilators, vaccines, testing, high-quality masks, and antiviral drugs), duty (e.g., do healthcare workers have a duty to treat?), priorities placed on positive and negative rights, and the rights of workers and industries co-opted toward public causes. Does one of these concepts fully cover the rest? Dewey argues that the lack of a coverall concept is the rule in ethics rather than the exception.

Justice and aggregate welfare frequently vie for primacy as bottom lines. For example, drivers of high-efficiency vehicles arguably pay less than their fair share of the gas taxes that fund highway infrastructure. In that one respect, green-driver penalties that exact fees to offset lower gas taxes, as in the US state of Virginia, may be fair. Yet such penalties do not incentivize buyers of low-emission vehicles, which may slow the transition to a greener transportation system. Or to take a less consequential example, anyone who has worked on administrative policies for allocating faculty workloads at a university is at least implicitly aware that an institution or department can purchase greater aggregate happiness at the price of some unfairness. One can also demand an exactingly rational fairness in workload at the cost of some unhappiness.

Each case above involves conflicting moral factors. Is the job of the theorist to discern which of these ways of organizing reflection is the most justified? That is, is the theorist's job to show which antecedently defended and (relatively) static principles should govern choice? Ethical monists have traditionally said yes.

A pragmatic alternative is to challenge the assumption that a good value theory suppresses variability. Dewey criticized the quest for a putatively more rational framework with which all ethical choices should conform. The still-prevailing tendency among moral theorists is to infer, and perhaps impose, a standardized framework without consultation. Instead, moral theorists can gain a foothold with particular conditions by uncovering and critically analyzing incongruous values without flattening them (cf. 1925/ 1929, LW 1:323). Moreover, they can anticipate consequences of pivoting on this or that value, and they can make emphatic cases regarding trade-offs. A vital role of ethical debate, on a pragmatic approach, is not to determine what we should do based on the right abstractions, but to clarify and advocate compensatory emphases that are most appropriate for intelligently transforming a particular context. If that is all that one is asserting by "the right way to think about X," then such a pragmatic outlook can generate possibilities that are concealed by the situational insensitivity of overly formal approaches.

For example, Broome's formal utilitarian notion in *Climate Matters* that "the good of the world is the arithmetic total of people's well-being" allows him to develop a project that contributes to social welfare. But from Dewey's perspective, Broome's project cannot determine in advance whether to adopt a policy by taking "a sort of weighted average across the portfolio of all the possible amounts of well-being that might result from our policy" (Broome 2012, 116). Utilitarian ethicists like Broome are distinctive for their aggregating emphasis, but they are representative of mainstream ethics in their monistic assumption that there is a right way to reason about morals. Broome's hidden premise is that there is a theoretically correct account of metaethics and normative morality that can and must be pre-given straightforwardly in terms of one and only one supreme root. As will be explored in Chapter 5, Dewey rejected this assumption as empirically false and morally shortsighted. As argued in Chapter 2, unleashing theoretical work from that hedgehoggish assumption could free it up to make greater contributions to democratic discourse and social learning.

J. Baird Callicott wittily argues that moral pluralism is too dissociative in its identity, analogous to "multiple personality disorder" (1999, 175). Far from being an antidote to the problematic perceptual gaps and avoidance behaviors that Callicott's analogy implies, moral monism's greatest risk is that it will exclude inquiry into tensions and concerns that are undetected or hidden by our idealizations. In this way, monism itself fosters perceptual gaps and can lead to well-intentioned myopia.

Building on his general theory of operative or experimental intelligence (e.g., 1929, LW 4; 1938, LW 12), Dewey contended that no matter how carefully elaborated one's supreme moral principle (e.g., Gewirth 1978), it will rarely focus one's attention on all of the relevant situational forces that one ought to note and deal with. His moral epistemology imbibed the spirit of James's *A Pluralistic Universe*: "The word 'and' trails after every sentence. Something always escapes. 'Ever not quite' has to be said of the best attempts made anywhere in the universe at attaining all-inclusiveness" (1977, 145). There is *relevantly* more to any situation than can be covered by a single principle, concept, or ideal, just as there is more to any person than what annoys us about them.

Pluralists, for their part, can disagree with each other just as vigorously as monists. But they are also aware that their diagnoses and prescriptions will likely fail to capture all that is objectively relevant, so they typically uphold nuanced perception and communicative problem-solving as virtues of inquiry.

Hypothetically, it may be that the simpler the moral problem, the more likely it is that reduction to a single category may ameliorate the situation. In turn, it may be that the more complicated the problem, the higher the risk of moral paralysis or fatalistic resignation, so that monistic simplification may sometimes rescue people from inaction. These hypotheses are prima facie plausible and worth exploring. But take note that they are pragmatic hypotheses, and they illustrate how readily pragmatic pluralism can accommodate without dismissing monistic insights.

What I am arguing is that contemporary conflicts and disturbances are rarely so superficial that a theoretically correct rational analysis could, even in principle under ideal conditions, sweep the path clear toward what is "truly" good, right, just, or virtuous (cf. Taylor 1982; Williams 1985). Traditional monistic theories can serve the imagination required for wise deliberation (1932, LW 7; Johnson 1993; Alexander 2013, chs. 6–7). Competing perspectives are potentially complementary; they may compensate for each other's concealments. But whatever we see with their help is situated within what is inconspicuous. Whatever they put us in touch with is situated within what is ungrasped (cf. 1925/ 1929, LW 1:44). Forgetting this, we pay for conceptual clarities by neglecting existential subject matter that troubled us to inquire in the first place.

If moral action is heterogeneous in its origins and operations, and typified by underlying tangles between irreducible forces, as analyzed in the next chapter, then ethical monism's usefulness to moral understanding is limited. That is fine. Indeed, as Appiah (2017) argues, the articulation of one-sided idealizations is a personal or collective help in specific contexts. Moreover, pluralists are not immune from obtuseness. The problems with traditional monism are that (1) it is more consistent than conscientious, and (2) the quest for a single rational ruler to impose order on deliberation—a plumb line of reason that will square our moral lives to the world—fastens the linchpin that rationalizes moral fundamentalism's one-dimensional consciousness.

Enabling one-way-ism, save perhaps as a conscious experimental strategy, oversimplifies imbroglios. Far from being an antidote to moral dissociative disorders, monism—especially in the rationalistic form of ideal theories—tends to obstruct inquiry into marginalized concerns that escape our otherwise useful abstractions. Even when we are aware, like Nozick, that we are "idealizing greatly" (1974, 151; cf. Appiah 2017, 119), we may be taken in by the siren song of armchair clarity at the cost of rendering actual problems more opaque.

Dewey consequently saw little place for winner-take-all disputes in theory or policy assessment (cf. Edenhofer and Kowarsch 2015). Of course, in sharp contrast with prototypical fundamentalists or groupthink zealots, monistic moral philosophers are professional critics of valuational systems. They believe that they have much to learn from those who disagree with them. But traditional monists hold that their moral house may, with renovations and touch-ups here and there, fully accommodate whatever they need to learn. Building on Dewey, I am arguing that it cannot. A monistic house of theory may meet selective practical needs very well, but this does not imply that it is "best" in an all-encompassing sense.

Conclusion

In his 1923 preface to *Scepticism and Animal Faith*, George Santayana criticized the unsoundness of "special schools of philosophy, each of which squints and overlooks half the facts and half the difficulties in its eagerness to find in some detail the key to the whole" (1955, v; cf. Atkins 2024). The quest by these "special schools" for a universal moral plumb line presents problems for ethics and politics, and these problems arise in part from the one-way premise that monistic moral theorists share with moral fundamentalists. Traditional theorizing's "zeal for a unitary view" (1930b, LW 5:288) oversimplifies and standardizes in a way that is ill-suited to the indeterminacy of complex practical conditions. The resulting cultural lag is troubling, but not merely because we persist in using benighted ideas. It is troublesome because overly simplistic, habituated outlooks are out of sync with real, unsettled, on-the-ground circumstances. To borrow Vandana Shiva's agricultural image, in ethical and political theorizing we need more polyculture, not more monoculture.

There is nothing anti-theoretical in these observations. I am raising a question about how to theorize more effectively, in a way that contributes to wiser decisions. What ethical theory can do, despite or because of its emphatic idealizations, is to help lay bare "the factors causing [problems] and thus make the choice more intelligent" (Dewey, in Koch 2010, 2241–2245). If the assertion "This theory is correct" is intended in an operative sense, as in "The map to the pub is correct," then it is a sensible ideal to strive for theories that help us to navigate moral life. Unfortunately, the "correctness" claimed for moral theories has too often been analogous to claiming there is a right map in cartography as some fixed and final charting of changeless territory, isolated from an inclusive context, specified purposes, and objective results (see 1938, LW 12:138–139, 399). If being theoretically correct in ethics implies, as a regulative ideal, a completely enlightened standpoint secured in advance of confronting struggles in particular contexts—an ideal standpoint from which our general habits of moral thinking will, with tweaks, be fully adequate—then the quest for it increases cultural lag (cf. Anderson 2009). It is increasingly essential that we place theories on a stronger footing if they are to contribute to a healthier, more just, and more sustainable future.

Dewey did not simply assert the platitude that each major historical ethical framework has some truth to it. As analyzed in the next chapter, he explored a hypothesis to clarify how often-conflicting basic values relate to one another and how they might be put into communication with each other without being reified as universal standards for adjudicating all situations. Two claims are central to the chapter: (1) Dewey argued that moral uncertainty is often a sign of conscientiousness, and (2) this uncertainty arises in part from conflicts between heterogeneous sources of moral action—irreducible basic factors in morals—to which reasonable agents ought to pay attention. He thereby showed how functionally isolated theories can be critically appraised within a wider normative context even as these theories retain their distinctive identities as idealized partial mappings of moral terrain. When we cling to partial mappings as though they are true "independent of what they lead to when used as directive principles" (1929, LW 4:221), we fuel moral fundamentalism and leave deliberation incomplete. But when normative models are reframed as revisable experiments in living, as what Dewey in *The Quest for Certainty* called instrumentalities of direction, then they can be progressively reformed.

5

Dewey's Independent Factors in Moral Action

Students in university ethics courses learn to differentiate the Kantian deontologist's question (What is my duty?) from the utilitarian consequentialist's question (Which actions help us do the most good?), and they distinguish both from the virtue theorist's question (Which character traits contribute to a flourishing human life?). Over the course of a term, encouraged by instructors who charitably push these and other theories to their limits, students typically get the sense that each framework has something on its radar that the others miss. This chapter argues Dewey's case in favor of their wisdom, even as it criticizes many of their professors for labeling a "relativist" or "skeptic" anyone who challenges the very idea of a framework that represents the essence of morality. To appropriate a line from Heisenberg, Dewey implied that what ethical theorists observe is not the moral situation *in itself*, but the situation exposed to our method of questioning (see 1958, 32).

Monism and Pluralism Revisited

As Kitcher observes, "Dewey thinks we sometimes do not need to resolve controversies but to understand their persistence in terms of the pulls of incompatible fundamental values" (2019, 12–13; cf. 1919, MW 11:42–47). The study of ethics can help to cultivate conditions for social inquiry into these conflicting forces. Dewey hoped to contribute to a culture of inquiry, and he had this goal in

Beyond Moral Fundamentalism. Steven Fesmire, Oxford University Press. © Oxford University Press 2024. DOI: 10.1093/9780197763919.003.0005

mind as he framed his central question as an ethical theorist from 1926 to 1932: Is there a single empirical source of moral action, or are there plural sources?

Dewey was asking what is today called a "meta-ethical" question, one asked independent of normative prescriptions or constraints regarding what specifically is good or bad, right or wrong, virtuous or vicious. The monistic theories he criticizes are helpfully referred to by Glen Newey as "thin-property" reductivist systems which "fail to save some important phenomena of the moral life" (Newey 1997, 291). In some ways akin to twenty-first-century "moral particularists" such as Jonathan Dancy (2017), Dewey argued that moral complications tangle and diverge in ways that elude complete predictability, and satisfactory resolutions are "never twice alike" (1922b, MW 14:146). "Every honest piece of inquiry is distinctive, individualized; it has its own incommensurable quality and performs its own unique service" (1922a, MW 13:300). The good is unique.

Dewey did not deny that moral life includes recurrent decisions that *can be generalized* across similar cases, though, like Dancy, he did not fully appreciate the extent of their moral import. He instead emphasized the extent to which "different wants are in themselves qualitative and incommensurable" (MW 15:265). As Kahneman and others have shown of "noisy" judgments (in criminal sentencing, diagnosing patients, insurance underwriting, university admissions, and the like), excessive variability in judgments can be morally inappropriate (Kahneman et al. 2021). The more recurrent (less singular) the decision, the more rule-bound it might justifiably be. Nevertheless, Dewey focused on more singular events that rouse moral deliberation, conditions unique enough that they are not fully controllable by the impositions of any generalized abstract principle.

In order to weave incompatible and relatively unprecedented elements into coherent moral choices, philosophers inspired by Dewey have argued that we need aesthetic values such as contextual sensitivity and creativity more than we need the right supply of pre-given principles (Johnson 1993; Fesmire 2003). For example, D. Micah Hester (2019) builds on what he calls Dewey's "soft" particularism. Theorizing through healthcare practices which employ principles as "methods of inquiry and forecast" (1922b, MW 14:164), Hester draws from his clinical background to defend a Dewey-inspired conception of healthcare as an art that uses science to heal living individuals, in contrast with atomistic or merely mechanical approaches.

In contrast with Dancy's position that the moral principles advocated by "generalists" (a.k.a. universalists) are at worst arbitrary, or at best a "crutch" (Dancy 2017), Dewey thought that our most generalizable principles have deep experiential roots. His strong pluralistic hypothesis was that moral problems require reconciliation and coordination of "heterogeneous elements" (in Koch 2010, 2270) that include "at least three independent variables in moral action" (1930b, LW 5:280) which "pull different ways" (Dewey, undated ms, 4). He did not mash these variables together in some hedgehoggish attempt to assimilate them and show how they are really integrated. Instead, he treated the variables as independent in the sense that one variable is neither logically derivable from another nor translatable without remainder into the terms of another. A metaethical implication is that, at least in their strident or "hard" forms, both the particularist and universalist overstate their cases (cf. Axtell 2023), as do both the moral realist and antirealist.

In this chapter I clarify and develop Dewey's hypothesis, from its inception in the 1920s to its elaboration in the early 1930s, that moral life has *at least* three distinct, nonarbitrary experiential roots that can neither be deduced from ultimate axiomatic principles nor encompassed in one ideal way to proceed. With the support of archival research, I intersperse the three root factors (and corresponding concepts) that Dewey emphasized in his essay "Three Independent Factors in Morals" (1930b) with his parallel chapters in the 1932 Ethics (chs. 11–13). By exposing Dewey's own generalizations to scrutiny, promises and limitations of his approach can be critically evaluated.

Three Independent Factors in Morals

On November 7, 1930, Dewey addressed the French Philosophical Society in Paris, giving what his French colleagues recognized as "a première of his new ideas" (quoted in LW 5:503). He hypothesized that each of the primary Western ethical systems, as he construed them, represents a distinctive and irreducible primary root of moral life, which theorists go on to universalize: Greek teleologists like Aristotle represent aspiration, Roman and German deontologists represent obligation, and British moral sentiment theorists like Adam Smith represent approbation. Each basic experiential root is expressed in that system's leading fundamental concept: conceptions of the good are rooted in aspiration, conceptions of duty are rooted in obligation, and conceptions of virtue are rooted in social approval (cf. Axtell and Olson 2009). Each major ethical system seeks to bring these divergent experiential roots wholly within the logical scope of its own category. They relegate other factors as subordinate and derivative.

For example, rationalistic deontologists like Kant derive virtues from duties. That is, Kant conceives a character trait like benevolence to be virtuous because it maps to what can be determined by autonomous reason to be right or obligatory. Meanwhile, Greek teleologists identify virtues as those traits of character that contribute to a good life. It is sensible to categorize Aristotle as a virtue theorist, per convention, but Dewey highlighted Aristotle's subordination of virtues to a eudaimonistic conception of the good. British moralists like Smith and Hume reversed this by subordinating goodness and duty to socially approved and disapproved character traits (complemented by a welfarist standard). Dewey contextualized all three of these systems within the wider scene of moral action. He contended that aspirations, obligations, and approbations are distinctive experiential/existential phenomena that often get tangled up with each other and cannot be fully blanketed by a single covering concept.

Sorbonne professor Charles Cestre immediately translated Dewey's (1930b) English presentation, along with highlights from the ensuing discussion, and published it in *Bulletin de la SFP* as "Trois facteurs indépendants en matière de morale."[1] Decades later, in 1966, Jo Ann Boydston translated the French article back into English for *Educational Theory* as "Three Independent Factors in Morals," which she eventually included in the critical edition of Dewey's works (LW 5:279–288).

Soon after Boydston published her back translation, an unpublished and undated typescript (mss102_53_3) was discovered in the Dewey archives at Southern Illinois University, titled in Dewey's hand "Conflict and Independent Variables in Morals" (Figure 5.1).[2] A copy of this typescript was available to Abraham Edel and Elizabeth Flowers, who introduced the 1985 critical edition of Dewey's 1932 *Ethics* (LW 7; cf. Edel 2001). Pages 1–5 and 13 of the typescript remain unpublished, though these pages clarify several substantive points about Dewey's ethical outlook and offer unique angles and metaphors. The first five pages were likely presented in 1926 to a philosophy club at Columbia University (1933.12.26 [07682]: Dewey to Horace S. Fries]). Pages 6–12 closely track "Trois facteurs indépendants en matière de morale," though Boydston decided not to include Dewey's substantive handwritten annotations for those pages in the critical edition. In what follows, I incorporate material from the unpublished typescript whenever it offers a unique angle, clarifies a point, or adds something philosophically substantive.

Assuming that Dewey was reworking the typescript for an English publication, why did he never follow through? A plausible reply can be inferred from the fact that he incorporated its basic insights into his chapters of the 1932 revision of the Dewey-Tufts *Ethics* textbook (LW 7, chs. 10–17). The "three roots" hypothesis in

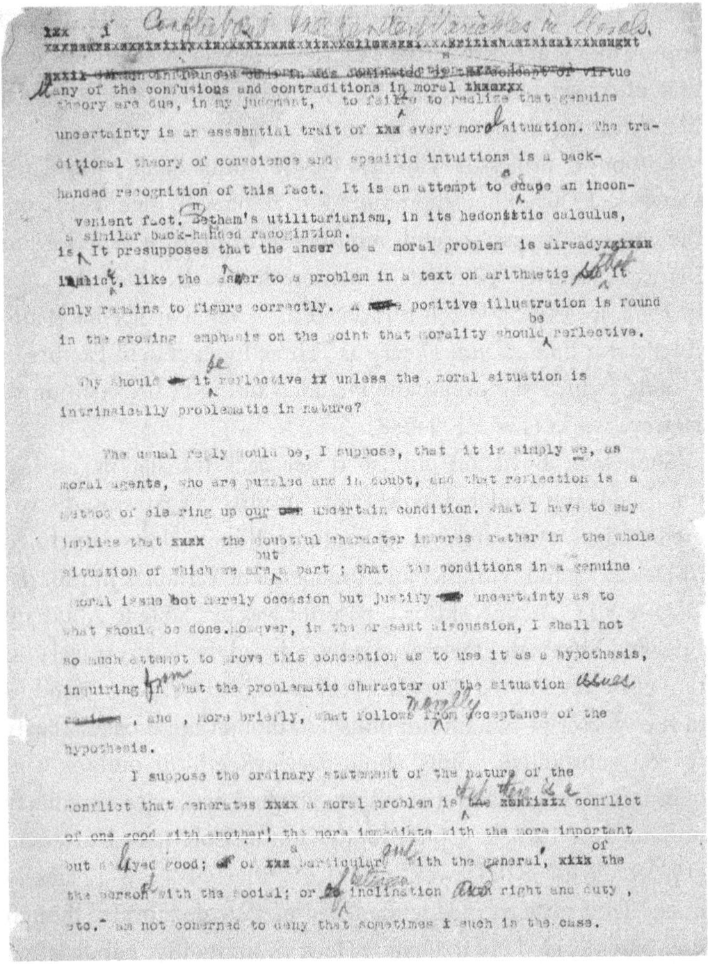
Many of the confusions and contradictions in moral theory are due, in my judgment, to failure to realize that genuine uncertainty is an essential trait of every moral situation. The traditional theory of conscience and specific intuitions is a back-handed recognition of this fact. It is an attempt to escape an inconvenient fact. Bentham's utilitarianism, in its hedonistic calculus, is a similar back-handed recognition. It presupposes that the answer to a moral problem is already at hand, like the answer to a problem in a text on arithmetic, so that it only remains to figure correctly. A positive illustration is found in the growing emphasis on the point that morality should be reflective.

Why should it be reflective unless the moral situation is intrinsically problematic in nature?

The usual reply would be, I suppose, that it is simply we, as moral agents, who are puzzled and in doubt, and that reflection is a method of clearing up our uncertain condition. What I have to say implies that the doubtful character inheres rather in the whole situation of which we are but a part; that the conditions in a genuine moral issue not merely occasion but justify uncertainty as to what should be done. However, in the present discussion, I shall not so much attempt to prove this conception as to use it as a hypothesis, inquiring from what the problematic character of the situation issues, and, more briefly, what follows from acceptance of the hypothesis.

I suppose the ordinary statement of the nature of the conflict that generates a moral problem is that there is a conflict of one good with another; the more immediate with the more important but delayed good; of a particular with the general, the person with the social; or of inclination with right and duty, etc. I am not concerned to deny that sometimes such is the case.

Figure 5.1
John Dewey. Undated manuscript (mss 102_53_3), 1. Used by permission of Special Collections Research Center and Center for Dewey Studies, Southern Illinois University Carbondale.

the 1930 presentation (Dewey 1930b) serves as an organizational chart or blueprint for those chapters, especially chapters 11–13.[3] But he incorporated the three roots in a less theoretical form that he judged to be better suited to the practical and pedagogical needs of undergraduate students (1933.12.26 [07682]: Dewey to Horace S. Fries). He set aside the theoretic key once it had served his pedagogical goal for the *Ethics*, which was to reforge historical theoretical tools in light of current moral needs so that students could use them to become more comprehensively conscientious in their deliberations and character development. Specifically, Dewey's goal in the 1932 *Ethics* was to help students become more perceptive of moral complexity, study and assess their own circumstances in light of prior systems, and competently use diverse theories as deliberative tools in predicaments that require practical coordination among disparate elements.

The theoretic key he left behind is among the most practically significant things Dewey ever wrote on ethics. Its significance has arguably increased as rampant moral fundamentalism and homogeneous narrowness continue to build walls of exclusionary oppression (see Collins 1998, 2019) and block the way to achieving social goals. These vices are often inadvertently validated by well-intentioned narrowness among traditional theorists. Instead of joining most monists in accepting the dogma that a defensible ethical theory must be a hierarchy that subdues variety among fundamental moral concepts, *or* merely venturing "an eclectic combination of the different theories" (LW 7:180), Dewey approached philosophical research into ethics in a way that refreshingly steered clear of an autocratic tendency to predefine and prejudge.

Is There a Single Conceptual Home Range of Moral Action?

In the 1930 presentation, Dewey (1930b) began his critical analysis of valuational systems with a simplified binary of independent factors before expanding to "at least" a trifecta. He operationalized the two most familiar "opposing systems of moral theory" by rejecting the false dilemma that confines them: either (a) what is morally Right derives from what is Good, or (b) what is morally Good derives from what is Right. If you choose (a), you get a teleological morality of ends, where right action is defined as the means to the supreme good of *eudaimonia* (as Aristotle argued), pleasure (as hedonists argue), self-realization, liberty (libertarianism), equality, sustainability, biotic integrity, peace, or the like. If you choose (b), you get a deontological morality of absolute rights and laws, where right action is prescribed by "juridical imperative."

Dewey argued that "neither of the two can derive from the other," that there is no "constant principle" tilting the balance "on the side of good or of law," and that both good and law are conceptions that "flow from independent springs" (LW 5:281). Thus, in moral education, learning to desire the good and learning to do one's duty are equally legitimate expectations, even though these may be at cross purposes and tug in different directions. Reflective morality consists in the capacity to determine a "practical middle footing" *between* relatively incommensurable claims, "a middle footing which leans as much to one side as to the other without following any rule which may be posed in advance" (281).

Moral situations, in Dewey's view, are not just *occasions* for uncertainty about what to do. Due to practically incompatible claims being made upon us, problematic moral situations more typically *justify* our uncertainty. "Moral experience is a genuine experience" of real, systemic conflicts (in Koch 2010, 2270), not just a matter of surface tension. We generally *ought* to be reflective because conflict is part and parcel of moral experience. And yet, Dewey argued, traditional theories have treated conflict as specious. Moral philosophers have acknowledged angst and indecision, but with their "Special Powers in their Special Armchairs" (Kitcher 2012, xix) they have for the most part postulated "one single principle as an explanation of moral life" (1930b, LW 5:280), an objectively correct standpoint from which we would, at least in principle (if for instance we ideally possessed all relevant facts), see that our initial hesitancy had been based on momentary ignorance.

If there is a unitary conceptual home range of moral action, Dewey argued, then moral conflict boils down to mere hesitancy on our part about what to choose. On that view, what is good or right is presumed to be *already* objectively good or right. No matter how fraught the situation, its goodness or rectitude is benignly waiting to be laid bare by intellectual analysis. But the evidence from actual moral experience, as I am seeking to illustrate in this book, suggests that we typically need time to think about morally uncertain situations because they require us to artfully reconcile conflicting factors that are best perceived and analyzed through multiple concepts.

Consequently, Dewey urged: "It is not without significance that uncertainty is felt most keenly by those who are called conscientious" (Dewey, undated ms).[4] Under the restrictive assumption legitimized by traditional theorizing, conflict and diversity are merely surficial and apparent (1930b, LW 5:279–288). Unity is presumed to lie beneath. A situation may at first *seem* to be a quagmire, the supposition runs, but rigorous examination, or complete data to feed into our utility calculations (Singer 2015), or comparison to an ideally just world (Rawls 1971), or perhaps comparison to an ideal egalitarian island of rational albeit hapless contractors (Dworkin 2000), would reveal that (a) there had been an objectively good, right, fair, or best path through the territory all along, and (b) the path's goodness, rightness, or fairness overrides other considerations when it comes to justification.

Forced to choose between tending a sick family member and attending a friend's wedding, Kantians traditionally grapple with competing duties in order to find the binding one. They sidestep downstream consequences as a moral red herring. Meanwhile, utilitarians calculate what does the most good when we give equal consideration for similar interests, independent of the ties that bind them to family and friends. Both exhibit the traditional monistic view that uncertainty is mostly as a "hesitation about choice" between the moral and the immoral (or less moral): we assume we must choose the most good (vs. lesser good or evil), will the obligatory (vs. giving way to appetite, inclination, and desire), or do the virtuous (vs. the vicious). "That is the necessary logical conclusion if moral action has only one source, if it ranges only within a single category" (1930b, LW 5:280). "*We* may be in doubt as to what the good or the right or the virtuous is in a complicated situation," Dewey wrote, but under the restrictive one-way assumption, "it is there and determination of it is at most a purely intellectual question, not a moral one. There is no conflict inhering in the situation" (Dewey, undated ms, 3).

Should an expectant mother of triplets selectively reduce to twins? Should we globally follow a principle of per capita equity for carbon emissions? Should an Orthodox Jew observe a religious duty to mourn in a large crowd during a resurgent pandemic that has disproportionately killed his fellows? To see and answer these questions through the lens of only one factor—say, as at bottom a matter of rights or duties not downstream consequences, of duty not virtue, of what is good not what is right, of what I should do and not what kind of person I should become—risks lopsided, partial, and exclusionary deliberation.

From Three Factors to Three Foundations: Hypostatization in Ethics

In a letter to Horace S. Fries (1933.12.26 [07682]) (Figure 5.2), Dewey identified the main conceptual shift he made between the 1908 first edition of *Ethics* (MW 5) and the 1932 revision. He had, he wrote, been committed in 1908 to a "socialized utilitarianism" that foreshortened moral action from the teleological perspective of good ends. This earlier consequentialist emphasis is apparent in *Outlines of a Critical Theory of Ethics* (1891, EW 2:238–388) and *The Study of Ethics: A Syllabus* (1894, EW 4: 219–362). *Human Nature and Conduct* (1922) reflected the view that moral life pivots on good ends, especially our responsibility to inclusively promote

320 "est 72nd St N Y City
Dec 26 '33

My dear Professor Fries.

I supposed my position in the early edition was that of a socialized utilitarianism; if I have made that point clearer in the last edition I am glad of it.

The material, my part, was prepared for first over a rathe r long period, the illness of Dr Tufts, and then preoccupations on my part postponed publication. The earlier matter was all revised in '31 and the part of Part III was all .... written for the first time then.

..as far as I can tell a large part of the change in the two edit- ions was made for reeducational reasons, the material of Part II I felt was too much couched in terms of ethical theories. I re-organized the material with a view to making the approach direct and criticism of theories secondary.

The theoretical change is in the direction of a sharper dis- tinction between different strands in .... morals. I wrote a paper abou 26 or 27 for a small philosophical club to which I belong on the independent variables in morals, the good, standard, approbation and, right and virtue and the ideas I expressed in that were the ones that expressed the theoretical change .I was a little surprised to find in going back over the early edition that the idea was at times implicit there; it must have been somewhere below express consciousness. I am not aware of any influence coming from Dr Sharp. The change was not connected with any change from agnostic to universalistic utilitarianism, but with a perception that there are three independent factors which have influences the development of morals that many of our moral problems come from the necessity of uniting them as when we act. I ?hey that in the early tradition I followed the tradition in making ends, the good, the basic idea, and in that sense the end was made primary. I

became convinced that in the actual development of morals the concepts of right had in fact played an independent role. I do not now reverse the roles but hold that it is a moral problem- one of a adjust-to adapt the concepts of right and virtue to that of the good and..theoretically, they are distinct and independent.

I am of course interested in what you say about your local situa tion. I hope you come through without too much friction.

Sincerely yours,

John Dewey

As far as I can recall any specific influence in changing my views it was reading more carefully the English moralists. I saw that they determined the good in terms of approbations or identified it with the virtuous; xxxx or course I knew that that determined it in terms of obligation. The consequence was that I was led to the idea of three independent concepts.

Figure 5.2

1933.12.26 (07682): John Dewey to Horace S. Fries. Published by permission of the Wisconsin Historical Society, Horace S. Fries papers, Mss 518, box 1, folder 6.

"growth of present action" (MW 14:194). By 1932, he told Fries, he had transitioned to a strong axiological pluralism that holistically maintains the intellectual distinctiveness of variables that are selectively—often helpfully—emphasized in the three leading concepts in Western ethics: good, duty, and virtue. This deeper metaethical pluralism was not a radical departure from Dewey's earlier outlook. Indeed, he told Fries that he was "a little surprised to find in going back over the early edition that the idea was at times implicit there; it must have been somewhere below express consciousness."

Edel proposes that Dewey respected the independence of each factor while making the content of each "responsible to the idea of the good" (2001, 11). Given Dewey's pervasive experimentalism and his emphasis on the ends-means continuum, it is fair for Edel to suggest that the good—as continuous personal growth and growing—is a nonreductive dominant emphasis in Dewey's mature ethics. This suggestion is also consistent with Dewey's naturalistic theory that moral cognition must be functionally organized to search for meaningful ways to meet needs by restoring dynamic equilibrium (Johnson 2019; cf. 1925/1929, LW 1:194; 1938a, LW 12:31–34). "Life grows," Dewey wrote in *Art As Experience*, "when a temporary falling out is a transition to a more extensive balance of the energies of the organism with those of the conditions under which it lives" (1934b, LW 10:20).

This nonreductive emphasis does not imply, however, that in his mature ethical theorizing Dewey was building a traditional closed system that prescribes and defends a growth-oriented consequentialism as the right way to think about moral choices. He strove for intellectual coherence, but his democratic tone was to let a thousand experiments in theorizing bloom, so long as they are mindful of means and consequences, are open and experimental in method, and reject hypostatization (clarified below). To illuminate moral life, with humility about what our inquiries may be obscuring, ethical theorizing must retravel, inspect, and resurvey the changing experiential terrain, and it must revise past conceptions accordingly. He concisely summed up this approach in *Experience and Nature*:

> All of the wit and subtlety of reflection and logic find scope in the elaboration and conveying of directions that intelligibly point out a course to be followed. Every system of philosophy presents the consequences of some such experiment. As experiments, each has contributed something of worth to our observation of the events and qualities of experienceable objects. Some harsh criticisms of traditional philosophy have already been suggested; others will doubtless follow. But the criticism is not directed at the experiments; it is aimed at the denial to them by the philosophic tradition of selective experimental quality, a denial which has isolated them from their actual context and function, and has thereby converted potential illuminations into arbitrary assertions. (1925/1929, LW 1:35–36)

Note, importantly, that in his mature writings Dewey at no point *reduced* moral life to a triumvirate of root sources. He did not have, nor did he seek, a universal, cover-all ethical theory in that respect, and he was extraordinarily adept at avoiding what he called hypostatization. *Hypostatization* includes a range of reification fallacies in which we get taken in by our own clarities. We mistake a functional abstraction—such as duty—for a preexisting basic entity, property, or relation. Then we forget its genesis as a result of selective analysis. The image is of medical hypostasis, a blockage that slows the flow of blood. In addition to proliferating supergaseous substances in traditional metaphysics, the fallacy violates Peirce's first principle of reason: it blocks the way of inquiry. It blocks inquiry by converting what was selectively taken from a situation-in-process into the whole of what may be found there, then disavowing the rest as extraneous. Dewey recognized this as "*the* philosophical fallacy" (see 1925/1929, LW 1:27–29), "the bias toward treating objects selected because of their value in some special context as the 'real," in a superior and invidious sense" (33). Whitehead analyzed the fallacy in terms of "misplaced concreteness," and in *The Concept of Nature* he accordingly admonished natural philosophers to "Seek simplicity and distrust it" (Whitehead 1920, 104; cf. Myers 2019 and Pappas 2008).

Dewey developed his simplified pluralistic typology of "at least three" independent factors in moral action in the 1920s as the organizing principle of his spring 1926 course, Ethical Theory, at Columbia University. Thanks to Donald Koch's editorial labors on *The Class Lectures of John Dewey* (2010), researchers have access to previously unpublished material unknown to Edel or Flowers, including clarificatory gems in Sidney Hook's class lecture notes on that 1926 course. Hook's notes take readers into the classroom as Dewey surveys the history of ethical theory to lay bare "certain categories found to be involved in judgments which men actually pass in the course of moral conduct and which concepts have become the foundation stones of theories about ethics" (in Koch 2010, 2230). The 1926 course—again, akin in its topic to a course in metaethics today in that it was "not concerned with what is specifically right, but with the category of right" (2230)—was organized around a hypothetical explanation for the variety of ethical theories. I draw from Hook's notes where helpful.

In the 1926 course, Dewey struggled with whether right and duty are fundamentally distinct concepts with different empirical origins. For example, he explored Sidgwick's notion in *Methods of Ethics* that the right is the universally binding "Rational Good" that we impartially and thus virtuously judge "from the point of view . . . of the universe," which Sidgwick contrasted with merely *natural*, nonmoral goods that we desire and fulfill due to our biological inheritance and particular circumstances (cf. Lazari-Radek and Singer 2014). Dewey told his students in the class's opening days:

These remarks [identifying good, right, duty, and virtue as fundamental concepts that enter into moral conduct] presuppose the possibility of a hierarchy of these different ideas, i.e., all deduced from a supreme one. But an alternative is possible, i.e., that none are derivative or subordinate. They may be independent variables, i.e., ideas representing facts which while they overlap, are still intellectually distinct so far as the meaning of the four terms is concerned. The originality in the [spring 1926] course will largely be concerned with the inability to find a single central notion from which the others can be derived or around which they can be organized. Two or three may be connected, but there are at least three independent variables. (in Koch 2010, 2231)

Contrary to moral fundamentalists, Dewey argued that moral problems arise naturally from conflicts inhering in situations, and that they do not come gift-wrapped with a correct formulation or a single justified course of action. In *Human Nature and Conduct* (1922b) he had focused on moral psychology, as with his description of deliberation as dramatic rehearsal of alternatives for mediating "conflict and entanglement of various incompatible impulses and habits" (MW 14:146). In 1926–1932, he broadened his scope to encompass the wider scene of moral action. This allowed him to situate the "socialized utilitarianism" of his earlier ethics within a wider telescoping perspective. "Three Independent Factors in Morals" is Dewey's resulting conceptual map of the diverse existential terrain of moral action. The essay foreshortens his mature ethical theory.

In the following three subsections, titled after chapters 11–13 of the 1932 *Ethics*, I draw on Dewey's unpublished and published sources from 1926 to 1932 to clarify and develop his analysis in "Three Independent Factors in Morals" (1930b) of good, duty, and virtue as distinct categories that in many cases express different experiential origins. In conversation with recent ethical and political theorists, I trace these traditional categories back to their generative roots.

Ends, the Good, and Wisdom

The Good as a leading category in reflective ethics arises from desires and aspirations. People have purposes they aim to realize; pervasive wants, drives, appetites, and needs that constantly demand to be satisfied. Yet what *seems* good at short range may not in fact *be* durably good, as when a student enjoys an evening of video games and shrugs off tomorrow's assignment. The isolated *satisfaction* we anticipate and crave may not be judged *satisfactory* when we take a wider view, so we need practice and wisdom to thoughtfully discriminate between the real good and the spurious mirage (cf. 1939b, LW 13).

Consequently, the teleological conception of goods that *approvably* speak to human cravings and aspirations is "neither arbitrary nor artificial" (1932, LW 7:309). When we make hasty choices without intelligent foresight, we just follow the strongest impulse and fulfill an inclination without taking its measure. We may desire something that is not, from a wider and longer-range angle, desirable, just as we may eat something that is not edible. "But when one foresees the consequences which may result from the fulfillment of desire, the situation changes" (1930b, LW 5:282). Intelligent foresight, however modest, involves judgment and comparison as we envision consequences ex ante and track them ex post.

As explored in Chapter 4, Dewey analyzed the human capacity to imaginatively rehearse alternative avenues for acting (e.g., 1922b, MW 14, ch. 16; cf. Fesmire 2003, Alexander 2013, and Johnson 2019). We dramatically rehearse in a developing social-historical context, and our judgments can be "examined, corrected, made more exact by judgments carried over from other situations; the results of previous estimates and actions are available as working materials" (1930b, LW 5:282).

In this way, we learn to organize and prioritize desires with an eye to their bearings, and this led historically to candidates for the "chief good," the summum bonum (Aristotle 1999, Book I), such as hedonistic pleasure, Epicurean wisdom, egoistic satisfaction, self-realization, and asceticism. When we set national, educational, and personal aspirations to accord with our worship of what James sardonically called "the bitch goddess, success" (in LW 2:161), we are laying plans for an overarching good, albeit one that most philosophers since Socrates have rejected as a sham (Plato 1992, Book I; Plato 1960).

Wherever the Good is the uppermost factor in philosophical theorizing, *reason* is conceived as "intelligent insight into complete and remote consequences of desire" (1932, LW 7:217). The envisioned action is right and virtuous because it is truly, objectively, farsightedly good; it is wrong and vicious because it is shortsightedly bad.

As a contemporary example, take Singer's hedonistic utilitarian approach to "effective altruism" in *The Most Good You Can Do* (2015), one of the most teachable books in contemporary practical ethics. For Singer, reason objectively calculates the best quantifiable way to "maximize the amount of good you do over your lifetime" (Singer 2015, 65; cf. 198 n. 10). Reason counters our emotive impulse to discount the lives of those who are physically or temporally distant. Singer argues that reason also checks our conflation of "warm glow giving," such as a donation to the Make-a-Wish Foundation, with cost-effective philanthropies like those recommended by The Life You Can Save, a charity that Singer himself founded in order to enable donors to find the charities that do the most good with each dollar they receive.[5] One need not be morally "on the clock" 24/7, as this would reach a point of diminishing returns. But weighing your options—say, alternatives for charitable giving—to maximize the true, objective good that you do is what it *is* to be moral.

Singer argues that if you can work for Goldman Sachs and donate your considerable discretionary cash to effective charities, you may do more life-saving and quality-of-life-improving good than if you strictly adhere to a deontological "do no harm" principle and refuse to participate in the capitalistic financial system due to its putative unfairness. Although Singer's specific line of argument has not been helped by dubious publicity for effective altruism by American entrepreneur Sam Bankman-Fried, convicted in the FTX cryptocurrency scandal (see Lewis-Kraus 2022), the general ethical idea is that the good that you do *justifies* your participation in the system, unless you could have aggregated more good in some other way. *If* struggling against structural inequalities by minimizing involvement in financial markets added up to the greater good, then it would be justified. But fighting for justice is not good "in itself" independent of its utility, Singer argues.

For Singer, answering a moral problem is analogous to answering a math problem. It requires us to calculate payoffs and pitfalls, debits and credits, and thereby determine the objective good (145). We assemble information and then calculate profits and losses, as if we were completing a moral accounting spreadsheet. This has given rise to a debate between "longtermists" and "shortermists" regarding the temporal scale of this accounting. For instance, what priority should an objective and impartial agent give to expenditures on decreasing existential risk from asteroids, climate change, and other threats, compared to expenditures for decreasing shorter-range suffering? Singer quotes Nick Bostrom, an Oxford utilitarian specializing in existential risk analysis, who deduces via utility calculations that it should be our highest global priority: "If benefiting humanity by increasing existential safety achieves expected good on a scale many orders of magnitude greater than that of alternative contributions, we would do well to focus on this most efficient philanthropy" (in Singer 2015, 174).

In the unpublished typescript, Dewey included such mathematizing, neo-Benthamite approaches in a sweeping criticism of traditional moral philosophies. He acknowledged that appeals to "the dictates of conscience," intuition, a moral calculus, moral law, or divine command give a nod to moral hesitancy and puzzlement. But they mask deep existential uncertainty when they presuppose "that the answer to a moral problem is already licit, like the answer to a problem in a text on arithmetic that it only remains to figure correctly" (undated ms, 1). Dewey held that moral problems typically bear little analogy to elementary arithmetic tasks, or even to being stumped by a very hard puzzle. "Deliberation is not then to be identified with calculation, or a quasi-mathematical reckoning" (1932, LW 7:275). When a child puzzles over the square root of 81, there is a clear-cut way to formulate the problem and a right solution to calculate, so the only real problem is temporary ignorance of the answer. Solving a jigsaw or sudoku puzzle may be difficult, but there is at most a superficial uncertainty that is resolvable. These are benign rather than wicked problems, in the trending lingo. In moral life, however, there are typically no objectively computable preexisting answers or timeless mechanisms for getting at them.

In reply to this Dewey-inspired critique, Singer has clarified his position on moral uncertainty. "As for the 'moral mathematics' that Dewey criticizes," Singer writes, "there is of course plenty of uncertainty in moral decisions, both in whether one has the right data going into the 'mechanism' and the right mechanism itself. Even among consequentialists, there is plenty of disagreement about what the exact mechanism should be" (personal communication).[6] Singer thus agrees that moral decision-making is accompanied by considerable uncertainty. As with the debate between longtermism and shortermism, Singer of course acknowledges that his own neo-Benthamite approach is thoughtfully contested by fellow consequentialists.

Singer's reply helpfully distinguishes his utilitarianism from Dewey's pragmatic pluralism. When Dewey wrote that "Genuine uncertainty is an essential trait of every moral situation" (Dewey, undated ms, 1), he was not merely remarking on the uncertainty that arises from the *difficulty* of a "puzzle," or to lack of *access* to relevant data to plug into our diagnostic machinery or algorithmic technology. He was contending that there simply *is* no exactly and irrecusably right mechanism, *not even in principle under ideal conditions*, for definitively formulating and finally answering quandaries about which moral choice to make among viable alternatives.

Practical deliberative mechanisms in ethics are nevertheless valuable, and their value is growing today in the field of machine intelligence. Dewey's pragmatic point was that they get their value as anticipatory tools. We use improvable intellectual instruments to enlighten judgment. These are forged in response to situational needs, evaluated and refined by how well they meet those needs. At their best, these instruments are "deliberately constituted by critical inquiry intended to produce objects that will operate as effective and economical means when they are needed" (1938a, LW 12:139). They may help to make our judgments less specious, exclusive, "arbitrary, capricious, unreasoned" (1925/1929, LW 1:320)

Even prior to the sophistication of twenty-first-century game-theoretic modeling, or debates about value-laden algorithms in artificial intelligence, Dewey should have emphasized that a utilitarian economic-mathematical balancing model can function well as a heuristic for specific purposes. We need reliable tools for the jobs at hand, and these evolve over time. Insofar as metrics and algorithms help to disclose the good of a situation by economizing deliberation, without occluding other morally relevant factors, then they are pragmatically valuable to that extent.[7]

When used to expand our dramatic rehearsals, utilitarian welfarist number-crunching can tamp down on irrational prejudices, challenge our unreflective disregard for those with relevantly similar interests, devise risk-benefit models, inform technological algorithms, and thereby help to advance social and animal welfare. Such strategies should be evaluated like any other tool, by the work they do. They are at least a counterweight to a do-nothing attitude about the welfare of others.

What Dewey challenged was the aggregating moralist's quest for a predetermined metric whereby we judiciously weigh matters so that the balance automatically tips toward the optimal outcome supported by a universal welfarist principle—that is, the most good we can do. More generally, the quest in teleological ethics for a cover-all metric that is "right" once and for all relies on the classic preconception of an *ultimate end* such as pleasure, a prescientific holdover that is not essential to constructing welfare models and assessments. Dewey's advice was to drain the theoretic bathwater while evaluating the functional-operational baby by its directive power. He wrote in the concluding pages of *Experience and Nature*:

> To discover and define once for all the *bonum* and the *summum bonum* in a way which rationally subserves all virtues and duties, is the traditional task of morals; to deny that moral theory has any such office will seem to many equivalent to denial of the possibility of moral philosophy. Yet in other things repeated failure of achievement is regarded as evidence that we are going at the affair in a wrong way. (1925/1929, LW 1:322)

Rights, Duty, and Loyalty

The way we express our concerns and make sense of problems is acquired through interaction with the physical, cultural, and interpersonal environments in which we are at home. Through their cultural medium, classic Greek theorists acquired their intellectual habit of pulling toward the good, just as Roman and British theorists later pulled respectively toward the dutiful and virtuous.

They all tailored theories to fit the demands of the situation as they understood it, and all assumed one size would fit all.

Dewey argued that the intimacy of the Greek polis supported teleological intelligence and the idea that laws reflect the rational ability of citizens to cooperatively set and achieve goals. Accordingly, theories tethered to the good made sense to classical Greek theorists. The far-flung hodgepodge of peoples in the Roman Empire, however, favored the historical development of centralized order and the imposition of demands. Consequently, in the transition from Greek teleology to Roman law, as exemplified by Stoic philosophers like Epictetus and Marcus Aurelius, compliance with authorized duty was placed at "the centre of moral theory" (1930b, LW 5:284).

The resulting deontological theories speak to a fact in everyday human behavior: we unavoidably make claims on each other through living together. This includes the control of desire and appetite, companionship and competition, cooperation and subordination. Our desires are impeded and regulated, sorted into the forbidden and the permitted. These demands and prohibitions appear arbitrary unless they square sufficiently with each other's practical purposes. So, Dewey proposed, "there finally develops a certain set or system of demands, more or less reciprocal according to social conditions, which are . . . responded to without overt revolt." In this way, he argued, authorized rights and duties evolved, and continue to evolve, through public demands and bans. These tie our hands independent of whether they promote aggregate welfare. "From the standpoint of those whose claims are recognized, these demands are rights; from the standpoint of those undergoing them they are duties." These publicly defined rights and duties constitute "the principle of authority, Jus, Recht, Droit, which is current" (284).

Dewey hypothesized, then, that duty as a leading concept in morals arose historically, and for better or worse is rooted still, in authoritative control of individual satisfactions and temptations within social relationships. As such, the concept of duty (along with the related concept of loyalty to what is *right*) is distinguishable from the concept of good. They are conceptually independent factors in morals. The concepts of duty and good may be conflated or appropriated, but they are independent both in their experiential origins and in their logical operations. They pivot on different elements: the good on aspiration, the right on exaction and obedience.

Because imperatives often inhibit the fulfillment of desires, the concept of duty is not "reducible to the conception of the good as satisfaction, even reasonable satisfaction, of desire" (1932, LW 7:214). As Kant argued, there is no moral quality in binding people's choices to an authority they deem arbitrary. Rights and duties are defined socially, but when reflectively justified they have a standing beyond merely inherited mores (165). For example, years ago, my young son was happily picking flowers in a public garden. We told him, "Don't pick the flowers." To him, his parents' curtailment of this good seemed to be an arbitrary imposition. Asked about this some years later, he concluded that it was reasonable for his liberty to be restrained in this way. What had begun as compliance had been converted into something with moral standing, something *right*. He now concurred. He acknowledged the ban on flower picking in public gardens as a *moral* demand that he and others should meet.

Taking these insights a step further, Dewey carefully distinguished the *origins* of root factors from their eventual *operations*. For example, that which operates as a good (to which one sincerely aspires) may have originated as a duty with which one had to comply. Today our son wants to help that garden flourish. What began as an alien requirement that thwarted his desire to grab flowers developed into something right to which he realized the wisdom of submitting, and it eventually became a good that he pursues absent any requirement. The same might eventually be said of his enforced responsibility to do schoolwork, a duty that can also originate in obedience to communal regulations, when he would understandably prefer to relax. When cultivating a garden or doing schoolwork enters one's personal aspirations, "it loses its quality of being right and authoritative and becomes simply a good" (1930b, LW 5:285).

To summarize, "the Good is that which attracts; the Right is that which asserts that we *ought* to be drawn by some object whether we are naturally attracted to it or not" (1932, LW 7:217). When the latter factor is foremost, *reason* (or a presumed innate faculty of conscience) is conceived as "a power which is opposed to desire and which imposes restrictions on its exercise through issuing commands" (217).

To whatever degree a deontologist is a monist, an act is ultimately good and virtuous *because* it is right; it is bad and vicious because it is wrong. It follows for the deontologist that there are no morally relevant aspects of virtue or good that cannot be organized under covering concepts of duty, right, law, and obligation. To will and be loyal to what is right *because it is right*, and not primarily because it is expedient, is consequently a popular way of framing moral judgments, and the conception of lawful duty (and compliance with constraints) is thus taken by many to be the universal foundation of ethics.[8]

In the 1932 *Ethics*, Dewey applied these insights to Kantian deontology. For Kantians, what is morally Good "is that which is Right, that which accords with law and the commands of duty" (214–216). Recent representatives are so varied as to defy easy generalization, including Rawls (1971), Donagan (1977), Gewirth (1978), Darwall (1983), and Korsgaard (1996). For example, central to his conception of justice as fairness, Rawls—while rejecting Kant's foundationalism, universalism, and strong version of monism—held with Kant that a deontological principle of right takes priority over consequentialist concepts of good (1971, 31; cf. Freeman 2007, 72). Rawls referenced Kant's *Critique of Practical Reason*: "the concept of good and evil must not be determined before the moral law . . , but only after it and by means of it" (Kant 2002, 37). Contrary to

Singer, Rawls argued that one should struggle against inequality or strive to change an unjust system *independent* of any welfarist purpose such as anticipated net utility.

For Kantians, the good is a path to the right, and the right gets its governing authority by reasonably obliging everyone. In Korsgaard's Kantian writings on the "source of normativity," moral obligations are assigned by first-person autonomous consciousness (1996; cf. Schaubroeck 2010). Fully complying with your obligations consistent with the categorical imperative, and thereby at least attitudinally intending to uphold the rights of others, is what it *is* to be moral.

Like many East Asian and contemporary environmental philosophies, Dewey criticized ethical theories that are based on first-person autonomous consciousness, and he rejected the traditional Kantian transcendental subject. I emerge as a differentiated locus of activity through interactions; I am not an antecedently existing entity. Hence the locus of ethics is fundamentally relational. As Stephen Darwall's (2006) relational deontology reveals, some contemporary Kantians converge with Dewey on this relational standpoint. (See Korsgaard 2007 for her critique of Darwall.)

As Roger Ames (2019) observes of the burgeoning dialogue between Confucian role ethics and American pragmatism, it is redundant in both traditions to postulate something extra-relational like Reason-ruled will to explain and support personal identity and moral conduct. Dewey recognized, at least as early as his 1896 critique of the stimulus-response reflex arc in psychology, that we achieve coordination *through* our relationships, not through exertions emanating from the inner space of mind. This is why relational virtuosity and moral imagination are irreplaceable for Dewey (Ames 2007 and 2019; see Chapter 2). If a generalized statement of the action I am considering cannot rationally be willed to be a universally binding law, then I should indeed pause to consider whether I am holding myself to a lower standard than I hold others. Reasonable social expectations bind me to do better. But the work of moral deliberation is not thereby complete.

Korsgaard would wonder how social expectations take on binding moral authority for Dewey. He does not single out autonomy as the anchorage for normativity, nor does he ground moral decision-making in rational demonstrations of axiomatic first principles. From Korsgaard's own Kantian perspective, in contrast with Darwall's "second-personal" relational standpoint, that is a moral nonstarter because it fails to ground the logical inference that others have a will and welfare of their own. For Korsgaard (1996), that inference is essential for establishing the objectively correct procedure and criterion—the categorical imperative—for resolving moral questions. She argues that any moral theory that fails to establish such a criterion surrenders the field to moral skeptics.

How, then, did Dewey reinterpret and operationalize the locus and ground of rightfulness so that moral commitments have normative force without falling back on God, the state, an inner law of pure practical reason, a preexisting law of nature, or at least the procedures of idealized rational actors? Does any moral theory that lacks a noncontingent, necessary ground of normative self-governance—an a priori anchorage that will never slip—amount to little more than a provincial clan morality, or perhaps a permission slip for wavering and dissolute behavior? From a neo-Kantian view, the pragmatic pluralist outlook has far too much leeway.

Dewey's general reply to this Kantian concern was that we have justified obligations not primarily because we possess a sophisticated theory of mind and are abstractly bound by the principle of consistency in our rational procedures, but mostly because relationships naturally bind us to each other and nature—as parents and children, spouses or partners, friends, and citizens. These are facts about human interactions, but they are not inquiry-independent "moral facts" that objectively determine the truth-value of moral claims (see end of Chapter 1). Dewey was not bound to that "substantive moral realist" assumption, which is Korsgaard's primary target. By starting with and returning to moral experience, he chose neither side of the current debate between moral realists and constructivists (cf. Pappas 2008).

Through our experience of relationships, which Noddings influentially discussed as relationships of care (2013), we are exposed to "the expectations of others and to the demands in which these expectations are made manifest" (1932, LW 7:218). Explicit and implicit claims upon our cares, Dewey argued, are "as natural as anything else in a world in which persons are not isolated from one another but live in constant association and interaction" (218). Of course, not all relational claims upon us are *moral* claims. For example, although children, friends, spouses, or citizens might be coerced into slavish conformity by despotic power, they experience this as a brute and arbitrary imposition without moral standing. Social expectations become moral claims because, even when inconvenient or exasperating, conscientious parents, friends, spouses, or citizens respond to relations of parenting, friendship, marriage, and citizenship as "expressions of the whole" to which they belong rather than merely as extrinsic impositions (218). They become ties that bind, and it is perfidy to turn our backs on them: "If we generalize such instances, we reach the conclusion that right, law, duty, arise from the relations which human beings intimately sustain to one another, and that their authoritative force springs from the very nature of the relation that binds people together" (219).

Moral life calls us to meet the demands of situations, and this requires us to perceive and comprehensively respond to more than our private hankerings. We are typically far from the only ones with a stake in our choices. But this does not on its own imply, with Korsgaard's first-person ideal theory standpoint, that normativity is singularly rooted in being consistent in our respect for others' autonomous consciousness. In Dewey's view, the libertine for whom nothing is forbidden fails to perceive and respond to the relationships bound up in the situation, and so fails morally. The word "duty" is apt for the many occasions, banal to momentous, in which our own narrow preferences run at cross purposes with relational demands that should not be shirked merely because they may be irksome, discomforting, inconvenient, or dangerous.

Akin to Dewey's relational outlook on the source of obligations, Bao Zhiming compares the model of moral agency in Confucian-influenced societies like China, Korea, and Japan with the familiar model of autonomy that has dominated Western law and ethics. He writes: "Ultimately, man is social, hence relational. . . . Man as an individual abstracted away from the social and political relationships he is born into never enters the picture of Confucius' ethical world" (in Becker 1991, 169). Individual and society emerge from each other; neither is derivative of the other. Nevertheless, Dewey consistently placed more emphasis than neo-Confucians on the realization of individual capacities. He was sharply critical of social organicism, especially in its extremes when "concrete individualities" are swallowed (MW 9:65), as arguably when hospital workers in Xi'an reportedly enforced China's zero-Covid policy during a 2021–2022 lockdown by refusing "to admit a man suffering from chest pains because he lived in a medium-risk district. He died of a heart attack" (Yuan 2022). Dewey's "emergent individualism" (1930a, LW 5:89) is reflected in his 1919–1920 series of letters and essays from Japan and China. He deeply appreciated Japanese aesthetics, but he criticized its feudal communitarianism for subordinating individuals to the emperor as the deferential symbol of communal life (1920, MW 12).

Dewey shared Japanese philosopher Tetsurō Watsuji's (1889–1960) opposition to ethical and political approaches that, as Watsuji wrote in *Rinrigaku*, "remove the human being from social groups, and deal with him as a self-sustaining being" (1996, 13). "The locus of ethical problems," Watsuji asserted, "lies not in the consciousness of the isolated individual, but precisely in the in-betweenness of person and person" (1996, 10). From either Watsuji's or Dewey's standpoint, anyone who aims with Korsgaard to analyze the source and ground of normative judgments errs by starting with a detached individual consciousness that apprehends and applies rational principles. Although Dewey was much closer to Korsgaard than to Watsuji in respecting individual agency and self-determination over loyalty to one's social group, he agreed with Watsuji's view that the standpoint of being situated or relationally placed should be the primary one (Ames 2019).[9]

Dewey also rejected the Kantian notion that there are objectively, demonstrably correct procedures for reasoning about moral questions. In his own theory of moral judgment and knowledge, he argued that the "comprehensive object" of moral choice is the option one foresees leading to a recovery of relative equilibrium, because it most reliably expresses and resolves the situation's conflicting factors (LW 7, ch. 14; cf. 1922b, MW 14:135). Personal inclinations will often run counter to this comprehensive object of choice. But akin to virtue theorists like Foot, and taking a cue from Hume and Smith, Dewey was skeptical of the traditional Kantian contention that our moral mettle is truly revealed when we are motivated to pursue the comprehensive object by the resolute force of reason independent of desire (Foot 1978, 161; cf. Trianosky 1990). Conscientious moral artistry does not rely on dispassionate pure reason (Kant), comparison to a world of fully compliant agents (Rawls), or detached moral bookishness (utilitarianism), though it may be informed by the orientations that posit these fictions. Even in situations in which the comprehensive object has its origins in dutiful compliance, it is a matter of moral significance for Dewey that we create conditions that increase its desirability as a (hypothesized) good, instead of being satisfied with cool, disinterested assent alone.

Some commentators have misrepresented Dewey's *mature* ethics as an ethics of self-realization. Not only would this be a monistic reduction, but also self-realization as an ideal may deaden people to the experiences of others so that we value them like pleasantries. Dewey's perspective was far from "happyism" (Salerno 2005). Kantians are right that we cannot rationally will a world of shoplifters, liars, cheaters, or sexual harassers; they are also right to call for an inner sentinel alert to the exceptions people make for themselves even as they demand honesty, fidelity, and respect from others. Who is better than Rawls, Appiah observes, for shining a light on the way we benefit from a practice while shirking to do our share in sustaining that practice for others? (2017, 203). Yet for Dewey, the general social demand to do our fair share arises from and is justified in practical experience, not by compliance with the first principles of idealized contractors.

Kantians typically reject Dewey's style of aspectual pragmatizing and operationalizing, just as they reject his nonideal starting point. They argue that it introduces extraneous considerations of expediency into moral discourse. Nevertheless, Dewey agreed with Kant that "to be truthful from duty is ... quite different from being truthful from fear of disadvantageous consequences" (Kant 1993, 15). Duty, right, and obligation are concepts that serve an experiential function as *one* of several constant and distinctive streams of moral action. Kant's rational and empirical mistake was to hypostatize this factor and sharply separate moral conduct from our natural aspirations and practical purposes, inferring that "All so-called moral interest consists solely in respect for the law" (14 n. 14). In so doing, Kant unjustifiably cleaved the rational *form* of morality (as the presumptive subject matter for philosophical theory) from the practical *functions* that, in Dewey's view, give rise to the demands of justice and authenticate moral theorizing.

Contemporary Kantians could be more cautious about perpetuating their predecessor's hypostatization, even as they helpfully disclose the ways we manipulate others by treating them as instruments to arbitrary purposes instead of respecting them as moral equals. The value of respect for persons, and hence of moral equality, are not "moral facts" that can be empirically demonstrated, but they do emerge nonarbitrarily from moral experience. We are all the better because Kantians proclaim it from the rooftops. Nevertheless, presuming that we can navigate moral life entirely by Kant's fixed stars is at best superfluous and at worst a green light for moral fundamentalism.

Approbation, the Standard, and Virtue

Dewey asserted in the 1930 presentation: "Empirically, there is a third independent variable in morals" centered on praise and blame, approval and disapproval, reward and punishment (1930b, LW 5:285). "Acts and dispositions generally approved form the original virtues; those condemned the original vices" (286). In all of their variability and inconsistency within and across social groups and political boundaries, approving and disapproving attitudes mark the virtuous as a basic factor in moral life.

This factor differs fundamentally from the deliberate pursuit of good ends (which virtue theorists regard as too intellectualistic) and the demand for dutiful compliance (which virtue theorists regard as too legalistic). Deontologists use praise and blame as sanctions for right and wrong, while teleological thinkers acknowledge the instrumental importance of social approval and disapproval (Dewey, undated ms, 10). "But as categories, as principles, the virtuous differs radically from the good and the right. Goods, I repeat, have to do with deliberation upon desires and purposes; the right and obligatory with demands that are socially authorized and backed; virtues with widespread approbation" (1930b, LW 5:286).

Virtue ethicists extend this initial emphasis—on acts and dispositions that are praiseworthy or blameworthy—to a rigorous search for consistency and coherence about which durable character traits *ought* to be approved or censured. Plainly, we cannot erect communal approbation into a universal moral standard, so what makes a virtue the subject of justifiable social validation? Any defensible answer requires a nonarbitrary standard of approbation to critique the "original," socially preestablished virtues so that more appropriate and defensible ones can be discovered and prescribed. Typically, virtue theorists turn, like Anscombe (1958), to some eudaimonistic conception of living well together.

In the 1933 letter to Fries (Figure 5.2), Dewey credited his mature genealogy of ethical theories to a careful rereading of eighteenth- and nineteenth-century British moral philosophers such as Hume, Smith, Bentham, Mill, and Sidgwick. I have shown how his typology complicates the standard categorization of Aristotle (1999) as a virtue ethicist, but a brief explanation is required to make sense of Dewey's unorthodox reading of Mill as more of a virtue theorist than an aggregator of pleasures. Dewey settled on a Jekyll-and-Hyde framing of the utilitarian tradition: it is better to be an inconsistent Millian than a consistent Benthamite. By understanding ethics in terms of scales for measuring private pleasures, the Benthamite strain of utilitarianism was mired in an untenable psychology that subjected Bentham's progressive reformist agenda to a battery of criticisms targeting hedonism. Although Mill, in Dewey's words, "never formally surrendered the hedonistic psychology," he received and renewed the torch of eighteenth-century moral sentiment theory by reframing ethics in terms of personal moral sentiments and the cultivation of character, with public welfare as the standard of approbation.

Mill explained his early distancing from Bentham's calculus, with its "hedons" of pleasure and "dolors" of pain, in his *Autobiography*: "I, for the first time, gave its proper place, among the prime necessities of human well-being, to the internal culture of the individual. I ceased to attach almost exclusive importance to the ordering of outward circumstances. . . . The cultivation of the feelings became one of the cardinal points in my ethical and philosophical creed" (in 1932, LW 7:244). On Dewey's reading, Mill understood that "the moral problem which confronts every person is how regard for general welfare, for happiness of others than himself, is to be made a regulative purpose in his conduct" (1932, LW 7:240–241). The standard by which we should appraise the value of social arrangements, then, lies in whether community members identify their own happiness with acting to advance the happiness of others. This approach decoupled utilitarianism from hedonism. Dewey concluded: "Although Mill never quite acknowledges it in words, a surrender of the hedonistic element in utilitarianism" enabled him to develop, or mostly develop, a welfarist standard that morally appraises institutions and actions to be good "not only because of their direct contribution to well-being but even more because they favor the development of the worthy dispositions from which issue noble enjoyments" (1932, LW 7:245). This standard is implicit in our approbations, for Mill.

Commentaries on Dewey's ethics, including some of my own, have tended to discuss utilitarianism of all stripes under the category of the good. But Dewey argued that this is a half-truth. Smith and other eighteenth-century sources of the utilitarian tradition were at bottom virtue theorists for whom morality is founded on sympathetic sentiments. In what follows, I clarify and further Dewey's analysis by integrating it with my own rereading of Smith and Hume.

Following the lead of Smith and Hume, Dewey discussed empathetic imagination in terms of sympathy, a subcategory of what Mead neutrally described as taking the attitude of another. Dewey defined sympathy as "entering by imagination into the situations of others" (1908b, MW 5:150), closely tracking (without citing) Smith's phrasing: "By the imagination we place ourselves in his situation" (1790, I.I.2). Sympathy names a type of immediate responsiveness and sensitivity without which not only would we be callous and indifferent, but there would not even be "an inducement to deliberate or material with which to deliberate" (1932, LW 7:269). In contrast with Kant's and Singer's (2015) view that a generous sympathy is unnecessary, even subversive, Dewey agreed with moral sentiment theorists that it is essential to moral action, while not on its own sufficient for moral artistry (see Fesmire 2003). Dewey held that disaffective conduct is cold-blooded and morally confining, a view that anticipated recent work in feminist ethics and in neuroscientific research such as Antonio Damasio's (1994, 1999). For Dewey, direct, spontaneous valuing such as sympathy is complemented and expanded in dramatic rehearsal (1932, LW 7:271; 1922b, MW 14:132–138), which focuses deliberation on the present yet expands attention beyond what is immediately experienced so that the lessons of the past and as-yet-unrealized potentialities "come home to us and have power to stir us" (1934a, LW 9:30).

Hume wrote in the *Treatise*, "Sympathy is the chief source of moral distinctions" (1978, 618). In *The Theory of Moral Sentiments*, Smith (1790) followed Hume in tracing the source of morals to the principle of sympathy. Sympathy brings approval, while antipathy brings disapproval. We approve because we sympathize, and whatever elicits this sentiment we call good. We disapprove because we feel antipathy, and whatever calls out this sentiment we deem bad. Dewey explained their view with a nod of approval: "Through sympathy the cold calculation of utilitarianism and the formal law of Kant are transported into vital and moving realities" (1932, LW 7: 271).

In their theories of moral judgment, Hume and Smith did not merely equate being praised with being praiseworthy. Nor is it *just* that we automatically feel antipathy toward, say, Iago's treachery in *Othello*. Rational appraisal plays a vital role. Dewey was especially attentive to the way in which, for Hume and Smith, our moral sentiments can be corrected and regulated by rational considerations. "In individuals, the exercise of sympathy in accordance with reason—i.e., from the standpoint of an impartial spectator, in Smith's conception—is the norm of virtuous action" (1935, LW 11:11).

Often neglected by scholars singling out Smith's (1790) influential treatment of sympathetic imagination, Smith discussed the "impartial spectator" in terms of prescriptions and approvals of the authoritative "judge within the breast" (VI.iii.17–19). He wrote:

When we first come into the world, from the natural desire to please, we accustom ourselves to every person we converse with. ... [Yet] the fairest and most equitable conduct must frequently obstruct the interests or thwart the inclinations of particular persons, who will seldom ... see that this conduct ... is perfectly suitable to our situation. In order to defend ourselves from such partial judgments, we ... conceive ourselves as acting in the presence of ... an impartial spectator who considers our conduct with the same indifference with which we regard that of other people. (Smith 1790, III.ii.36; cf. Frierson 2006, 148–149)

Hence, for Smith in *The Theory of Moral Sentiments*, the job of reason in moral judgment is to inform and secure the correctives of an impartial standard of approbation so that it plays a formative role in critically reflective ends. For Smith, Dewey explains, reason seeks a nonarbitrary standard that does not merely bow to customary esteem or ridicule, "a *standard* upon the basis of which approbation and disapprobation, esteem and disesteem, *should* be awarded" (1932, LW 7:255).

This problem of identifying nonarbitrary standards is uppermost in moral sentiment theory, Dewey argued, "even when the writer seems to be discussing some other question" (1930b, LW 5:286). Again, within sentiment theory what is good or dutiful is derived from what our sentiments approve as virtuous and disapprove as vicious. What we spontaneously sympathize with and favor, according to Hume and Smith, are benevolent actions that serve others. Meanwhile, ill will spontaneously arouses antipathy. They argue that ethical theory extrapolates from this and gives its seal of rational approval to the implicit standard in such natural judgments. On their view, Dewey clarifies, "the Good must be defined in terms of impulses that further general welfare since they are the ones naturally approved" (Dewey, undated ms, 10). According to Smith, this is the natural, conscious, and nonarbitrary criterion that we arrive at when, in his words, we take up the standpoint of a fully informed impartial spectator.

In this way, moral sentiment theorists accounted for aspiration (for the good) and compliance (with duty) in terms of what they took to be *the more fundamental fact* of approval and disapproval (i.e., the virtuous and vicious). Lamentably though predictably, their next step was to hypostatize this into the universal foundation stone of ethics. Mid-nineteenth-century British utilitarianism's inheritance of this legacy is especially evident in Mill's focus on social sympathy. But in Dewey's view, Mill illogically tried to combine "Dr. Jekyll" with "Mr. Hyde": (a) sympathy for the commonwealth as the legitimate natural standard implicit in social approval (or reproach) of dispositions, practices, and institutions with (b) the hedonistic idea that individual pleasure is the summum bonum.

To summarize Dewey's analysis of virtue: for monistic theories rooted in the third factor, a practice or disposition such as nonanger (Nussbaum 2016), generosity, courage, honesty, industriousness, curiosity, perseverance, or compassion is deemed good and dutiful because our moral sentiments approve it as virtuous (and ought legitimately to approve it when considered from an impartial perspective). Meanwhile, a predisposition toward miserliness or retaliatory payback is bad and wrong because it is vicious (and rationally merits disapproval). To the degree that virtue theorists are monists—Michael Gill (2011) argues that Hume was a pluralist of sorts, at least with respect to fundamental conflicts among moral ends—they infer that basic concepts such as goodness, welfare, duty, and right can be systematically organized without remainder under a conception of virtuous character traits. They take these traits to be those we should approve because these virtues contribute to a rationally defensible conception of living and being well. Monistic virtue theorists hold that cultivating stable traits that are as virtuous as possible is what it ultimately *is* to be moral. Or, to update Dewey's analysis, the virtue theorist must at least fictionalize (see Alfano 2013) reliably stable character traits. Situational psychologists and ethical theorists are currently debating whether we are capable of exhibiting these traits in the trans-contextual way that is required by strong monistic virtue theories (e.g., Appiah 2008, ch. 2).

Conclusion

If a hospital uses doctors and patients mostly as a means for keeping beds filled at 80 percent capacity, this is disrespectful in the Kantian sense. It also worsens public health and condones a vicious loss of fellow feeling. Dewey's hypothesis was that none of these moral concepts—a duty to respect persons, consequences for public welfare, cultivation of sympathetic regard—operates as the bottom line that can accommodate all that is of moral worth in the rest. Hence, no single factor of moral life is the overriding source of moral justification, including Dewey's signature emphasis on the good of lifelong growth.

Moral deliberation is a reflective excursion into what is possible. As explored in Chapters 2 and 4, when these excursions begin with a practical predicament instead of a theoretical abstraction, we discover that diverse factors are already in tension with each other. Dewey states this most clearly in the unpublished typescript: "The three concepts in question represent forces that have different roots, not a common and single one. Because these forces pull different ways there is a genuine conflict—and a problematic quality pervades the whole situation" (Dewey, undated ms, 3). Our foremost practical need in moral life is to diversify fine-tuned habits that enable us to comprehensively navigate dynamic tensions without paving over them. Theories and practices that open a nonassimilative communicative field, however uneasy or frictional (Medina 2013a), between conflicting irreducible forces can help to disclose and co-create common ground, inform wiser deliberations, and weave a tapestry from diverse strands of our moral selves. They may help us to achieve Berlin's "uneasy equilibrium" for democratic discourse (1998, 19).

Dewey consequently sought to analyze the main categories through which long-lived ethical theories have concentrated attention on these forces. He did not fancy that we could become, as comedy writer Michael Schur quips, "Perfectly Virtuous and Flourishing and Deontologically Pure Happiness-Generating Super People" (Schur 2022, 165). But he did think that we can put conflicting factors in communication for the sake of more adaptive and mutually traversable choices, policies, and institutions.

The three primitive strands that Dewey analyzed are conceptually distinct and have independent sources, but in actual moral life they intertwine and "cut across one another" (1930b, LW 5:287). For moral deliberation to be at all comprehensive, it must search for a way to creatively reconcile variables to each other, by weaving them into choices that more or less satisfactorily express the tensions that originally set the problem at hand.

Striving for systematic coherence can be a philosophic virtue, and selecting some factor of moral action as central and uppermost often has great instrumental value. But when we hypostatize this factor, then treat it as the necessary and sufficient starting point for moral inquiry as well as the foundational bedrock for justification, we make a move that is both irrational and troubling. Singling out any one value as a trump despite a plurality of relevant concerns tracks the same pattern as the hypostatization of basic moral factors into foundation stones. It induces a similar myopia, as when environmental policymakers presume that economic criteria have supremacy over other key values (aesthetic, spiritual, recreational, ecological, etc.) (Norton 2005; 2015). When linked to essentialism, such hypostatization also fuels injustice. For example, in Intellectual Disability: Ethics, Dehumanization, and a New Moral Community (2013), Heather Keith and Kenneth Keith draw from Dewey's theory of intelligence as a function rather than an unchanging entity to chart an empathetic course beyond the notion that our rational grappling power is humanity's defining essence (Keith and Keith 2020).

The need to avoid moral myopia and to privilege more adaptive virtues of inquiry is why Dewey concluded "Three Independent Factors in Morals" with a call for our moral imaginations to become more perceptive and responsive to situations. Along the same lines, Johnson in *Morality for Humans* (2014) makes a compelling case for Dewey's sense of conscientiousness as a durable virtue of inquiry. Conscientiousness, for Johnson, is characterized by openness, self-awareness, self-criticism, and imagination of possibilities. Dewey's insights on this virtue from the early 1930s, together with recent scholarship inspired by his pluralistic and nonreductive approach, can be criticized and supplemented with contemporary research on Du Boisian "double consciousness" (2015), or better, Jose Medina's "kaleidoscopic consciousness" (2013a, 200), standing democratically in the frictional intersections of communities that are contextualized by race, class, gender, ethnicity, sexuality, religion, nationality, and culture (cf. Heldke 2019).

Dewey took seriously that classic monistic philosophies were forged culturally as idealized tools to interpret and deal with social situations. Our old love of clean edges between houses of moral theory cannot be intellectualized away, nor perhaps should it. But the durable value of these theories can be liberated by research that gets over both the quest for, and the tone of, finality in favor of developing experimental projects with distinctive sets of emphases, angles, and inferences. As Appiah observes, identities are woven like fabrics (2018a, 102), so identification with an ethical tradition need not be defined by unrevisable essential doctrines.

For example, Kant's corpus, on the whole, was more empirically informed and humane than is revealed in standard readings (see Louden 2002). To my knowledge, Kantian pluralism has yet to be substantively defended in the strong sense of pluralism being developed here. Nevertheless, a modified, nonabsolutistic, broadly Kantian pluralism in ethics, bringing rough conformity to duty to the forefront, has been plausibly defended as more than an oxymoron (Hill 2000). The Kantian publicity test, with its rejection of double standards and demand for reasonable consistency, gains its practical power independent of Kant's thin monistic reduction. Meanwhile, pluralistic contractarian methods are actively being developed through engagement with methodological pragmatists (e.g., Moehler 2020). As Neiman (2008) observes, we do not have to flee to an otherworldly metric or fancied preestablished harmony to see that "sometimes morality and self-interest part company" (20).

The monistic Kantian inference that morality is thus *nothing but* autonomous willing in accord with universal law, or that conformity with duty is what morality essentially *is* (unlimited by the purpose at hand and wholly apart from whatever damage we imprudently though dutifully do), flows not from logic but from a hidden premise of theoretical correctness. That premise persists wherever anticonsequentialism is declared the victor in a theoretic prizefight, or wherever consequentialists overlook the practical bearings of dispositions. We enable this premise, or give it a free pass, at the *cost* of creating footholds to secure dignity and respect.

In the discussion that followed his 1930 presentation in Paris, published alongside the lecture, Dewey allowed that "he exaggerated, for purposes of discussion, the differences among the three factors, that indeed moral theories do touch on these three factors more or less, but what he wanted to emphasize was the fact that each particular moral theory takes one of them as central and that is what becomes the important point, while the other factors are only secondary" (1930b, LW 5:503). Dewey doubtless hoped to inspire theoretical projects reconciling (without collapsing) diverse empirical factors of moral action. Such projects could change the terms of debate within and across ethical traditions. A more pragmatic and pluralistic future for ethics would approach historical theories, traditional codes of conduct, and legal history as resources for social inquiry, not as finalities to be endorsed or dismissed wholesale (1932, LW 7:179; cf. Koch 2010). Rejecting zero-sum theorizing would open a door for research reconstructing classic philosophies as proximate and compensatory emphases for meeting problems and remaking experience.

Again, Dewey nowhere *reduced* moral life to a trifecta of independent factors. His point was to emphasize that, having long ago unseated the monarch of *custom*, moral philosophers continue to contest which monarch of *reason* shall rule from the old throne and issue truths about how we ought to diagnose and answer moral questions (cf. 1920, MW 12:172–186). To help delegitimize the monistic mentality that props up moral fundamentalism, what philosophers could do, in contrast, is to surrender the monarchical quest altogether so that we might cooperatively "attend more fully to the concrete elements entering into the situations" in which we must act (1930b, LW 5:288).

Conclusion

Moral fundamentalism is among our greatest obstacles to fostering inquiry and decision-making that can meet contemporary predicaments. To grow beyond it, we need to educate for democracy. Intellectual leaders grappling with this need are enjoined in an uphill struggle against a toxic combination of hyper-individualism, anti-naturalistic distrust of experimental intelligence, anti-intellectual rancor, hyper-politicization, demagoguery, and reckless pandering, all steeped in centuries of one-way moral and political habits. The culturally lagging assumption of a unitary experiential and conceptual locus of moral action unintentionally—but not blamelessly—validates, or at least gives free passage to, the one-way premise of moral fundamentalism. By cultivating a context for inquiry, communication, and debate across discordant values, we can deal more responsibly with wickedly complex problems without relapsing into fundamentalism. The best we can individually do to nurture this context is to make democracy a way of daily life. I have primarily focused on implications of this way of life for the way we theorize and educate about ethics, politics, and policy. I have argued that a pluralistic approach to making decisions helps to move us beyond a homogenizing mentality that conceals the plurality of values, meanings, concerns, and purposes.

Dewey averred in "What I Believe" (1930c) that, as the single-right-way assumption gives way, democratic participation can become "a means to a fuller and more significant future experience" (LW 5:272). Democratic participation is essential to effective decision-making about intractable problems within complex systems, and this amplifies the need to reflect on appropriate educational values. Yet even as we witness an exponential increase in the need for social learning and communication across differences, techno-industrial countries such as the United States favor a workforce-training model of prepackaged content delivery. I have argued and illustrated that we can educate better.

In these and other non-ideal conditions, Dewey's pragmatic pluralism exemplifies his democratizing alternative to the kind of theorizing that prolongs the quest for a universal moral plumb line. If there are several generative roots of moral action, then one implication is that any theory that rests on *the* objectively correct moral conception will be inadequate to the heterogeneity of moral experience. Dewey argued that principles, metrics, standards, and unitary ideals are helps, but they do not perfectly square people's judgments to the circumstances they face. The quest for a universal foundation of ethics—whether procedurally constructed or "foundational" in the now old-fashioned Cartesian sense of an immovable bedrock for securing knowledge claims about values—cannot deliver on its promise. That promise was to single out, in Thompson's phrasing, "the most fully justified course of action, even in situations where beneficial outcomes are offset by costs, or where rights and duties conflict" (Thompson 2016, 70).

Dewey's meta-ethical hypothesis provides a blueprint for interpreting his deeply pluralistic, fallibilistic, and pragmatic approach to ethics. Proponents of the primary ethical systems miss, at least in their explicit theorizing, the *irreducible* tensions that constantly underlie moral action, as when binding social demands conflict with aspirations for goods. If Dewey's hypothesis is borne out, then it is not possible to theoretically settle moral problems in advance of their occurrence. This is because each variable in moral action "has a different origin and mode of operation," so "they can be at cross purposes and exercise divergent forces in the formation of judgment." Dewey concludes, "The essence of the moral situation is an internal and intrinsic conflict; the necessity for judgment and for choice comes from the fact that one has to manage forces with no common denominator" (1930b, LW 5:280).

As Dewey reframed his ethics in the mid-1920s to early 1930s, while working with James Tufts to complete a major revision of their bestselling 1908 *Ethics* textbook, his central questions were as follows: when we are morally conflicted, is this a superficial hesitancy that would dissolve if only we could conduct our reasoning rightly, marshal enough data, consult our inborn moral sense, or pray harder? Or is the experience of moral conflict often rooted in something more intractable, a conflict *intrinsic* to the situation itself? Should we strive for a one-size-fits-all approach that organizes moral cognition under a single concept? Do the traditional covering concepts of good, right, and virtue arise from the same experiential source, or do they express distinctive origins? If leading moral categories express independent forces with different empirical roots, do these roots ultimately jibe well with each other (i.e., are they fully compatible)? Or do they more typically get at cross purposes, often pulling us in different yet seemingly legitimate directions, leaving us in a muddle about what to choose? If the primitive springs of moral action are disparate forces, then how can we practically manage and evaluate the normative claims they make on us?

As discussed, Dewey's stab at answering these questions pivoted on the non-prescriptive thesis that there are "independent variables in moral action" (1930b, LW 5:280), these diverse experiential factors are in tension with each other, and they are reducible neither to an ideal starting point for moral inquiry nor to a changeless universal foundation.

How might a pragmatic and pluralistic approach to ethical theorizing add something to informal and incidental moral reflection? I have argued that even as we continue to identify ourselves with diverse ethical traditions, scrutinizing principles to guide wiser choices, we should nevertheless shift, or at least expand, priorities. Dewey did not explicitly spell out implications of his pluralistic ethics and politics for redirecting theorizing, but recommendations can be extrapolated by marrying his writings with a sampling of contemporary pragmatic pluralists who are steeped in his general outlook. Weaving together five thematic strands of this book, some priorities that may help contemporary ethical and sociopolitical theorizing meet tangled situations and recover from cultural lag include these:

1. Lay bare, classify, and analyze experiential entanglements between diverse and often discordant elements of moral life within a wider "framework of moral conceptions" that puts these elements in communication (1932, LW 7:309; cf. 1925/ 1929, LW 1:323). When analyzing the conditions in which aspirations, obligations, and approbations appear, along with other elements on which contemporary conceptions pivot, theorists may strive for an ideal of communicative friction (Medina 2013a), instead of defaulting to the mainstream attempt to unify and standardize what may be independent variables (e.g., Pappas 2008; Frega and Levine 2020).

2. Place these diverse elements in an experimental context in which norms—such as responsibility, self-respect, and authenticity, in Dworkin's defense of being a "hedgehog" for justice (2011)—gain practical traction amid the frictions and tangles of non-ideal conditions that are diagnosed through democratic colloquy (e.g., Norton 2005; Medina 2013a; Thompson 2015; Norton 2015; Minteer et al. 2018; Pappas 2019; McKenna 2020).

3. Empirically investigate and assess the hypothesis that we can experimentally work out together what is ameliorative and deleterious, while anticipating that progress relative to one dimension of a problem may be retrograde in another (e.g., Norton 2005, 2015; Kitcher 2014; Johnson 2014; Thompson 2015; Light 2017; Weston 2017).

4. Interpret, evaluate, and criticize moral, political, educational, and legal conceptions that lag behind twenty-first-century conditions, while debating and recommending values and cross-cultural resources that would help us better meet those troubled conditions (e.g., Fesmire 2003, 2012, 2023; Glaude 2008; Rogers 2008; Keith and Keith 2013; Alexander 2013; Weston 2017; Behuniak 2019a; Heldke 2019; Hester 2019; Misak 2019; Saito 2019a; Stuhr 2019; Sullivan 2019; Tan 2019; Waks 2019; Ames 2020; McKenna 2020; Johnson and Schulkin 2023; Stroud 2023; Axtell 2023; Henning 2023).

5. Expand prospects for social learning and for convergence on policy and action (e.g., Lee 1993; Minteer 2011; Norton 2015; Thompson 2015; Light 2017; McKenna 2018, 2020).

There is a familiar accusation that pragmatic pluralism is too compromising, conciliatory, and spineless to guide action, with the implication that theorists must fall back on defending antecedent principles as their overriding focus. This might at least alleviate some of the anxiety of choice and uncertainty, and it might provide a counterweight to fatalistic resignation in the face of daunting complexity. These are pragmatic concerns. *If* upheld by the verdict of experience, these concerns could warrant a strategic default orientation around monistic principles, at least for specified purposes. I have argued that the verdict of contemporary moral and political experience rules against thin, reductive forms of ethical monism. Nevertheless, far from turning its back on ethical traditions, a pragmatic and pluralistic approach can contribute to an open and more adaptive future for traditions that are growing beyond their lagging hypostatizing tendencies. Relative merits aside, moral life can potentially be aided by any rigorously defensible ethical approach that substantiates, sustains, and deepens the courage of conviction, so long as it does not relapse to moral fundamentalism.

Static utopias are fictions, but we would be better off experimenting with how far we can go toward creating a shared context for frank, if uneasy, communication and inquiry that counterbalances both moral fundamentalism and the reactionary relativistic extreme that is fundamentalism's inverted image. Opposing "their" fundamentalism with ours perpetuates the root problem. We need a more genuinely radical approach that is not Pollyannaish. We need democratic engagement and resistance without puritanical zealotry, courage in mediating troubles without certainty, bold action without fatalistic resignation or paralyzing guilt, and moral clarity without oversimplification.

Moral fundamentalist habits, along with the single-right-way assumption that unduly reinforces them, are obstacles to cooperative problem-solving. If philosophers and other public intellectuals are to speak to shared problems in a way that furthers colloquy across identities, social positions, and political boundaries, critical engagement with Dewey's democratic and pragmatic pluralism would be salutary.

Notes

Chapter 1

1. I concur with Scott Aikin and Robert Talisse (2017) that these terms are distinct. For clarification of terms, in light of Talisse and Aikin's critiques of pragmatic pluralism, see the final section of this chapter, "Some Technical Distinctions."
2. A public philosophy version of the moral fundamentalist pledge appeared in Fesmire (2019b).

Chapter 2

1. This illustration draws in revised form from my *Dewey* (Fesmire 2015), ch. 4.
2. Nevertheless, with regard to public deliberation and citizenship education, we can help people be better pluralists without convincing them to be naturalists.
3. Hardin was not a pragmatist in his approach to ethics, as evidenced by his armchair deduction of an empirically unwarranted and morally ill-considered "lifeboat ethics."
4. In the main, contemporary climate ethicists focus on assessing policy options and making prescriptions. This is unsurprising, as much of the agenda for climate ethics has been set by meetings responsive to the UN Framework Convention on Climate Change. However, an exclusive focus on policy assessments would take the "practical" too narrowly. Despite the import of debating policies, this chapter does not, for instance, weigh in on controversies regarding Stern vs. Nordhaus on ethically appropriate ways to discount future costs and benefits of climate action, or the relative prioritization of adaptation and abatement, or how best to assess expected future value in lieu of an excessively moralistic precautionary principle.
5. Andrew Light, January 2016 videoconference with my Middlebury College class The Pragmatists and Environmental Pragmatism, and March 2017 videoconference with my Green Mountain College class Climate Justice. What follows is also drawn in part from personal communication.
6. Norton's and Light's articulations of pragmatic pluralism differ from those developed by philosophers who work more overtly in the American tradition that included Dewey. McDonald's edited volume *Pragmatism and Environmentalism* (2012) offers a good representation of the latter. Cf. McKenna and Light's edited volume *Animal Pragmatism* (2004) and Henning 2023.
7. Leffers clarifies that for Addams, "it would not make sense to talk about having an ethical position independent of relationship to self, other, or community. At this within-relationship-matrix of her position we find a dynamic principle of respect for self and others" (Leffers 1993, 73). In Dewey's words in *Human Nature and Conduct*, "what sort of self is in the making" must be identified with the question "what kind of world is in the making" (1922b, MW 14:150). For Addams and Dewey, it was not enough merely to passively affirm, with Kant, that all humans should be equally respected for their innate dignity. We must actively establish conditions in which capacities are fulfilled instead of being arrested by denied opportunities and socially imposed limits.

8. As Shane Ralston argues, Dewey had no context-free theory of "deliberative democracy" as an end point for governance (2010, 31).
9. Relevant biases include the "availability heuristic" (the well-studied bias of falling back on mental shortcuts that readily come to mind [e.g., Kahneman et al. 2021]) and the illusion of objectivity (the error of assuming one's own perspective objectively captures reality, while one's adversaries are biased and irrational [Ross 2018]).
10. For reasons such as these, Norton (2015) advocates renewed emphasis on the education of facilitators to more effectively separate the diagnostic wheat from the chaff in public inquiries.

Chapter 3

1. Green Mountain College, founded in 1834, closed June 2019 because of financial troubles.
2. I moderated the student forum in which the slaughter decision was vetted, and I am drawing from my own detailed notes about events surrounding Bill and Lou. In the interest of intellectual disclosure: my own family's default diet is vegetarian, and the idea of giving Bill (the uninjured ox) a living retirement had both an intuitive and rational "pull" for us.
3. Wilson's address, "The Meaning of a Liberal Education," was originally published in *High School Teachers Association of New York*, volume 3, 1908–1909.

Chapter 4

1. A version of this analogy first appeared in Fesmire 2015, 118–119.
2. It would be fruitful, though beyond the scope of this book, to compare and contrast Dewey's form of pluralism with other contemporary styles from the 1920s–1930s, such as W. D. Ross's (1930) intuitionist pluralism in *The Right and the Good*.
3. Haidt (2016) hypothesizes five moral foundations that operate as underlying universal intuitions: care/harm, fairness/cheating, loyalty/betrayal, authority/subversion, sanctity/degradation. Dewey cautioned against universal instinct theories, and Haidt's theory could be strengthened by restatement in terms other than innate and universal modular foundations. For development of this line of criticism, see Johnson (2014).
4. Appiah (2017) makes a melioristic plea for "partial compliance" theories.
5. Peirce's insight heralded a pragmatic functionalist conception of logic that in the next century would be pitted against Bertrand Russell's structuralist approach (see Burke 2019).
6. Dewey's later involvement in the outlawry-of-war movement of the 1920s, known as the Kellogg-Briand Pact, helped ensure that war would be unprofitable (see Hathaway and Shapiro 2017).
7. I am indebted to the late Richard Bernstein for this insight (personal communication).

Chapter 5

1. Originally published as "Trois facteurs indépendants en matière de morale," trans. Charles Cestre, in *Bulletin de la SFP* 30 (October–December 1930): 118–127.
2. This typescript was subsequently misplaced, then retrieved in 2016 in a careful search by staff at Morris Library, Special Collections, Southern Illinois University at Carbondale.
3. The 1932 *Ethics* chapters are titled "Ends, the Good, and Wisdom" (ch. 11), "Right, Duty, and Loyalty" (ch. 12), and "Approbation, the Standard, and Virtue" (ch. 13).
4. Dewey's typos silently corrected throughout.
5. https://www.thelifeyoucansave.org/; accessed October 17, 2023.

6. Personal communication from Peter Singer, October 26, 2020. Used with permission.
7. This may serve as a pragmatic argument favoring monism in some situations. But remember the ends-means continuum (Chapter 2): always ask what else we have done by making hegemonic moral decisions.
8. Of course, there are many hybrid ethical theories that defy tidy categorization. Rule utilitarianism, for example, operates in the main via compliance with universal rules, albeit rules theoretically justified on welfarist grounds: if you aspire to maximize the good, then conform to the rule.
9. Dewey and Watsuji mutually regarded ethics as "dealing with matters arising between person and person," person and society, and person and nature (Watsuji 1996, 10). Dewey also shared Watsuji's antizealotry and rejection of absolute moral bedrocks. However, deep tonal and conceptual differences are revealed as they flesh out this "betweenness." Watsuji retained elements of feudal communitarianism by subordinating individuals to the emperor as the unifying symbol of communal life. The state, as reported by his most famous student Yuasa Yasuo, thus became for Watsuji "the ultimate standard of value" (in Watsuji 1996, 315). In sharp contrast, Dewey prioritized communicative interaction between individuals that secures "flexible readjustment" of social institutions (1916, MW 9, ch. 7).

Works Cited

Abramowitz, Alan I., and Steven W. Webster. 2018. "Negative Partisanship: Why Americans Dislike Parties But Behave Like Rabid Partisans." *Political Psychology* 39 (Suppl 1): 119–135.

Ackerman-Leist, Philip. 2017. "Cultivating Values on the College Farm." *Pacific Standard*, June 14. https://psmag.com/environment/cultivating-values-on-the-college-farm-or-revisionist-history-has-no-future-64488; accessed April 14, 2024. .

Addams, Jane. 2002a. *Democracy and Social Ethics*. Urbana: University of Illinois Press.

Addams, Jane. 2002b. *Peace and Bread in Time of War*. Urbana: University of Illinois Press.

Aikin, Scott F., and Robert B. Talisse. 2017. *Pragmatism, Pluralism, and the Nature of Philosophy*. New York: Routledge.

Alexander, Natalia Rogach, and Philip Kitcher. 2021. "Educating Democratic Character." *Moral Philosophy and Politics* 8, no. 1:51–80.

Alexander, Thomas M. 1987. *John Dewey's Theory of Art, Experience, and Nature*. Albany: SUNY Press.

Alexander, Thomas M. 2013. *The Human Eros*. New York: Fordham University Press.

Alexander, Thomas M. 2019. "Dewey's Naturalistic Metaphysics." In Steven Fesmire (ed.), *The Oxford Handbook of Dewey*, 25–52. New York: Oxford University Press.

Alfano, Mark. 2013. *Character as Moral Fiction*. New York: Cambridge University Press.

Ames, Roger T. 2007. "'The Way Is Made in the Walking': Responsibility as Relational Virtuosity." In Barbara Darling-Smith (ed.), *Responsibility*, 41–61. Lanham, MD: Lexington Books.

Ames, Roger T. 2019. "Dewey and Confucian Philosophy." In Steven Fesmire (ed.), *The Oxford Handbook of Dewey*, 553–574. New York: Oxford University Press.

Ames, Roger T. 2020. *Confucian Role Ethics*. Albany: SUNY Press.

Anders, George. 2017. *You Can Do Anything: The Surprising Power of a "Useless" Liberal Arts Education*. Boston: Little, Brown.

Anderson, Elizabeth. 2009. "Toward a Non-ideal, Relational Methodology for Political Philosophy: Comments on Schwartzman's *Challenging Liberalism*." *Hypatia* 24, no. 4:130–145.

Anderson, Elizabeth. 2013. *The Imperative of Integration*. Princeton, NJ: Princeton University Press.

Anscombe, G. E. M. 1958. "Modern Moral Philosophy." *Philosophy* 33, no. 124:10.

Appiah, Kwame Anthony. 2008. *Experiments in Ethics*. Cambridge, MA: Harvard University Press.

Appiah, Kwame Anthony. 2010. "Relativism and Cross-Cultural Understanding." In Michael Krausz (ed.), *Relativism: A Contemporary Anthology*, 488–500. New York: Columbia University Press.

Appiah, Kwame Anthony. 2017. *As If: Idealization and Ideals*. Cambridge, MA: Harvard University Press.

Appiah, Kwame Anthony. 2018a. *The Lies That Bind: Rethinking Identity*. New York: W. W. Norton.

Appiah, Kwame Anthony. 2018b. "Go Ahead, Speak for Yourself." *New York Times*, August 10. https://www.nytimes.com/2018/08/10/opinion/sunday/speak-for-yourself.html; accessed April 14, 2024.

Aristotle. 1999. *Nicomachean Ethics*. Trans. Terence Irwin. Indianapolis, IN: Hackett.

Atkins, Richard. 2024. "Pragmatism and Ignorance." In Robert Lane (ed.), *Pragmatism Revisited*. Cambridge: Cambridge University Press, Forthcoming.

Atkinson, Robert D., et al. 2011. *Climate Pragmatism: Innovation, Resilience, and No Regrets*. Breakthrough Institute and Information Technology and Innovation Foundation. https://itif.org/files/2011-climate-pragmatism.pdf?_ga = 2.19041 912.1321589747.1578504042-1849958892.1578504042; accessed April 14, 2024.

Auxier, Randall E., and John R. Shook. 2019. "Idealism and Religion in Dewey's Philosophy." In Steven Fesmire (ed.), *The Oxford Handbook of Dewey*, 651–674. New York: Oxford University Press.

Axtell, Guy. 2023. "Partiality Traps and Our Need for Risk-Aware Ethics and Epistemology." In Eric J. Silverman (ed.), *Virtuous and Vicious Partiality*, 133–163. New York: Routledge.

Axtell, Guy, and Philip Olson. 2009. "Three Independent Factors in Epistemology." *Contemporary Pragmatism* 6, no. 2:89–109.

Baca, Alex, Patrick McAnaney, and Jenny Schuetz. 2019. "'Gentle' Density Can Save Our Neighborhoods." Brookings, December 4. https://www.brookings.edu/research/gentle-density-can-save-our-neighborhoods/; accessed April 14, 2024.

Baker, Robert. 1998. "A Theory of International Bioethics: Multiculturalism, Postmodernism, and the Bankruptcy of Fundamentalism." *Kennedy Institute of Ethics Journal* 8, no. 3:201–231.

Baldwin, James. 1985. *The Price of the Ticket: Collected Nonfiction, 1948–1985*. New York: St. Martin's Press.

Becker, Carl. 1991. "Language and Logic in Modern Japan." *Communication & Cognition* 24, no. 2:167–177.

Behuniak, Jim. 2019a. *John Dewey and Daoist Thought*. Vol. 1 of *Experiments in Intra-cultural Philosophy*. Albany: SUNY Press.

Behuniak, Jim. 2019b. *John Dewey and Confucian Thought*. Vol. 2 of *Experiments in Intra-cultural Philosophy*. Albany: SUNY Press.

Bergman, Ronen. 2018a. *Rise and Kill First*. New York: Penguin.

Bergman, Ronen. 2018b. "Journalist Details Israel's 'Secret History' of Targeted Assassinations." National Public Radio, January 31. https://www.npr.org/2018/

01/31/582099085/journalist-details-israels-secret-history-of-targeted-assassi
nations; accessed April 14, 2024.

Berlin, Isaiah. 1953. *The Hedgehog and the Fox.* New York: Simon and Schuster.

Berlin, Isaiah. 1998. *The Crooked Timber of Humanity.* Princeton, NJ: Princeton University Press.

Bernstein, Richard J. 1966. *John Dewey.* New York: Washington Square Press.

Boisvert, Raymond D., and Lisa Heldke. 2016. *Philosophers at Table: On Food and Being Human.* London: Reaktion Books.

Broome, John. 2012. *Climate Matters.* New York: W.W. Norton.

Bump, Philip. 2015. "Scott Walker Moved to Drop 'Search for Truth' from the University of Wisconsin Mission. His Office Claims It Was an Error." *Washington Post,* February 4. https://www.washingtonpost.com/news/the-fix/wp/2015/02/04/scott-walker-wants-to-drop-search-for-truth-from-the-university-of-wisconsin-mission-heres-why/; accessed April 14, 2024.

Burke, F. Thomas. 2019. "Dewey's Chicago-Functionalist Conception of Logic." In Steven Fesmire (ed.), *The Oxford Handbook of Dewey,* 507–536. New York: Oxford University Press.

Callicott, J. Baird. 1999. *Beyond the Land Ethic.* Albany: SUNY Press.

Campbell, James. 2019. "John Dewey's Debt to William James." In Steven Fesmire (ed.), *The Oxford Handbook of Dewey,* 615–628. New York: Oxford University Press.

Caney, Simon. 2005. "Cosmopolitan Justice, Responsibility, and Global Climate Change." *Leiden Journal of International Law* 18:747–775.

Carson, Rachel. 1962. *Silent Spring.* Boston: Houghton Mifflin.

Carter, Jacoby Adeshei. 2024. "Pragmatism and the Black Intellectual Tradition." In Robert Lane (ed.), *Pragmatism Revisited.* Cambridge: Cambridge University Press. Forthcoming.

Carter, Jimmy. 2005. *Our Endangered Values: America's Moral Crisis.* New York: Simon & Schuster.

Carver, Rebecca L., and Richard P. Enfield. 2006. "John Dewey's Philosophy of Education Is Alive and Well." *Education and Culture* 22, no. 1:55–67.

Coeckelbergh, Mark. 2021. "Cascading Morality after Dewey: A Proposal for a Pluralist Meta-ethics with a Subsidiarity Hierarchy." *Contemporary Pragmatism* 18, no. 1:18–35.

Colapietro, Vincent. 2019. "Pragmatist Portraits of Experimental Intelligence by Peirce, James, Dewey, and Others." In Steven Fesmire (ed.), *The Oxford Handbook of Dewey,* 75–98. New York: Oxford University Press.

Collins, Billy. 2005. *The Trouble with Poetry and Other Poems.* New York: Random House.

Collins, Patricia Hill. 1998. "It's All in the Family: Intersections of Gender, Race, and Nation." *Hypatia* 13, no. 3:62–82.

Collins, Patricia Hill. 2019. *Intersectionality as Critical Social Theory.* Durham, NC: Duke University Press.

Crenshaw, Kimberlé. 2017. *On Intersectionality: Essential Writings.* New York: New Press.

Cronon, William. 1996. "The Trouble with Wilderness, or, Getting Back to the Wrong Nature." In *Uncommon Ground: Rethinking the Human Place in Nature*, 69–90. New York: W.W. Norton.

Damasio, Antonio R. 1994. *Descartes' Error: Emotion, Reason, and the Human Brain*. New York: Avon Books.

Damasio, Antonio R. 1999. *The Feeling of What Happens: Body and Emotion in the Making of Consciousness*. Fort Worth: Harcourt Brace.

Dancy, Jonathan. 2017. "Moral Particularism." In Edward N. Zalta and Uri Nodelman (eds.), *Stanford Encyclopedia of Philosophy*, Winter 2017 ed. https://plato.stanford.edu/entries/moral-particularism/; accessed April 14, 2024.

Darwall, Stephen L. 1983. *Impartial Reason*. Ithaca, NY: Cornell University Press.

Darwall, Stephen L. 2006. *The Second-Person Standpoint: Morality, Respect, and Accountability*. Cambridge, MA: Harvard University Press.

Dea, Shannon. 2024. "The Way of Inquiry: Pragmatism, Academic Freedom and the Duty of Care." In Robert Lane (ed.), *Pragmatism Revisited*. Cambridge: Cambridge University Press. Forthcoming.

Deen, Phillip. 2019. "Dewey, Habermas, and the Unfinished Project of Modernity in *Unmodern Philosophy and Modern Philosophy*." In Steven Fesmire (ed.), *The Oxford Handbook of Dewey*, 537–550. New York: Oxford University Press.

Descartes, René. 1968. *Discourse on Method*. Trans. F. E. Sutcliffe. New York: Penguin Books.

Dewey, John. Undated ms (mss102_53_3). "Conflict and Independent Variables in Morals." Morris Library, Special Collections, Southern Illinois University, Carbondale.

Dewey, John. 1908a. "Does Reality Possess a Practical Character?" MW 4:125–142.

Dewey, John, and James H. Tufts. 1908b. *Ethics*. MW 5.

Dewey, John. 1915a. *German Philosophy and Politics*. MW 8:135–204.

Dewey, John. 1915b. "Education versus Trade-Training: Reply to David Snedden." MW 8:411–413.

Dewey, John. 1916. *Democracy and Education*. MW 9.

Dewey, John. 1917. "The Need for a Recovery of Philosophy." MW 10:3–48.

Dewey, John. 1919. "Philosophy and Democracy." MW 11:41–53.

Dewey, John. 1920. *Reconstruction in Philosophy*. MW 12.

Dewey, John. 1922a. "Individuality, Equality and Superiority." MW 13:295–300.

Dewey, John. 1922b. *Human Nature and Conduct*. MW 14.

Dewey, John. 1925. "Practical Democracy." LW 2:213–221.

Dewey, John. 1925/1929. *Experience and Nature*. LW 1.

Dewey, John. 1926. "William James in Nineteen Twenty-Six." LW 2:158–162.

Dewey, John. 1927. *The Public and Its Problems*. LW 2:235–372.

Dewey, John. 1929. *The Quest for Certainty*. LW 4.

Dewey, John. 1930a. *Individualism, Old and New*. LW 5:44–123.

Dewey, John. 1930b. "Three Independent Factors in Morals." LW 5:279–288, 496–503.

Dewey, John. 1930c. "What I Believe." LW 5:267–278.

Dewey, John. 1930d. "In Response." LW 5:418–423.

Dewey, John, and James H. Tufts. 1932. *Ethics*. 2nd ed. LW 7.

Dewey, John. 1933a. "The Social-Economic Situation and Education." LW 8:43–76.

Dewey, John. 1933b. *How We Think.* LW 8:105–352.

Dewey, John. 1934a. *A Common Faith.* LW 9:1–58.

Dewey, John. 1934b. *Art as Experience.* LW 10.

Dewey, John. 1935. *Liberalism and Social Action.* LW 11:1–67.

Dewey, John. 1938a. *Logic: The Theory of Inquiry.* LW 12.

Dewey, John. 1938b. "Democracy and Education in the World of Today." LW 13:294–303.

Dewey, John. 1939a. *Freedom and Culture.* LW 13:63–188.

Dewey, John. 1939b. *Theory of Valuation.* LW 13:189–254.

Dewey, John. 1945a. "The Revolt against Science." LW 15:188–191.

Dewey, John. 1945b. "Democratic versus Coercive International Organization: The Realism of Jane Addams." LW 15:192–198.

Dewey, John. 1945c. "Dualism and the Split Atom: Science and Morals in the Atomic Age." LW 15:199–203.

Dewey, John. 1949. "Has Philosophy a Future?" LW 16:360–363.

Dewey, John. 1950. "On Philosophical Synthesis." LW 17:35–36.

Dewey, John. 2012. *Unmodern Philosophy and Modern Philosophy.* Ed. Philip Deen. Carbondale: Southern Illinois University Press.

Donagan, Alan. 1977. *The Theory of Morality.* Chicago: University of Chicago Press.

Dougherty, Mike, and Katya Schwenk. 2020. "What Humanities Cuts Could Mean for UVM." In *VTDigger,* December 13. https://vtdigger.org/2020/12/13/the-deeper-dig-what-humanities-cuts-could-mean-for-uvm/; accessed April 14, 2024.

Du Bois, W. E. B. 2015. *The Souls of Black Folk.* New Haven, CT: Yale University Press.

Dworkin, Ronald. 2000. *Sovereign Virtue: The Theory and Practice of Equality.* Cambridge, MA: Harvard University Press.

Dworkin, Ronald. 2011. *Justice for Hedgehogs.* Cambridge, MA: Harvard University Press.

Edel, Abraham. 2001. *Ethical Theory and Social Change: The Evolution of John Dewey's Ethics, 1908–1932.* Piscataway, NJ: Transaction.

Edenhofer, Ottmar, and Martin Kowarsch. 2015. "Cartography of Pathways: A New Model for Environmental Policy Assessments." *Environmental Science & Policy* 51:56–64.

Elgin, Catherine Z. 1997. *Between the Absolute and the Arbitrary.* Ithaca, NY: Cornell University Press.

Eliot, George. 1876/2002. *Daniel Deronda.* New York: Random House.

Emerson, Ralph Waldo. 1851. "The Fugitive Slave Law." https://quod.lib.umich.edu/e/emerson/4957107.0011.001/1:11?rgn = div1;view = fulltext; accessed April 14, 2024.

Emerson, Ralph Waldo. 1965. "Self-Reliance." In *Selected Writings of Ralph Waldo Emerson,* 257–280. New York: Penguin.

English, Andrea R., and Christina Doddington. 2019. "Dewey, Aesthetic Experience, and Education for Humanity." In Steven Fesmire (ed.), *The Oxford Handbook of Dewey,* 411–441. New York: Oxford University Press.

Farmer, Paul. 2004. "An Anthropology of Structural Violence." *Current Anthropology* 45, no. 3: 305–325.

Fesmire, Steven. 2003. *John Dewey and Moral Imagination: Pragmatism in Ethics.* Bloomington: Indiana University Press.

Fesmire, Steven. 2010. "Ecological Imagination." *Environmental Ethics* 32, no. 2:183–203.

Fesmire, Steven. 2012. "Ecological Imagination in Moral Education, East and West." *Contemporary Pragmatism* 9, no. 1:205–222.

Fesmire, Steven. 2015. *Dewey.* New York: Routledge.

Fesmire, Steven. 2016. "Democracy and the Industrial Imagination in American Education." *Education and Culture* 32, no. 1:53–61.

Fesmire, Steven. 2019a. "Beyond Moral Fundamentalism: John Dewey's Pragmatic Pluralism in Ethics and Politics." In Steven Fesmire (ed.), *The Oxford Handbook of Dewey,* 209–234. New York: Oxford University Press.

Fesmire, Steven. 2019b. "Ethics for Moral Fundamentalists." *Inside Higher Ed,* April 9. https://www.insidehighered.com/advice/2019/04/09/teaching-const ructive-discourse-current-environment-opinion; accessed April 14, 2024.

Fesmire, Steven. 2020. "Pragmatist Ethics and Climate Change." In Dale E. Miller and Ben Eggleston (eds.), *Moral Theory and Climate Change: Ethical Perspectives on a Warming Planet,* 215–237. New York: Routledge.

Fesmire, Steven, ed. 2023. *The Oxford Handbook of Dewey.* New York: Oxford University Press.

Fisher, Max. 2021. "Europe's Vaccine Ethics Call: Do No Harm and Let More Die?" *New York Times,* March 19. https://www.nytimes.com/2021/03/19/world/eur ope/europe-vaccine-astrazeneca-interpreter.html; accessed April 14, 2024.

Foot, Philippa. 1978. *Virtues and Vices and Other Essays in Moral Philosophy.* Berkeley: University of California Press.

Francione, Gary L. 2021. *Why Veganism Matters: The Moral Value of Animals.* New York: Columbia University Press.

Franks, Benjamin, Stuart Hanscomb, and Sean F. Johnston. 2017. *Environmental Ethics and Behavioural Change.* London: Routledge.

Freeman, Samuel. 2007. *Justice and the Social Contract: Essays in Rawlsian Political Philosophy.* Oxford: Oxford University Press.

Frega, Roberto. 2010. "What Pragmatism Means by Public Reason." *Etica & Politica / Ethics & Politics* 12, no. 1:28–51.

Frega, Roberto, and Steven Levine (eds.). 2021. *John Dewey's Ethical Theory: The 1932 "Ethics".* New York: Routledge.

Frierson, Patrick. 2006. "Applying Adam Smith: A Step towards Smithian Environmental Virtue Ethics." In Leonidas Montes and Eric Schliesser (eds.), *New Voices on Adam Smith,* 140-168. New York: Routledge.

Funke, Joachim. 2010. "Complex Problem Solving: A Case for Complex Cognition?" *Cognitive Processing* 11, no. 2:133–142.

Galston, William A. 2021. "Covid 19 Vaccinations: Why Are Some States and Localities So Much More Successful?" Brookings, January 21. https://www. brookings.edu/articles/covid-19-vaccinations-why-are-some-states-and-localit ies-so-much-more-successful/; accessed April 14, 2024.

Gardiner, Stephen M. 2011. *A Perfect Moral Storm: The Ethical Tragedy of Climate Change.* Oxford: Oxford University Press.

Gardiner, Stephen M. 2017. "Climate Ethics in a Dark and Dangerous Time." *Ethics* 127:430–465.

Garrison, Jim. 2012. "Individuality, Equality, and Creative Democracy—the Task before Us." *American Journal of Education* 118, no. 3:369–379.

Garrison, Jim. 2019. "Derridean Poststructuralism, Deweyan Pragmatism, and Education." In Steven Fesmire (ed.), *The Oxford Handbook of Dewey*, 351–372. New York: Oxford University Press.

Gaus, Gerald. 2016. *The Tyranny of the Ideal: Justice in a Diverse Society.* Princeton, NJ: Princeton University Press.

Gewirth, Alan. 1978. *Reason and Morality.* Chicago: University of Chicago Press.

Gill, Michael B. 2011. "Humean Moral Pluralism." *History of Philosophy Quarterly* 28, no. 1:45–64.

Gilpin, Donald. 2020. "Eddie Glaude Jr. Responds with Hope in 'an Incredibly Dark and Challenging Time.'" *Princeton Magazine.* http://www.princetonm agazine.com/eddie-glaude-jr-responds-with-hope-in-an-incredibly-dark-and-challenging-time/; accessed April 14, 2024.

Glaude, Eddie S., Jr. 2007. *In a Shade of Blue: Pragmatism and the Politics of Black America.* Chicago: University of Chicago Press.

Glaude, Eddie S, Jr. 2016. *Democracy in Black: How Race Still Enslaves the American Soul.* New York: Crown.

Glaude, Eddie S., Jr. 2020. *Begin Again: Baldwin's America and Its Urgent Lessons for Our Own.* New York: Crown.

Godfrey-Smith, Peter. 2019. "Dewey and Anti-representationalism." In Steven Fesmire (ed.), *The Oxford Handbook of Dewey*, 151–171. New York: Oxford University Press.

Gray, John. 1996. *Isaiah Berlin.* Princeton, NJ: Princeton University Press.

Greene, Joshua. 2013. *Moral Tribes.* New York: Penguin.

Haas, Peter M. 1990. *Saving the Mediterranean: The Politics of International Environmental Cooperation.* New York: Columbia University Press.

Haidt, Jonathan. 2012. *The Righteous Mind: Why Good People Are Divided by Politics and Religion.* New York: Pantheon.

Haidt, Jonathan. 2016. http://moralfoundations.org/; accessed April 14, 2024.

Haidt, Jonathan, and Fredrik Bjorklund. 2008. "Social Intuitionists Answer Six Questions about Moral Psychology." In Walter Sinnott-Armstrong (ed.), *Moral Psychology, Vol. 2, The Cognitive Science of Morality: Intuition and Diversity*, 181–218. Cambridge, MA: MIT Press.

Hammer, Espen. 2019. "Dewey, Adorno, and the Purpose of Art." In Steven Fesmire (ed.), *The Oxford Handbook of Dewey*, 471–488. New York: Oxford University Press.

Hanstedt, Paul. 2018. *Creating Wicked Students: Designing Courses for a Complex World.* New York: Routledge.

Hardin, Garrett. 1985. "Human Ecology: The Subversive, Conservative Science." *American Zoologist* 25, no. 2:469–476.

Haskins, Casey. 2019. "Dewey's *Art as Experience* in the Landscape of Twenty-First-Century Aesthetics." In Steven Fesmire (ed.), *The Oxford Handbook of Dewey*, 445–470. New York: Oxford University Press.

Hathaway, Oona A., and Scott J. Shapiro. 2017. *The Internationalists: How a Radical Plan to Outlaw War Remade the World*. New York: Simon & Schuster.

Hauser, Marc. 2006. *Moral Minds: How Nature Designed Our Universal Sense of Right and Wrong*. New York: HarperCollins.

HBR Editors. 2014. "How Companies Can Profit from a 'Growth Mindset.'" *Harvard Business Review*, November. https://hbr.org/2014/11/how-compan ies-can-profit-from-a-growth-mindset, accessed April 14, 2024.

Heisenberg, Werner. 1958. *Physics and Philosophy: The Revolution in Modern Science*. New York: HarperCollins.

Heldke, Lisa. 2019. "Dewey and Pragmatist Feminist Philosophy." In Steven Fesmire (ed.), *The Oxford Handbook of Dewey*, 271–290. New York: Oxford University Press.

Hester, D. Micah. 2019. "Dewey and Bioethics." In Steven Fesmire (ed.), *The Oxford Handbook of Dewey*, 733–745. New York: Oxford University Press.

Hickman, Larry A. 1990. *John Dewey's Pragmatic Technology*. Bloomington: Indiana University Press.

Hickman, Larry A. 2019. "Dewey, Pragmatism, Technology." In Steven Fesmire (ed.), *The Oxford Handbook of Dewey*, 491–506. New York: Oxford University Press.

Hildebrand, David L. 2019. "Dewey, Rorty, and Brandom: The Challenges of Linguistic Neopragmatism." In Steven Fesmire (ed.), *The Oxford Handbook of Dewey*, 99–130. New York: Oxford University Press.

Hill, Thomas E. 2000. *Respect, Pluralism, and Justice: Kantian Perspectives*. Oxford: Oxford University Press.

Horwitz, Tony. 2013. "150 Years of Misunderstanding the Civil War." *The Atlantic*, June 19. https://www.theatlantic.com/national/archive/2013/06/150-years-of-misunderstanding-the-civil-war/277022/; accessed April 14, 2024.

Hourdequin, Marion. 2014. *Environmental Ethics*. London: Bloomsbury.

Huebner, Daniel R. 2019. "Mead, Dewey, and Their Influence in the Social Sciences." In Steven Fesmire (ed.), *The Oxford Handbook of Dewey*, 629–650. New York: Oxford University Press.

Hume, David. 1978. *A Treatise of Human Nature*. Ed. L. A. Selby-Bigge. Oxford: Clarendon Press.

Hutchinson J. B., and L. F. Barrett. 2019. "The Power of Predictions: An Emerging Paradigm for Psychological Research." *Current Directions in Psychological Sciences* 28, no. 3:280–291.

Isaacson, Walter. 2017. *Leonardo Da Vinci*. New York: Simon & Schuster.

James, William. 1977. *A Pluralistic Universe*. In *The Works of William James*, vol. 4, ed. Frederick H. Burkhardt, Fredson Bowers, and Ignas K. Skrupskelis. Cambridge, MA: Harvard University Press.

James, William. 1979. *The Will to Believe and Other Essays in Popular Philosophy*. In *The Works of William James*, vol. 6, ed. Frederick H. Burkhardt, Fredson Bowers, and Ignas K. Skrupskelis. Cambridge, MA: Harvard University Press.

Jamieson, Dale. 2014. *Reason in a Dark Time: Why the Struggle against Climate Change Failed—and What It Means for Our Future*. New York: Oxford University Press.

Jessop, Bob. 2018. "On Academic Capitalism." *Critical Policy Studies* 12, no. 1:104–109.

Johnson, Mark. 1993. *Moral Imagination: Implications of Cognitive Science for Ethics.* Chicago: University of Chicago Press.

Johnson, Mark. 2014. *Morality for Humans: Ethical Understanding from the Perspective of Cognitive Science.* Chicago: University of Chicago Press.

Johnson, Mark. 2019. "Dewey's Radical Conception of Moral Cognition." In Steven Fesmire (ed.), *The Oxford Handbook of Dewey,* 175–194. New York: Oxford University Press.

Johnson, Mark, and Jay Schulkin. 2023. *Mind in Nature: John Dewey, Cognitive Science, and a Naturalistic Philosophy for Living.* Cambridge, MA: MIT Press.

Johnson, Steven. 2021. "How Humanity Gave Itself an Extra Life." *New York Times,* April 21. https://www.nytimes.com/2021/04/27/magazine/global-life-span.html; accessed April 14, 2024.

Jotzo, Frank. 2016. "The Climate Change Authority's Gamble on Political Pragmatism." *The Conversation.* https://theconversation.com/the-climate-change-authoritys-gamble-on-political-pragmatism-64745, accessed April 14, 2024.

Kahneman, Daniel, Olivier Sibony, and Cass R. Sunstein. 2021. *Noise: A Flaw in Human Judgment.* New York: Little, Brown Spark.

Kant, Immanuel. 1993. *Grounding for the Metaphysics of Morals.* Trans. James W. Ellington. Indianapolis, IN: Hackett.

Kant, Immanuel. 2002. *Critique of Practical Reason.* Trans. Werner Pluhar. Indianapolis, IN: Hackett.

Karsten, Jack, and Darrell M. West. 2016. "Inside the Social Media Echo Chamber." Brookings, December 9. https://www.brookings.edu/blog/techtank/2016/12/09/inside-the-social-media-echo-chamber/; accessed April 14, 2024.

Keith, Heather E., and Kenneth D. Keith. 2013. *Intellectual Disability: Ethics, Dehumanization, and a New Moral Community.* Chichester: Wiley-Blackwell.

Keith, Heather E., and Kenneth D. Keith. 2020. *Lives and Legacies of People with Intellectual Disability.* Silver Spring, MD: American Association on Intellectual and Developmental Disabilities.

Kitcher, Philip. 2012. *Preludes to Pragmatism: Toward a Reconstruction of Philosophy.* Oxford: Oxford University Press.

Kitcher, Philip. 2014. *The Ethical Project.* Cambridge, MA: Harvard University Press.

Kitcher, Philip. 2019. "Dewey's Conception of Philosophy." In Steven Fesmire (ed.), *The Oxford Handbook of Dewey,* 3–21. New York: Oxford University Press.

Kitcher, Philip. 2021. *Moral Progress.* New York: Oxford University Press.

Kitcher, Philip, and Evelyn Fox Keller. 2017. *The Seasons Alter.* New York: Liveright.

Koch, Donald, ed. 2010. *The Class Lectures of John Dewey.* Vol. 2, Ethical Theory (1926). Class Lecture Notes by Sidney Hook. Charlottesville, VA: InteLex Corp., 2230–2284.

Kolbert, Elizabeth. 2021. *Under a White Sky: The Nature of the Future.* New York: Crown.

Korsgaard, Christine M. 1996. *The Sources of Normativity.* Cambridge: Cambridge University Press.

Korsgaard, Christine M. 2007. "Autonomy and the Second Person Within: A Commentary on Stephen Darwall's *The Second-Person Standpoint.*" *Ethics* 118 (October): 8–23.

Korsgaard, Christine M. 2014. University of Groningen Interview on Ethics and Morality. https://www.youtube.com/watch?v = jzBLPDt-Bl0; accessed April 14, 2024.

Krugman, Paul. 2013. "Rubio and the Zombies." *New York Times,* February 14. https://www.nytimes.com/2013/02/15/opinion/krugman-rubio-and-the-zombies.html, accessed April 14, 2024.

Labaree, David. 2010. "How Dewey Lost: The Victory of David Snedden and Social Efficiency in the Reform of American Education." In D. Tröhler, T. Schlag, and F. Osterwalder (eds.), *Pragmatism and Modernities,* 163–188. Rotterdam: Sense Publishers.

Lasch, Christopher. 1991. *The Culture of Narcissism.* Rev. ed. New York: W.W. Norton.

Latour, Bruno. 1993. *We Have Never Been Modern.* Trans. Catherine Porter. Cambridge, MA: Harvard University Press.

Lazari-Radek, Katarzyna de, and Peter Singer. 2014. *The Point of View of the Universe: Sidgwick and Contemporary Ethics.* Oxford: Oxford University Press.

Lee, Kai. 1993. *Compass and Gyroscope: Integrating Science and Politics for the Environment.* Washington, D.C.: Island Press.

Leffers, M. Regina. 1993. "Pragmatists Jane Addams and John Dewey Inform the Ethic of Care." *Hypatia* 8, no. 2:64–77.

Lekan, Todd. 2022. *William James and the Moral Life: Responsible Self-Fashioning.* New York: Routledge.

Leland, Christine H., and Wendy C. Kasten. 2002. "Literacy Education for the 21st Century: It's Time to Close the Factory." *Reading & Writing Quarterly* 18:5–15.

Leonhardt, David. 2021. "Underselling the Vaccine." *New York Times,* January 18. https://www.nytimes.com/2021/01/18/briefing/donald-trump-pardon-phil-spector-coronavirus-deaths.html; accessed April 14, 2024.

Leopold, Aldo. 1966. "Thinking Like a Mountain." In *A Sand County Almanac,* 137–141. New York: Random House.

Lewis-Kraus, Gideon. 2022. "The Reluctant Prophet of Effective Altruism." *New Yorker,* August 15. https://www.newyorker.com/magazine/2022/08/15/the-reluctant-prophet-of-effective-altruism; accessed April 14, 2024.

Light, Andrew. 2013. "An Equity Hurdle in International Climate Negotiations." *Philosophy and Public Policy Quarterly* 31, no. 1:28–35.

Light, Andrew. 2017. "Climate Diplomacy." In Stephen M. Gardiner and Allen Thompson (eds.), *The Oxford Handbook of Environmental Ethics,* 487–500. London: Oxford University Press.

Light, Andrew, and Eric Katz, eds. 1996. *Environmental Pragmatism.* London: Routledge.

Lippmann, Walter. 1922. *Public Opinion.* New York: Harcourt, Brace.

Lippmann, Walter. 1925. *The Phantom Public.* New York: Macmillan.

Lippmann, Walter. 1955. *The Public Philosophy.* Boston: Little, Brown.

Louden, Robert B. 2002. *Kant's Impure Ethics: From Rational Beings to Human Beings.* Oxford: Oxford University Press.

Lovejoy, Arthur O. 1908. "The Thirteen Pragmatisms." *Journal of Philosophy, Psychology and Scientific Methods* 5, no. 1:5–12.

Margolis, Joseph. 2019. "Pragmatist Innovations, Actual and Proposed: Dewey, Peirce, and the Pittsburgh School." In Steven Fesmire (ed.), *The Oxford Handbook of Dewey*, 131–150. New York: Oxford University Press.

Marshall, Megan. 2014. *Margaret Fuller.* New York: Mariner Books.

McAfee, Noëlle. 2019. "Dewey and Public Philosophy." In Steven Fesmire (ed.), *The Oxford Handbook of Dewey*, 697–712. New York: Oxford University Press.

McDermott, Morna. 2013. "The Corporate Model of Schooling: How High-Stakes Testing Dehumanizes Education." *Counterpoints* 451:78–95.

McDonald, Hugh, ed. 2012. *Pragmatism and Environmentalism.* New York: Rodopi.

McIntyre, Alison. 2023. "Doctrine of Double Effect." In Edward N. Zalta and Uri Nodelman (eds.), *The Stanford Encyclopedia of Philosophy*, Fall 2023 ed. https://plato.stanford.edu/archives/fall2023/entries/double-effect/; accessed April 10, 2024.

McKenna, Erin. 2018. *Livestock: Food, Fiber, and Friends.* Athens: University of Georgia Press.

McKenna, Erin. 2020. *Living with Animals: Rights, Responsibilities, and Respect.* Mitchellville, MD: Rowman & Littlefield.

McKenna, Erin, and Andrew Light, eds. 2004. *Animal Pragmatism.* Bloomington: Indiana University Press.

McKenna, Erin, and Scott Pratt. 2019. "Philosophy and the Mirror of Culture: On the Future and Function of Dewey Scholarship." In Steven Fesmire (ed.), *The Oxford Handbook of Dewey*, 675–693. New York: Oxford University Press.

Mead, George Herbert. 1930. "The Philosophies of Royce, James, and Dewey in Their American Setting." In *John Dewey*, 104–105. Cambridge, MA: Harvard University Press.

Medina, José. 2013a. *The Epistemology of Resistance: Gender and Racial Oppression, Epistemic Injustice, and Resistant Imaginations.* New York: Oxford University Press.

Medina, José. 2013b. "Color Blindness, Meta-ignorance, and the Racial Imagination." *Critical Philosophy of Race* 1, no. 1:38–67.

Mill, John Stuart. 1986. *On Liberty.* Amherst, NY: Prometheus Books.

Mills, Charles W. 2005. "'Ideal Theory' as Ideology." *Hypatia* 20, no. 3:165–184.

Mills, Charles W. 2017. *Black Rights / White Wrongs: The Critique of Racial Liberalism.* New York: Oxford University Press.

Minteer, Ben A. 2011. *Refounding Environmental Ethics.* Philadelphia: Temple University Press.

Minteer, Ben A., and James P. Collins. 2005. "Ecological Ethics: Building a New Tool Kit for Ecologists and Biodiversity Managers." *Conservation Biology* 19:1803–1812.

Minteer, Ben A., Jane Maienschein, and James P. Collins, eds. 2018. *The Ark and Beyond: The Evolution of Zoo and Aquarium Conservation.* Chicago: University of Chicago Press.

Misak, Cheryl. 2019. "Dewey on the Authority and Legitimacy of Law." In Steven Fesmire (ed.), *The Oxford Handbook of Dewey*, 195–208. New York: Oxford University Press.

Moehler, Michael. 2020. "Contractarian and Climate Change." In Dale E. Miller and Ben Eggleston (eds.), *Moral Theory and Climate Change: Ethical Perspectives on a Warming Planet*, 139–156. New York: Routledge.

Moellendorf, Darrel. 2014. *The Moral Challenge of Dangerous Climate Change*. Cambridge: Cambridge University Press.

Moore, G. E. 1929. *Principia Ethica*. Cambridge: Cambridge University Press.

Morton, Adam. 2012. *Bounded Thinking: Intellectual Virtues for Limited Agents*. New York: Oxford University Press.

Mostajir, Parysa Clare. 2022. " 'Conjoint Communicated Experience': Art as an Instrument of Democracy." *The Pluralist* 17, no. 1:25–33.

Murphy, Deirdre, with Steven Fesmire, Philip Ackerman-Leist, and David Ondria. 2013. "We Are What We Think about What We Eat: Raising the Veil that Separates Us from Our Food." *Transformations* 23, no. 2:117–129, 183–186.

Myers, William T. 2019. "Dewey, Whitehead, and Process Metaphysics." In Steven Fesmire (ed.), *The Oxford Handbook of Dewey*, 53–74. New York: Oxford University Press.

Ne'eman, Ari. 2020. "I Will Not Apologize for My Needs." *New York Times*, March 23. https://www.nytimes.com/2020/03/23/opinion/coronavirus-ventilators-tri age-disability.html; accessed April 14, 2024.

Neiman, Susan. 2008. *Moral Clarity: A Guide for Grown-Up Idealists*. Princeton, NJ: Princeton University Press.

Newey, Glen. 1997. "Against Thin-Property Reductivism: Toleration as Supererogatory." *Journal of Value Inquiry* 31, no. 2:231–249.

Niebuhr, Reinhold. 1932. *Moral Man and Immoral Society: A Study in Ethics and Politics*. New York: Scribners.

Niemeyer, Simon. 2013. "Democracy and Climate Change: What Can Deliberative Democracy Contribute?" *Australian Journal of Politics and History* 59, no. 3:430–449.

Noddings, Nel. 2013. *Caring: A Relational Approach to Ethics and Moral Education*. 2nd ed. Berkeley: University of California Press.

Noddings, Nel. 2019. "Dewey and the Quest for Certainty in Education." In Steven Fesmire (ed.), *The Oxford Handbook of Dewey*, 335–350. New York: Oxford University Press.

Nordgren, Loran, and David Schonthal. 2021. *The Human Element: Overcoming the Resistance That Awaits New Ideas*. Hoboken, NJ: John Wiley & Sons.

Norton, Bryan G. 1991. *Toward Unity among Environmentalists*. Oxford: Oxford University Press.

Norton, Bryan G. 2002. "A Pragmatist Epistemology for Adaptive Management." In F. W. Jozef Keulartz et al. (eds.), *Pragmatist Ethics for a Technological Culture*, 171–190. Dordrecht: Springer.

Norton, Bryan G. 2005. *Sustainability: A Philosophy of Adaptive Ecosystem Management*. Chicago: University of Chicago Press.

Norton, Bryan G. 2015. *Sustainable Values, Sustainable Change: A Guide to Environmental Decision Making*. Chicago: University of Chicago Press.

Novack, George. 1937. "Trotsky's Views on Dialectal Materialism." https://www.marxists.org/archive/novack/works/history/ch14.htm; accessed April 14, 2024.

Nozick, Robert. 1974. *Anarchy, State, and Utopia*. New York: Basic Books.

Nussbaum, Martha C. 1990. *Love's Knowledge: Essays on Philosophy and Literature*. New York: Oxford University Press.

Nussbaum, Martha C. 1999. *Sex and Social Justice*. New York: Oxford University Press.

Nussbaum, Martha C. 2016. *Anger and Forgiveness: Resentment, Generosity, Justice*. New York: Oxford University Press.

Pappas, Gregory Fernando. 2008. *John Dewey's Ethics: Democracy as Experience*. Bloomington: Indiana University Press.

Pappas, Gregory Fernando. 2011. "Introduction." In Gregory Pappas (ed.), *Pragmatism in the Americas*, 1–16. New York: Fordham University Press.

Pappas, Gregory Fernando. 2019. "The Starting Point of Dewey's Ethics and Sociopolitical Philosophy." In Steven Fesmire (ed.), *The Oxford Handbook of Dewey*, 235–253. New York: Oxford University Press.

Parfit, Derek. 1984. *Reasons and Persons*. Oxford: Clarendon Press.

Paris, William Michael. 2016. "Assata Shakur, Mamphela Ramphele, and the Developing of Resistant Imaginations." *Critical Philosophy of Race* 4, no. 2:205–220.

Parker, Mike. 2009. *Map Addict*. London: Collins.

Peels, Rik. 2022. "On Defining 'Fundamentalism.'" *Religious Studies* 59, no. 4:1–19. https://www.cambridge.org/core/journals/religious-studies/article/on-defining-fundamentalism/5AAF2188C7E7414347D9C2CDA2B4335C; accessed April 14, 2024.

Peirce, Charles S. 1992. *The Essential Peirce*. Vol. 1. Bloomington: Indiana University Press.

Plato. 1960. *Gorgias*. Trans. Walter Hamilton. New York: Penguin.

Plato. 1992. *Republic*. Trans. G. M. A. Grube and C. D. C. Reeve. Indianapolis, IN: Hackett.

Pollan, Michael. 2006. *The Omnivore's Dilemma*. New York: Penguin.

Putnam, Hilary. 2004. *Ethics without Ontology*. Cambridge, MA: Harvard University Press.

Putnam, Hilary. 2011. "Reflections on Pragmatism." In John R. Shook and Paul Kurtz (eds.), *Dewey's Enduring Impact: Essays on America's Philosopher*, 43–56. Amherst, NY: Prometheus Books.

Putnam, Robert. 2000. *Bowling Alone: The Collapse and Revival of American Community*. New York: Simon & Schuster.

Ralston, Shane. 2010. "Dewey Theory of Moral (and Political) Deliberation Unfiltered." *Education and Culture* 26, no. 1:23–43.

Rawls, John. 1971. *A Theory of Justice*. Cambridge, MA: Harvard University Press.

Rawls, John. 1993. *Political Liberalism*. New York: Columbia University Press.

Regan, Tom, 1985. *The Case for Animal Rights*. Berkeley: University of California Press.

Rittell, Horst, and Melvin Webber. 1973. "Dilemmas in a General Theory of Planning." *Policy Sciences* 4:155–169.

Rogers, Melvin. 2008. *The Undiscovered Dewey*. New York: Columbia University Press.

Rorty, Richard. 1999. *Achieving Our Country: Leftist Thought in Twentieth-Century America*, Cambridge, MA: Harvard University Press.

Rosenbaum, Stuart. 2015. *Recovering Integrity: Moral Thought in American Pragmatism.* Lanham, MD: Lexington Books.

Ross, Lee. 2018. "From the Fundamental Attribution Error to the Truly Fundamental Attribution Error and Beyond: My Research Journey." *Perspectives on Psychological Science* 13, no. 6:750–769.

Ross, W. D. 1930. *The Right and the Good.* Oxford: Oxford University Press.

Rothwell, Jonathan, and Sonal Desai. 2020. "How Misinformation Is Distorting Covid Policies and Behaviors." Brookings, December 22. https://www.brooki ngs.edu/research/how-misinformation-is-distorting-covid-policies-and-behaviors/; accessed April 14, 2024.

Rubinstein, Dana. 2021. "After Unused Vaccines Are Thrown in Trash, Cuomo Loosens Rule." *New York Times,* January 10. https://www.nytimes.com/2021/01/10/nyregion/new-york-vaccine-guidelines.html; accessed April 14, 2024.

Saito, Naoko. 2019a. *American Philosophy in Translation.* Mitchellville, MD: Rowman & Littlefield.

Saito, Naoko. 2019b. "Two Way Internationalization: Education, Translation, and Transformation in Dewey and Cavell." In Steven Fesmire (ed.), *The Oxford Handbook of Dewey,* 575–594. New York: Oxford University Press.

Salerno, Steve. 2005. *Sham: How the Self-Help Movement Made America Helpless.* New York: Crown Forum.

Sandel, Michael. 1998. *Democracy's Discontent: America in Search of a Public Philosophy.* Cambridge, MA: Harvard University Press.

Santayana, George. 1955. *Scepticism and Animal Faith.* New York: Dover.

Sarkar, Sahotra, and Ben A. Minteer, eds. 2018. *A Sustainable Philosophy: The Work of Bryan Norton.* New York: Springer.

Schaubroeck, Katrien. 2010. Interview with Christine Korsgaard. *Leuven Philosophy Newsletter* 17:51–56. www.people.fas.harvard.edu/~korsgaar/Scha ubroeck.Korsgaard.pdf; accessed April 14, 2024.

Schur, Michael. 2022. *How to Be Perfect: The Correct Answer to Every Moral Question.* New York: Simon & Schuster.

Scriven, Michael. 2000. "Evaluation Ideologies." In D. L. Stufflebeam, G. F. Madaus, T. Kellaghan (eds.) *Evaluation Models.* Evaluation in Education and Human Services, vol. 49, 249–278. Dordrecht: Springer.

Seal, Andrew. 2018. "How the University Became Neoliberal." *Chronicle of Higher Education,* June 8. https://www.chronicle.com/article/how-the-university-bec ame-neoliberal/; accessed April 14, 2024.

Sen, Amartya. 2009. *The Idea of Justice.* Cambridge, MA: Harvard University Press.

Shapiro, Judith. 2001. *Mao's War against Nature: Politics and the Environment in Revolutionary China.* Cambridge: Cambridge University Press.

Sherif, Muzafer, et al. 1988. *The Robbers Cave Experiment: Intergroup Conflict and Cooperation.* Middletown, CT: Wesleyan University Press.

Silverman, Eric J., ed. 2023. *Virtuous and Vicious Partiality.* New York: Routledge.

Singer, Peter. 2004. *One World: The Ethics of Globalization.* New Haven, CT: Yale University Press.

Singer, Peter. 2015. *The Most Good You Can Do: How Effective Altruism Is Changing Ideas about Living Ethically.* New Haven, CT: Yale University Press.

Smith, Adam. 1790. *The Theory of Moral Sentiments*, 6th edition. London: A. Strahan.

Smith, Courtland L., Jennifer Gilden, Brent S. Steel, and Karina Mrakovcich. 1998. "Sailing the Shoals of Adaptive Management: The Case of Salmon in the Pacific Northwest." *Environmental Management* 22:671–681.

Stamant, James. 2012. "Hawthorne's and Emerson's Differing Perspectives on Political Violence." *South Central Review* 29, nos. 1–2:86–105.

Stocker, Michael. 1975. "The Schizophrenia of Modern Ethical Theories." *Journal of Philosophy* 73, no. 14:453–466.

Striano, Maura. 2019. "Dewey, the Ethics of Democracy, and the Challenge of Social Inclusion in Education." In Steven Fesmire (ed.), *The Oxford Handbook of Dewey*, 373–392. New York: Oxford University Press.

Stroud, Scott R. 2023. *The Evolution of Pragmatism in India: Ambedkar, Dewey, and the Rhetoric of Reconstruction*. Chicago: University of Chicago Press.

Stross, Randall. 2017. *A Practical Education: Why Liberal Arts Majors Make Great Employees*. Stanford, CA: Redwood Press.

Stuhr, John J. 2019. "Dewey's Pragmatic Politics: Power, Limits, and Realism about Democracy as a Way of Life." In Steven Fesmire (ed.), *The Oxford Handbook of Dewey*, 291–312. New York: Oxford University Press.

Sullivan, Shannon. 2019. "Dewey and Du Bois on Race and Colonialism." In Steven Fesmire (ed.), *The Oxford Handbook of Dewey*, 257–270. New York: Oxford University Press.

Tabuchi, Hiroko. 2022. "He's an Outspoken Defender of Meat. Industry Funds His Research, Files Show." *New York Times*, October 31. https://www.nytimes.com/2022/10/31/climate/frank-mitloehner-uc-davis.html; accessed April 14, 2024.

Talisse, Robert B., and Scott F. Aikin. 2005. "Why Pragmatists Cannot Be Pluralists." *Transactions of the Charles S. Peirce Society* 41, no. 1:101–118.

Talisse, Robert B. 2019. *Overdoing Democracy*. New York: Oxford University Press.

Tan, Sor-hoon. 2019. "Experimental Democracy for China: Dewey's Method." In Steven Fesmire (ed.), *The Oxford Handbook of Dewey*, 595–611. New York: Oxford University Press.

Taylor, Charles. 1982. "The Diversity of Goods." In Amartya Sen and Bernard Williams (eds.), *Utilitarianism and Beyond*. Cambridge: Cambridge University Press, 129–135.

Thompson, Paul B. 2010. *The Agrarian Vision: Sustainability and Environmental Ethics*. Lexington: University Press of Kentucky.

Thompson, Paul B. 2015. *From Field to Fork: Food Ethics for Everyone*. Oxford: Oxford University Press.

Thompson, Paul B. 2016. "The Emergence of Food Ethics." *Food Ethics* 1, no. 1:61–74.

Thompson, Paul B., and Zachary Piso. 2019. "Dewey and Environmental Philosophy." In Steven Fesmire (ed.), *The Oxford Handbook of Dewey*, 713–732. New York: Oxford University Press.

Thompson, Paul B., and Kyle Whyte. 2012. "What Happens to Environmental Philosophy in a Wicked World?" *Journal of Agricultural and Environmental Ethics* 25, no. 4:485–498.

Throop, William. 2017. "Learning Our Way toward Resilience." In Daniel Lerch (ed.), *The Community Resilience Reader*, 247–260. Washington, DC: Island Press.

Tillich, Paul. 1957. *The Dynamics of Faith*. New York: Harper & Row.

Trianosky, Gregory. 1990. "What is Virtue Ethics All About?" *American Philosophical Quarterly* 27, no. 4:335–344.

Valentini, Laura. 2012. "Ideal vs. Non-ideal Theory: A Conceptual Map." *Philosophy Compass* 7, no. 9:654–664.

Van Vugt, M. 2009. "Averting the Tragedy of the Commons: Using Social Psychological Science to Protect the Environment." *Current Directions in Psychological Science* 18, no. 3:169–173.

Waks, Leonard J. 2019. "Dewey and Higher Education." In Steven Fesmire (ed.), *The Oxford Handbook of Dewey*, 393–410. New York: Oxford University Press.

Walls, Laura Dassow. 2017. *Henry David Thoreau: A Life*. Chicago: University of Chicago Press.

Wang, Jessica Ching-Sze. 2007. *John Dewey in China*. Albany: SUNY Press.

Watsuji, Tetsuro. 1996. *Watsuji Tetsurō's Rinrigaku: Ethics in Japan*. Trans. Yamamoto Seisaku and Robert E. Carter. Albany: SUNY Press.

Watterson, Bill. 1988. *Calvin and Hobbes*. London: Sphere Books.

West, Cornel. 1989. *The American Evasion of Philosophy*. Madison: University of Wisconsin Press.

Westbrook, Robert. 2005. *Democratic Hope: Pragmatism and the Politics of Truth*. Ithaca, NY: Cornell University Press.

Weston, Anthony. 1991. "On Callicott's Case against Moral Pluralism." *Environmental Ethics* 13, no. 3: 283–286.

Weston, Anthony. 2017. *A 21st Century Ethical Toolbox*. 4th ed. New York: Oxford University Press.

Whipps, Judy D. 2019. "Dewey, Addams, and Design Thinking: Pragmatist Feminist Innovation for Democratic Change." In Steven Fesmire (ed.), *The Oxford Handbook of Dewey*, 313–332. New York: Oxford University Press.

Whitehead, Alfred North. 1920. *The Concept of Nature*. Cambridge: Cambridge University Press.

Williams, Bernard. 1985. *Ethics and the Limits of Philosophy*. Cambridge, MA: Harvard University Press.

Williams, Bernard. 1995. "The Point of View of the Universe: Sidgwick and the Ambitions of Ethics." In *Making Sense of Humanity: And Other Philosophical Papers, 1982–1993*, 153–171. Cambridge: Cambridge University Press.

Williams, Daniel. 2021. "Motivated Ignorance: A Challenge for Science Communication and Democracy." Hastings Center, January 19. https://www.thehastingscenter.org/motivated-ignorance-a-challenge-for-science-communication-and-democracy/; accessed April 14, 2024.

Wilson, Woodrow. 1909. "The Meaning of a Liberal Education." In *Wikisource*. https://en.wikisource.org/wiki/The_Meaning_of_a_Liberal_Education; accessed April 14, 2024.

Yuan, Li. 2022. "The Army of Millions Who Enforce China's Zero-Covid Policy, at All Costs," *New York Times*, January 12. https://www.nytimes.com/2022/01/12/business/china-zero-covid-policy-xian.html; accessed April 14, 2024.

Index

Figures are indicated by an italic *f* following the page/paragraph number

educating for democracy and, 87,
100, 110–15
environmental pragmatism and, 56–
61, 76–84
failings of, 79
imagination and, 27
moral fundamentalism and, 4–5, 19–
20, 186–91
moral meaning of democracy and,
112
participatory social learning and,
76–84
as personal way of life, 80
populism and, 81–82
pragmatic pluralism and, 34–35, 187
threats to, 4–5
deontology
Dewey's relation to, 24, 151–
52, 168–69
do not harm principle and, 162
ends justify the means and, 61–62
ideal theory and, 134
independent factors in moral action
and, 145, 148–49, 166, 168–
69, 174–75
pragmatism and, 44–45, 61–62
Derrida, Jacques, 123
Descartes, René, 105–6, 119–20, 194
Dewey, John
on academic specialization, 107–8
on aesthetic dimensions of education,
113–14
alienation from competent inquiry
and, 87–88
anticipation of contemporary research
by, 133
APA presidency of, 133
on approbation, 175
atomic bombings and, 6
Columbia University teaching
experiences of, 158
on commercial interests, 96–97
on conceptual home range for moral
action and, 151–52
consequentialism and, 42, 61–
62, 154–56
cultural lag and, 6–7

democratic decision-making and, 24–
25, 27–28, 56–61, 76–84, 111–12
democratic faith and, 13–14, 27–28, 84
democratic radicalism of, 56–61
deontology and, 24, 151–52, 168–69
development of prior theory by, 52
on disagreement, 20
on dogmatizing, 29–30
educating for democracy and, 88–89,
95–97, 99–101, 104, 107–9, 110–11,
113–14, 117–18
ends justify the means principle and,
61–62
ends-means continuum and, 56–57, 58
environmental pragmatism and,
43, 47–48
on essence of moral situation, 187–88
ethical and sociopolitical theory
and, 125–26, 129–34, 157–58,
159, 173–74
existential roots of moral categories
and, 37–38
on experimental method, 124
farm experiences of, 99
on fine arts, 114
flu pandemic of 1918-1920 and, 17
French Philosophical Society address
and, 148
on fundamental principle of
democracy, 61
generosity and, 7
on good and right, 168
on happiness found in intellectual
curiosity, 80
Hull House experiences of, 80
ideal of sovereign and omnicompetent
citizen and, 77–78
ills of democracy and, 27–28
on imagination, 102
on impatience, 26–27
on importance of cultural context, 20
on independent factors in moral
action, 181–82, 184–85
inevitability of unintended
consequences and, 52
on instrumentalist aspect of his
philosophy, 115

ethical and sociopolitical theory (*cont.*)
  Dewey's approach to, 125–26, 129–34, 157–58, 159, 173–74
  distinctiveness of moral problems and, 125–26
  dual-process theory and, 133–34
  ethical project and, 126–27
  experimental method and, 124–29
  Fugitive Slave Law and, 134–36
  heuristic proceduralism and, 194
  historical ethical systems and, 143–44
  imagination and, 133–34
  making intelligent choices and, 132–34
  mature writings of Dewey on, 157–58, 159, 173–74
  monism and, 137–42
  moral fundamentalism and, 120–21, 141–42, 143–44
  moral psychology of Dewey and, 129–34
  moral uncertainty and, 143–44
  non-ideal theory and, 121–24
  overview of, 119–21, 142–44
  perspective-free ethics rejected and, 128–29
  pluralism and, 121–24
  pragmatism as non-ideal theory and, 124–29
  supreme moral principles and, 121, 136–37, 139–40
  unaffected world and, 126
  value and, 135–42
Ethics (Dewey), 149–51, 159–60, 168–69, 173–74, 188
Experience and Nature (Dewey), 49, 82–83, 124, 157, 165
experimental method, 47–48, 57, 59, 124–29

faculty role in educating for democracy, 90, 92–93, 97, 107–8
fallibilism, 12–13, 35, 121
Fesmire, Steven, 73
fine arts education, 112–14, 117–18
Fleming, Alexander, 54
Flowers, Elizabeth, 149, 158
foundationalism, 168–69, 187–88

Franks, Benjamin, 72–73
Freedom and Culture (Dewey), 26–27
Frega, Roberto, 69
Fries, Horace S., 154–56, 176
Fuerst, Ilyse Morgenstein, 101–2
Fugitive Slave Law, 134–35
Funke, Joachim, 92

Gardiner, Stephen, 18
Garrison, Jim, 123
Gaus, Gerald, 122
Gephardt, Richard, 80
Gewirth, Alan, 168–69
Gill, Michael, 180–81
Glaude, Eddie, Jr., 21, 25–26
the good, 148–49, 151–52, 153–56, 164–67, 168–69, 175, 177
Great Leap Forward (1958-62), 58
Greek teleologists, 148–49, 166
Green Mountain College, 88, 99–100, 116
Grounding for the Metaphysics of Morals (Kant), 50

Haidt, Jonathan, 4–5, 121, 194n.3
Hardin, Garrett, 62–63
"Hedgehog and the Fox, The" (Berlin), 35–36, 64–65
Heldke, Lisa, 29, 44–45
Hester, D. Micah, 146–47
"How Companies Can Profit from a 'Growth Mindset'" (Dweck), 115
Hull House, 80
Human Nature and Conduct (Dewey), 75–76, 130, 159, 193n.7
Hume, David
  Dewey influenced by, 124, 176–78
  imagination and, 177–78
  as pluralist, 180–81
  sympathy and, 177–80
Hu Shih, 24–25

identity, 12, 13, 79–80, 91, 133–34, 140, 169
imagination
  democratic decision-making and, 27
  Dewey on, 102
  dual-process theory and, 133